The Princeton Review®

ACT® SCIENCE PREP

The Staff of The Princeton Review

PrincetonReview.com

Penguin Random House

The Princeton Review
110 East 42nd Street, 7th Floor
New York, NY 10017
Email: editorialsupport@review.com

Published in the United States by Penguin Random
House LLC, New York.

Terms of Service: The Princeton Review Online Companion Tools ("Student Tools") for retail books are available for only the two most recent editions of that book. Student Tools may be activated only once per eligible book purchased for a total of 24 months of access. Activation of Student Tools more than once per book is in direct violation of these Terms of Service and may result in discontinuation of access to Student Tools Services.

Some material in this book was previously published as *Math and Science Workout for the ACT, 4th Edition,* a trade paperback published by Penguin Random House LLC in 2019.

ISBN: 978-0-525-57036-3
eBook ISBN: 978-0-525-57040-0
ISSN: 2691-7173

ACT is a registered trademark of ACT, Inc.

The Princeton Review is not affiliated with Princeton University.

The material in this book is up-to-date at the time of publication. However, changes may have been instituted by the testing body in the test after this book was published.

If there are any important late-breaking developments, changes, or corrections to the materials in this book, we will post that information online in the Student Tools. Register your book and check your Student Tools to see if there are any updates posted there.

Editor: Meave Shelton, Alexa Schmitt Bugler
Production Editors: Liz Dacey and Sarah Litt
Production Artist: Jennifer Chapman, Jason Ullmeyer

Printed in the United States of America.

10 9 8 7 6 5 4 3 2 1

The Princeton Review Publishing Team
Rob Franek, Editor-in-Chief
David Soto, Senior Director, Data Operations
Stephen Koch, Senior Manager, Data Operations
Deborah Weber, Director of Production
Jason Ullmeyer, Production Design Manager
Jennifer Chapman, Senior Production Artist
Selena Coppock, Director of Editorial
Orion McBean, Senior Editor
Aaron Riccio, Senior Editor
Meave Shelton, Senior Editor
Chris Chimera, Editor
Patricia Murphy, Editor
Laura Rose, Editor
Alexa Schmitt Bugler, Editorial Assistant

Penguin Random House Publishing Team
Tom Russell, VP, Publisher
Alison Stoltzfus, Senior Director, Publishing
Brett Wright, Senior Editor
Emily Hoffman, Assistant Managing Editor
Ellen Reed, Production Manager
Suzanne Lee, Designer
Eugenia Lo, Publishing Assistant

Acknowledgments

The Princeton Review would like to extend very special thanks to Catherine Eason Healey for her effort, insight, and expertise in creating this title.

Special thanks are also due to Aaron Lindh, Emily Baumbach, Gabrielle Budzon, Sara Soriano, Jess Thomas, and Shannon Thompson.

The Princeton Review also applauds the efforts of the Production team, from the eagle-eyed scrutiny of Liz Dacey and Sarah Litt to the layout wizardry of Jennifer Chapman.

Finally, special thanks to Adam Robinson, who conceived of and perfected the Joe Bloggs approach to standardized tests, and many of the other successful techniques used by The Princeton Review.

—Amy Minster
Content Director, High School Programs

Contents

Get More (Free) Content vi

Part I: Orientation 1

1 Introduction to the Science Test 3

    Welcome 4

    Fun Facts About the ACT 4

    Strategies 7

2 How to Approach the ACT Online Test 11

Part II: Science 27

3 The ACT Science Test 29

    Fun Facts About the Science Test 30

    Personal Order of Difficulty (POOD) 31

    Now Passages 31

    Pacing 32

    Process of Elimination (POE) 32

    The Basic Approach 33

    Later Passages 43

4 Science Reading Strategy 45

5 Now Passages 55

6 Later Passages 79

7 Science Reading Passages 99

Part III: Science Practice Tests 111

8 Science Practice Test 1 113

9 Science Practice Test 1: Answers and Explanations 127

10 Science Practice Test 2 139

11 Science Practice Test 2: Answers and Explanations 153

12 Science Practice Test 3 165

13 Science Practice Test 3: Answers and Explanations 179

14 Science Practice Test 4 193

15 Science Practice Test 4: Answers and Explanations 207

Part IV: College Admissions Insider 219

Get More (Free) Content
at PrincetonReview.com/prep

As easy as 1·2·3

1 Go to PrincetonReview.com/prep or scan the **QR code** and enter the following ISBN for your book:
9780525570363

2 Answer a few simple questions to set up an exclusive Princeton Review account. *(If you already have one, you can just log in.)*

3 Enjoy access to your **FREE** content!

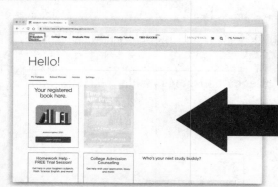

Once you've registered, you can...

- Get our take on any recent or pending updates to the ACT

- Take a full-length practice ACT

- Get valuable advice about the college application process, including tips for writing a great essay and where to apply for financial aid

- If you're still choosing between colleges, use our searchable rankings of *The Best 388 Colleges* to find out more information about your dream school

- Check to see if there have been any corrections or updates to this edition

Need to report a potential **content** issue?

Contact **EditorialSupport@review.com** and include:

- full title of the book
- ISBN
- page number

Need to report a **technical** issue?

Contact **TPRStudentTech@review.com** and provide:

- your full name
- email address used to register the book
- full book title and ISBN
- Operating system (Mac/PC) and browser (Chrome, Firefox, Safari, etc.)

Look For These Icons Throughout The Book

 ONLINE ARTICLES

 PROVEN TECHNIQUES

 APPLIED STRATEGIES

 OTHER REFERENCES

CONSIDERING AN ACT® PREP COURSE?

Pick the Option That's Right For You

OUR MOST POPULAR!

ACT COURSE

- 24/7 on-demand tutoring
- 36+ hours of classroom instruction
- Review and practice books

ACT TUTORING

- 18-hours of customized tutoring package
- Expert tutors matched to your goals
- Interactive score reports to track progress

ACT SELF-PACED

- 1-year access to online materials
- Practice drills for self studying

www.PrincetonReview.com | 1-800-2-REVIEW

Part I
Orientation

Chapter 1
Introduction to the Science Test

WELCOME

The ACT can be an important part of college admissions. Many schools require or recommend their applicants submit either SAT or ACT scores. It's worth keeping in mind, though, that the importance of these tests will vary among the many colleges and universities in the United States. If you haven't already, make sure to research whether the ACT is required or recommended for admission to the schools you plan to apply to.

For more on admissions, see The Princeton Review's *The Best 388 Colleges* or visit our website, PrincetonReview.com.

During the COVID-19 pandemic, many schools went test-optional to account for the numerous students whose SAT and ACT tests were canceled. Some of those schools have returned to requiring test scores, while others have not yet but still may. For the most up-to-date information on the schools you are interested in, check out their admissions websites.

Even if ACT scores are optional, you may still want to submit them if you think your great ACT scores will boost your chances of acceptance. Furthermore, ACT scores are often used for scholarships, so it can be worth putting time into preparing for the test if you can save a good amount on your college education in return.

When colleges require standardized test scores, they will accept either SAT or ACT scores. The expert advice of The Princeton Review is to take whichever test you do better on and focus your efforts on preparing for that one.

Because you bought this book, we assume you've already made the decision to boost your ACT score. This book provides a strategic and efficient way to improve your scores, specifically on the Science test. For a more thorough review of content and exhaustive practice, we recommend purchasing the latest editions of *ACT Prep* and our *ACT Practice Questions* book.

FUN FACTS ABOUT THE ACT

The ACT is nothing like the science tests you take in school. All of the content review and strategies we teach in the following lessons are based on the specific structure and format of the ACT. Before you can beat a test, you have to know how it's built.

If you feel like you need help with the other subjects, check out our companion books, *ACT Reading Prep, ACT English Prep*, and *ACT Math Prep*.

Structure

The ACT is made up of four multiple-choice tests and an optional Writing test.

The five tests are always given in the same order.

English	Math	Reading	Science	Writing
45 minutes	60 minutes	35 minutes	35 minutes	40 minutes
75 questions	60 questions	40 questions	40 questions	1 essay

Scoring

When students and schools talk about ACT scores, they mean the composite score, a range of 1–36. The composite is an average of the four multiple-choice tests, each scored on the same 1–36 scale: Ideas and Analysis, Development and Support, Organization, and Language Use and Conventions. If you take the Writing test, you'll also receive an additional Writing score on a scale of 2–12. The Writing score is an average of four 2–12 subscores. Neither the Writing test score nor the combined English Language Arts score affects the composite.

Students also receive subscores in addition to their (1–36) composite ACT score. These indicators are designed to measure student performance and predict career readiness, as well as competency in STEM (Science, Technology, Engineering, Mathematics) and English language arts. ACT believes that these additional scores will give students better insight into their strengths and how those strengths can be harnessed for success in college and beyond. In addition to the 1–36 score for each of the tests and their composite score, students now see score breakdowns in the following categories:

- **STEM score.** This score will show you how well you did on the Math and Science portions of the test.
- **Progress Toward Career Readiness indicator.** The ACT would have you believe this indicator measures how prepared you are for a career, but really it just measures how prepared you are to take yet another test: the ACT National Career Readiness Certificate™.
- **English Language Arts score.** If you take the Writing test, this score will give you a combined score for the English, Reading, and Writing tests.
- **Text Complexity Progress indicator**. This score will tell you how well you fared on those hard passages throughout the test.

There is also a section on the score report that breaks each section down into categories and tells you both how many questions there were in each category and how many of them you got correct. Some of these categories can be useful in helping you know what you need to study: for example, if you missed a lot of questions in the "Geometry" category, you should brush up your Geometry skills. But if you did poorly in the "Integration of Knowledge and Ideas" category, it's not quite as obvious what you need to study. Don't worry about these scores though—they're there because they align with federal academic standards, and school districts that use the ACT for standardized testing for all juniors want those scores, but college don't typically look at them for admissions purposes.

It's All About the Composite

Whether you look at your score online or wait to get it in the mail, the biggest number on the page is always the composite. While admissions offices will certainly see the individual scores of all five tests (and their subscores), schools will use the composite to evaluate your application, and that's why, in the end, it's the only one that matters.

The composite is an average. Let the full weight of that sink in. Do you need to bring up all four scores equally to raise your composite? Do you need to be a superstar in all four tests? Should you focus more on your weaknesses than your strengths? No, no, and absolutely not. The best way to improve your composite is to shore up your weaknesses but exploit your strengths as much as possible.

> To improve your ACT score, use your strengths to lift the composite score as high as possible.

You don't need to be a rock star on all four tests. Identify two, maybe three tests, and focus on raising those scores as much as you can to raise your composite. Work on your weakest scores to keep them from pulling you down. Think of it this way: if you had only one hour to devote to practice the week before the ACT, spend that hour on your best subjects.

Single-Section Tests and Superscoring

The people who write the ACT have announced their intention to allow students to take one, two, or three individual sections in a day, as opposed to needing to take the entire test. You will need to have taken the full ACT before using this option, and single-section tests will only be offered on the computer.

Unfortunately, plans to offer single-section retesting were delayed by the COVID-19 pandemic, and as of the publication of this book, a date for the rollout has not been announced. We encourage you to check the ACT website, www.act.org, for the most up-to-date information about the availability of single-section retesting when it is eventually offered.

One piece of good news is that ACT has begun Superscoring. If you take the ACT more than once, ACT will automatically take your highest English, Math, Reading, and Science scores and average them together to calculate a new "Superscore" composite.

Sounds great, right? We think it is—this gives you the opportunity to show your best ACT score to schools. Now, colleges and universities still have the option as to whether to accept the Superscore, but for the schools that let you Superscore, this is all positive for you.

Science Scores

The Science test can be frustrating for science fans and non-science fans alike. It's not unusual for students that excel in science and math at school to find that Math is one of their highest scores and Science is one of their lowest scores. There are good reasons for this. The Math test, perhaps deceptively so, resembles school tests more than the other three. Science feels the most different, and many students are intimidated by both the content and format.

Many students find improving scores on the Science test to be more difficult than the other sections. Unlike the Math or English test, there are no rules or content to master through rigorous practice. The Science test is designed to test your reasoning skills using passage-based information, not tap specific outside knowledge. Who knows what specific topics will appear on the next ACT? On the goods-news front, however, The Princeton Review can teach you a smart, effective approach designed to maximize your performance every time, regardless of content. It can be tough to change your ways, but dedicated practice with a strategic method can prevent the Science score from pulling down that composite.

Time

How often do you take a final exam in school that gives you *at most* a minute per question? Probably never. The ACT isn't a school test, and you can't approach it as if it is. While speed and accuracy depend on individual skills and grasp of content, almost all students struggle to finish the Science test on time. The more you treat the test the same way you would a school final, the less likely you are to finish, much less finish with the greatest accuracy. The Princeton Review's strategies are all based on this time crunch. There's a difference between knowing *how* to do a question under the best of circumstance and getting it *right* with a ticking clock and glowering proctor in the room.

STRATEGIES

You will raise your ACT score by working smarter, not harder, and a smart test-taker is a strategic test-taker. You will target specific content to review, you will apply an effective and efficient approach, and you will employ the common sense that frequently deserts many others when they pick up a number 2 pencil.

Each test on the ACT demands a different approach, and even the most universal strategies vary in their applications. In the chapters that follow, we'll discuss these terms in greater detail customized to Science.

Personal Order of Difficulty (POOD)

If time is going to run out, would you rather it run out on the most difficult questions or on the easiest questions? Of course you want it to run out on the points you are less likely to get right. The trick is to find all of the easiest questions and get them done first.

Now

Does a question look okay? Do you know how to do it? Do it *Now*.

Later

Does a question make you go, "hmm"? If you can't find a way to get your pencil moving right away, consider leaving it and coming back *Later*. Circle the question number for easy reference to return.

> **The Best Way to Bubble In**
> Work one page at a time, circling your answers right on the booklet. Transfer a page's worth of answers to the answer sheet. It's better to stay focused on working questions rather than disrupt your concentration to find where you left off on the answer sheet. You'll be more accurate at both tasks. Do not wait to the end, however, to transfer all the answers of that test on your answer sheet. Go one page at a time.

Never

Test-taker, know thyself. Know the topics that are most difficult for you, and learn the signs that flash danger. Don't waste time on questions you should *Never* do. Instead, use more time to answer the Now and Later questions accurately.

Letter of the Day (LOTD)

Just because you don't *work* a question doesn't mean you don't *answer* it. There is no penalty for wrong answers on the ACT, so you should never leave any blanks on your answer sheet. When you guess on Never questions, pick your favorite two-letter combo of answers and stick with it. For example, always choose A/F or C/H. If you're consistent, you're statistically more likely to pick up more points.

Note: if you are taking the ACT on a computer, all of the questions will have answer choices A, B, C, D (or A, B, C, D, E on the Math test). On the paper-and-pencil ACT, every other question will have answer choices F, G, H, J (or F, G, H, J, K on the Math test).

Process of Elimination (POE)

In a perfect world, you'll know how to work all of your Now and Later questions, quickly and accurately, circling the correct answer among the choices. The ACT is *not* a perfect world. But even with a ticking clock and a number 2 pencil in your sweaty hand, wrong answers can be obvious. Sometimes POE is a great Plan B, but it is actually the best way to find the correct answer on many questions on the Science test. And even when you can't narrow the answers to only one, using POE to get rid of at least one or two wrong answers will substantially increase your odds of getting a question right.

The Power of POE
Very often, the quickest way to the correct answer is to eliminate the wrong answer choices rather than focusing on finding the right one.

Pacing

The ACT may be designed for you to run out of time, but you can't rush through it as quickly as possible. All you'll do is make careless errors on easy questions you should get right and spend way too much time on difficult ones you're unlikely to get right.

To hit your target score, you have to know approximately how many raw points you need. Use the entire time allotted where it will do the most good. Go slowly enough to avoid careless errors on Now questions, but go quickly enough to get to as many Later questions as you need to hit your goal.

On each test of the ACT, the number of correct answers converts to a scaled score of 1–36. ACT works hard to adjust the scale of each test at each administration as necessary to make all scaled scores comparable, smoothing out any differences in level of difficulty across test dates. Thus, there is no truth to any one test date being "easier" than the others, but you can expect to see slight variations in the scale from test to test.

This is the scale from the 2021-2022 free test ACT makes available on its website, ACT.org. We're going to use it to explain how to pick a target score and pace yourself.

Science Pacing

Scale Score	Raw Score	Scale Score	Raw Score	Scale Score	Raw Score
36	38-40	24	26-27	12	9
35	37	23	25	11	8
34	36	22	23-24	10	7
33	35	21	22	9	6
32	34	20	20-21	8	5
31	—	19	19	7	4
30	33	18	17-18	6	3
29	32	17	15-16	5	—
28	31	16	13-14	4	2
27	—	15	12	3	1
26	30	14	11	2	—
25	28-29	13	10	1	0

The Science test has larger swings in difficulty levels between test administrations than the other subjects, so the scoring scale can vary significantly from one test to another. As a result, it's hard to predict exactly how many questions you will need to get correct to reach your goal score.

Here's one example scenario. Let's say your goal score on the Science is a 24. Find 24 in the scaled score column and you'll see that on the test that this scale is based on, you'd need 26–27 raw points. This could be done by devoting your time to the questions in 5 of the 6 passages and guessing LOTD on the remaining 6 or 7 questions. Even allowing for 4 or 5 mistakes in the 5 passages you work, you could still hit your target score. However, if the Science test you're faced with is easier, then it could require 29 raw points to get a 24. On the other hand, if the test you're faced with is harder, then might only require 26 raw points to get a scale score of 24. The chart is useful to give you a general guideline of how many questions you need to answer correctly, but keep in mind that it varies.

If you find yourself faced with a particularly difficult set of passages, you might be disheartened that you are unable to get through questions as quickly as you had hoped. Don't let that discourage you and distract you from the remaining questions! The important thing to remember is that if the test is harder, the scoring curve will even out the difference. Your job is to make sure that you are using your time wisely and picking the best passages and questions for Now. We will focus on this strategy in the lesson that follows.

Our advice is to be aggressive. Spend the time needed on the easiest passages first, but keep moving to get to your targeted raw score. Use the chart below to figure out approximately how many passages to work.

Target Score	# of Passages to Attempt
< 20	4 passages
20–23	4–5 passages
24–27	5–6 passages
> 27	6 passages

Be Ruthless

The worst mistake a test-taker can make is to throw good time after bad. You read a question and don't understand it, so you read it again. And again. If you stare at it really hard, you know you're going to just *see* it. And you can't move on, because really, after spending all that time, it would be a waste not to keep at it, right? Actually, that way of thinking couldn't be more wrong.

You can't let one tough question drag you down. Instead, the best way to improve your ACT score is to follow our advice.

1. Use the techniques and strategies in the lessons to work efficiently and accurately through all your Now and Later questions.
2. Know your Never questions and use your LOTD.
3. Know when to move on. Use POE and guess from what's left.

Now move on to the lessons and learn the best way to approach the content.

Chapter 2
How to Approach the ACT Online Test

In this chapter, you'll learn what to expect on the ACT Online Test, including how to apply its computer-based features and our strategies to the question types in each section—English, Math, Reading, Science, and Writing.

If your ACT will be pencil-and-paper, skip this chapter.

At the time of this book's printing, the option to take the ACT online at a testing center was postponed. ACT also plans to offer at-home online testing, although an exact rollout date has not yet been announced. For up-to-date news on both options, check the ACT website.

WHAT IS THE ACT ONLINE TEST?

The ACT Online Test is the ACT that you take on a computer, rather than with a pencil and paper. Despite the name, you can't take the ACT from the comfort of your own home; instead, you'll have to go to a testing center (possibly your high school) and take the test on one of the center's computers.

ACT has indicated that eventually students in the United States will have the option of taking the ACT Online Test instead of the traditional pencil-and-paper version. Students choosing this option will get their scores in about two to three business days (e.g., take the test on Saturday, have your score the next Wednesday). However, at the time of this printing, no specific timeline was available.

WHO TAKES THE ACT ONLINE TEST?

ACT has been offering versions of the ACT on computer since about 2016. The first students to take the ACT on the computer were students taking the test at school. Schools and school districts decided whether to give the test on the computer.

As of September 2018, all students taking the ACT outside of the United States take the test on a computer (except for those students with accommodations requiring the use of a traditional pencil-and-paper test).

ACT has indicated that eventually students in the United States will have the option of taking the ACT Online Test instead of the traditional pencil-and-paper version. Students choosing this option will get their scores in about two to three business days (e.g., take the test on Saturday, have your score the next Wednesday). However, at the time of this printing, no specific timeline was available.

Single-Section Retesting is an incredible option for students. However, colleges still have the option to accept or not accept these new scores. Research your target schools early so you know your options!

Single-Section Retesting

If you are happy with the score you receive from a single test administration, you will still have the option to send just that score to colleges. If your score in one section is not as high as you'd like, you will eventually have a chance to correct that. Students who have already taken the full ACT may choose to take one, two, or three sections again using Single-Section Retesting. ACT will then produce a "superscore" consisting of your best results in all tests (English, Math, Reading, Science, and Writing (if you took it)). Note that not all colleges accept a super-scored ACT, so do your research before taking advantage of this option.

ACT ONLINE TEST FEATURES

So, besides the obvious fact that it's taken on a computer, what are the differences between taking the ACT on the computer and taking it on paper? Let's start with what you can't do on the ACT Online Test. You can't "write" on the screen in a freehand way. You're limited in how you're able to mark the answer choices, and each question appears on its own screen (so you can't see multiple questions at one glance). You will also be given a small "whiteboard" and dry erase pen with which to make notes and do work.

So, what features does the ACT Online Test have?

- Timer
    - You can hide the timer by clicking on it.
    - There is a 5-minute warning toward the end of each test. There is no audible signal at the 5-minute warning, only a small indicator in the upper-right corner of the screen.
- Nav tool
    - You can use this tool to navigate directly to any question in the section.
    - The Nav tool blocks the current question when opened.
    - It also shows what questions you have flagged and/or left blank.
    - You can flag questions in this menu.
- Question numbers at the bottom of the screen
    - You can click on these numbers to navigate directly to any question in the section.
    - These numbers also indicate whether a question has been flagged and/or left blank.
- Flag tool
    - You can flag a question on the question screen itself or by using the Nav tool.
    - Flagging a question has no effect besides marking the question for your own purposes.
- Answer Eliminator
    - Answer choices can be "crossed-off" on-screen.
    - An answer choice that's been eliminated cannot be chosen and must be "un-crossed-off" first by clicking the answer choice.
- Magnifier
    - You can use this to magnify specific parts of the screen.
- Line Mask
    - This tool covers part of the screen. There is an adjustable window you can use to limit what you can see.
    - This is an excellent tool if you need an aid to help you focus on specific parts of the text or figure.
    - However, not everyone will find this tool useful, so do not feel obligated to use it!
    - Note that you cannot highlight the text in the window of the Line Mask.
- Answer Mask
    - This tool hides the answer choices of a question.
    - Answers can be revealed one at a time.
- Screen Zoom
    - This tool changes the zoom of the entire screen (as opposed to the magnifier, which magnifies only one part of the screen).
    - Your screen zoom setting will remain the same from question to question.
- Highlighter
    - You can use this tool to highlight parts of passage text, question text, or answer text.
    - You cannot highlight within figures.
    - If you highlight in a passage with multiple questions, your highlights will only show up on that question. (In other words, if you highlight, for example, question 1 of a Reading passage, questions 2–10 of that same passage will not

show those highlights.)
- o Turning off the highlighter tool removes your highlights.
- Shortcuts:

Keybind	Function	Keybind	Function
Ctrl + H	Toggle Help	Ctrl + Enter	Answer Question
Ctrl + F	Flag Item	Alt + M	Toggle Magnifier
Ctrl + I	Item Navigation	Alt + H	Toggle Highlighter
Alt + P	Previous Question	Alt + E	Toggle Answer Eliminator
Alt + N	Next Question	Alt + A	Toggle Answer Masking
A-E or 1-5	Select Alternative	Alt + L	Toggle Line Masking

- The Writing test is typed, rather than written by hand.

You will also be given a small "whiteboard" and dry erase pen with which to make notes and do work.

HOW TO APPROACH THE ACT ONLINE TEST

The strategies mentioned in this chapter are thoroughly discussed in our comprehensive guide, *ACT Prep*, so be sure to pick up a copy of that book if you have not already done so. These approaches were created in reference to the pencil-and-paper format, but they still apply to the ACT Online Test with some adjustments. This chapter assumes your familiarity with these strategies and will show you how to make the best use of them given the tools available in the computer-based format.

You will also want to incorporate some computer-based practice into your prep plan. ACT's website has practice sections for each of the four multiple-choice parts of the test and for the essay. We recommend that you do those sections toward the end of your preparation (and close to your test date) to give yourself an opportunity to practice what you've learned on a platform similar to the one you'll be using on the day of the test.

Remember!
Your goal is to get the best possible score on the ACT. ACT's goal is to assign a number to you that (supposedly) means something to colleges. Focus on your goal!

If you are planning to take the ACT online, you should practice as if you're doing all your work on the computer, even when you're working in a physical book. Use a highlighter, but don't use the highlighter on any figures (as the ACT Online Test won't let you do so). Use your pencil to eliminate answer choices and have a separate sheet of paper or a whiteboard to do any work you need to do, instead of writing on the problem itself.

Also, remember that our approaches work. Don't get misled by ACT's instructions on the day of the test—their way of approaching the test won't give you the best results!

Overall

Your Personal Order of Difficulty (POOD) and Pacing goals will be the same on the ACT Online Test as on the pencil-and-paper version. Because it is easy to change your answers, put in your Letter of the Day (LOTD) when skipping a Later or Never question. Use the Flag tool on the Later questions so you can jump back easily (using either the navigation bar at the bottom of the screen or the Nav tool).

Process of Elimination (POE) is still a vital approach. On both the paper-and-pencil ACT and the ACT Online test, there are more wrong answers than correct ones. Eliminating one you know are wrong helps you to save time, avoid trap answers, and make a better guess if you have to. On the ACT Online Test, you cannot write on the test, but you can use the Highlighter tool. Turn on these tools (and the Line Mask, if desired) at the beginning of the English section and use them throughout.

ENGLISH

The Basic Approaches to both Proofreader and Editor questions are the same on the computerized and the paper versions of the ACT. When you decide to skip a question to come back to it Later (for example, a question asking for the introduction to the topic of the passage before you've read any part of the passage), flag the question so you can easily jump back to it before moving on to the next passage. When you have five minutes remaining, flag your current question and use the Nav tool to make sure you've put in your LOTD for any questions that you haven't done, then return to your spot and work until time runs out.

When you work Proofreader questions, you can use the Highlighter tool to help you focus on the key parts of the text. Let's see an example:

> For a comprehensive review of all sections of the ACT and the strategies mentioned throughout this chapter, check out our book, *ACT Prep*.

Sneaking down the corridor, the agent, taking

care not to alert the guards, spotting the locked door.

- **A.** NO CHANGE
- **B.** spot
- **C.** are spotting
- **D.** spots

> Use the tools available to help you focus on the key portions of the text. Practice with a highlighter when you're working on paper (instead of underlining with your pencil).

Here's How to Crack It

Verbs are changing in the answer choices, so the question is testing subject/verb agreement. The verb must be consistent with the subject. *The agent* is the subject; highlight it:

Sneaking down the corridor, the agent, taking

care not to alert the guards, spotting the locked door.

- **A.** NO CHANGE
- **B.** spot
- **C.** are spotting
- **D.** spots

The agent is singular, so the verb must be singular. Eliminate (B) and (C), as both are plural. *Spotting* cannot be the main verb of a sentence, so eliminate (A). The correct answer is (D).

Similarly, the Highlighter tool is helpful on Editor questions. Use the tool on both the passage and the question to help you focus on the relevant parts of each.

As it's name suggests, the Indian fantail is not native to North America. In fact, its establishment here was quite accidental. In 1926, the San Diego Zoo acquired four pythons from India for its reptile exhibit. The long trip from India required, that, the pythons be provided with food for the journey, and a group of unfortunate fantails was shipped for just that purpose. Two lucky fantails survived, and their beautiful appearance caused the San Diego Zoo to keep and breed them for the public to see. Eventually, some of the animals escaped captivity and developed populations in the wild, all thanks to those two birds!

Given that all the choices are true, which one provides the most relevant and specific information at this point in the essay?

- A. NO CHANGE
- B. and they have quite an appetite.
- C. because no one wanted them to starve.
- D. and they are quite picky in what they'll eat.

Here's How to Crack It

The question asks for the *most relevant and specific information*. Highlight those words in the question. The first sentence of the paragraph focuses on the *Indian fantail*, and the sentence after the underlined portion discusses *(t)wo lucky fantails*. The final sentence discusses *the animals* that escaped. Highlight these words in the paragraph.

Your screen should look like this:

As it's name suggests, the Indian fantail is not native to North America. In fact, its establishment here was quite accidental. In 1926, the San Diego Zoo acquired four pythons from India for its reptile exhibit. The long trip from India required, that, the pythons be provided with food for the journey, and a group of unfortunate fantails was shipped for just that purpose. Two lucky fantails survived, and their beautiful appearance caused the San Diego Zoo to keep and breed them for the public to see. Eventually, some of the animals escaped captivity and developed populations in the wild, all thanks to those two birds!

Given that all the choices are true, which one provides the most relevant and specific information at this point in the essay?

- A. NO CHANGE
- B. and they have quite an appetite.
- C. because no one wanted them to starve.
- D. and they are quite picky in what they'll eat.

Use POE, focusing on whether the choice is consistent with the highlights in the passage. The sentence as written discusses *a group of unfortunate fantails*; keep (A). Choices (B), (C), and (D) do not talk about the Indian fantail; instead, they focus on the pythons. This is inconsistent with the goal of the sentence and the content of the paragraph; eliminate those answers. The correct answer is (A).

Finally, you can't write in the passage, so you'll need to approach the Vertical Line Test slightly differently. On the paper-and-pencil ACT, you would use this strategy for questions about punctuation, drawing a vertical line where the punctuation breaks up the ideas in the text. On the computerized ACT, you should use the whiteboard to handle these questions.

I'm not searching for a ghost or yeti, my phantom is the Indian fantail. These beautiful creatures are members of the pigeon family, but you could not tell that by looking at them.

- A. NO CHANGE
- B. yeti: my phantom
- C. yeti my phantom
- D. yeti, since this

Here's How to Crack It

Punctuation is changing in the answer choices, so the question is testing STOP and GO punctuation. There is Half-Stop punctuation in (B), so use the Vertical Line Test. You cannot draw a line in the text, so draw a "t" on your whiteboard, with "yeti" in the bottom-left and "my" in the bottom-right:

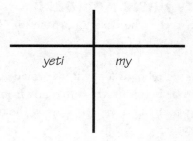

Read each part of the sentence and determine whether it is complete or incomplete. *I'm not searching for a ghost or yeti* is a complete idea; write "C" in the upper-left of the "t." *My phantom is the Indian fantail* is also a complete idea; write "C" (for "complete") in the upper-right of the "t." Your board should look like this:

Eliminate any answer that cannot link two complete ideas. Both (A) and (C) use GO punctuation, which cannot link complete ideas; eliminate (A) and (C). Choice (D) adds *since*, which makes the idea to the right of the line incomplete. However, *since* is used to show time or causation, which does not work in the context of the sentence. Eliminate (D). The correct answer is (B).

MATH

First off, you'll still need to bring your calculator to the ACT Online Test—which is a good thing! You're already comfortable with your personal calculator, so there will be one less thing to worry about on the day of the test.

> **Write it down!**
> It is tempting to do all your work in your head. Don't fall into this trap! It's easier to make mistakes when you're not writing down your work, and you'll often have to "go back" if you don't have something written down. Use your whiteboard!

When choosing questions to do Later, flag the question so you can easily navigate back to it after doing your Now questions. Do put in your LOTD when doing so; you don't want to accidently leave a question blank! When you get the five-minute warning, finish the question you're working on, flag it (so you can find your spot easily), then put in your LOTD for every unanswered question. Then you can go back to working until time runs out.

Use the Highlighter tool to highlight what the question is actually asking, especially in Word Problems. Of course, you'll want to use your whiteboard when working the steps of a math problem (don't do the work in your head!).

ACT Online Geometry Basic Approach

Because you can't write on the screen, the Basic Approach for Geometry questions needs a few slight tweaks:

1. Draw the figure on your whiteboard (copy if it's provided; draw it yourself otherwise). If the figure would be better drawn differently from the way ACT has drawn it (for instance, a similar triangles question), redraw the figure in a way that will help you answer the question.

2. Label the figure you drew on your whiteboard with the information from both ACT's figure and the question.

3. Write down any formulas you need and fill in the information you know.

Let's see how that works on a question.

In the figure below, triangle *ABC* is similar to triangle *DEF*. What is the length of *EF* ?

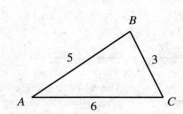
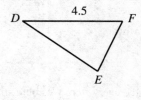

A. 1.5
B. 2.25
C. 3
D. 4
E. 4.5

Here's How to Crack It

The question asks for the length of *EF*, so highlight that in the question. Follow the Geometry Basic Approach. Start by drawing the figure on your whiteboard. Because the triangles are similar, redraw triangle *DEF* to be oriented the same way as *ABC*. Label your figure with the given information.

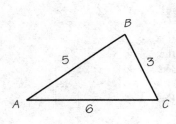
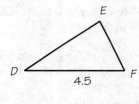

Write down the equation you need and fill in the necessary information. *AC* corresponds to *DF*, and *BC* corresponds to *EF*. Set up a proportion: $\frac{AC}{DF} = \frac{BC}{EF}$. Fill in the information from your figure: $\frac{6}{4.5} = \frac{3}{x}$, where *x* is equal to *EF*. Cross-multiply to get $6x = 3(4.5)$, or $6x = 13.5$. Divide both sides by 6 to get $x = 2.25$. The correct answer is (B).

READING

First off, there are a few differences between the pencil-and-paper ACT and the ACT Online Test. In the ACT Online Test, there are no line references; rather, the relevant part of the text is highlighted. The passage will also "jump" to the highlighted text if it's off the screen when you go to that question. This may disorient you at first: be prepared for this to happen.

Let's see an example.

...protested every step. We could still run, but, Hook worried, for how long? In a cross-country race, only a team's top five runners score, and we weren't those five. Our job was to finish ahead of as many of our rival teams' top fives as we could.

Leah was a senior that year, my freshman year. All season, she'd been counting down to this last race, praying her body wouldn't say *No*. She and I joked that we needed to go to the Knee Store and pick out new knees, ones that wouldn't crack and pop and burn all the time. It was hard to watch a teammate in that much pain, but Leah was a trooper, never slacking from workouts, never stopping to walk, never losing sight of the next person in front of her to catch.

The crack of the starter's pistol sent us surging out of that little crop of trees and onto the race course. I hollered, "See you at the Knee Store!" Behind me, she laughed.

The pack stayed tight through the first quarter-mile, and I was surrounded by so many bodies I couldn't think. I just ran, putting one foot in front of the other, trying not to fall. Trying to look beyond the jostling mass surrounding me, I could barely...

The narrator's references to the Knee Store primarily serve to suggest that:

- **A.** Leah wishes to buy better knee supports.
- **B.** the narrator and Leah use humor to cope with their pain.
- **C.** the narrator desires to learn more about her injury.
- **D.** Leah's injuries, unlike the narrator's, have become unbearable.

> Reading on a computer screen can be disorienting. Practice by reading articles or other passages on the computer when possible.

Here's How to Crack It

The question asks what the *references to the Knee Store...suggest*. The references to the *Knee Store* are highlighted in the text. Note that the text has shifted down to the highlighted portions. The window indicates that Leah and the narrator *joked that we needed to go to the Knee Store*. Leah *laughed* after the narrator referred to the Knee Store. Therefore, the answer should be consistent with joking and laughing. Choice (A) takes the reference too literally; eliminate (A). "Humor" is consistent with the text's references to *joked* and *laughed*; keep (B). There's no indication of the narrator's goal to *learn more about her injury*, nor does the text support the idea that Leah's injuries *have become unbearable*, eliminate (C) and (D). The correct answer is (B).

When you have five minutes remaining, flag your current question and use the Nav tool to make sure you've put in your LOTD for any questions that you haven't done. Then return to your spot and work until time runs out. If you've just started or finished a passage, click through the questions to look for Easy to Find questions in the remaining time, and don't forget to put in your LOTD for any question you don't answer!

The biggest difference between the ACT Online Test and the paper-and-pencil ACT is that you can only see one question on the screen at a time. Rather than looking over the questions at a glance, you must click from question to question. This feature means that the Reading Basic Approach (covered below) needs to be modified in order to be as time efficient as possible.

ACT Online Reading Basic Approach

1. **Preview**
   Read only the blurb—do not go through and map the questions. Instead, write the question numbers on your whiteboard to prepare to Work the Passage.

2. **Work the Passage**
   This step is *even more* optional on the ACT Online Test than on the pencil-and-paper ACT. You haven't mapped the questions, and your highlights only show up on one question. If you do decide to Work the Passage, ensure that you're getting through the passage in 2–3 minutes. More likely, you'll find it best to just skip this step and move on to the questions after reading the blurb and setting up your whiteboard.

> You don't get points for reading—only for answering questions correctly. Determine whether Working the Passage helps you answer questions correctly and quickly.

3. **Select and Understand a Question**
   When Selecting a Question, if a question is Easy to Find (a portion of the text is highlighted or you Worked the Passage and know where in the passage the content you need is), do it Now. Understand the question, then move on to Step 4. If the question is not Easy to Find (in other words, you don't immediately know where in the passage to go), write down the question's lead words on your whiteboard next to the question number. Include EXCEPT/LEAST/NOT if the question includes those words. If there are no lead words, flag the question.

   After you do all the questions with highlights, then Work the Passage, scanning actively for your lead words. Once you find a lead word, do the corresponding question. After answering the questions with lead words, finish with the flagged questions.

4. **Read What You Need**
   Find the 5–10 lines you need to answer the question. Remember that only the quotation will be highlighted—the answer is not necessarily highlighted. You must read the lines before and after the highlighted portion to ensure that you find the correct answer to the question. If you find the Line Mask tool helpful, use it to frame your window.

5. **Predict the Correct Answer**
   As you read, look for evidence for the answer to the question in your window and highlight it using the highlighter tool. (You can highlight text that ACT has already highlighted—the color will change to "your" highlighting color.) As always, base your prediction on the words in the passage as much as possible.

6. **Use POE**
   Use the Answer Eliminator tool to narrow the answer choices down to one answer. If the question is an EXCEPT/LEAST/NOT question, instead write ABCD on your whiteboard and mark each answer T or F for True or False (or Y or N for Yes or No) and choose the odd one out.

Dual Reading Approach

The questions for Dual Reading passages are grouped with the questions about Passage A, then those about Passage B, then those about both passages. Each question should be labeled with an indicator for the passage the question refers to. Work each passage separately, answering all the Passage A questions you plan to answer before moving onto the Passage B questions.

You should also write down the Golden Thread of each passage on your whiteboard—either after Working the Passage or after finishing the questions on that passage. That will aid you in answering the questions about both passages.

SCIENCE

The overall approach to the Science test is the same on the ACT Online Test as it is on the traditional pencil-and-paper version. There are a few small adjustments to make, but the overall strategy remains the same.

The Flag tool is very important when identifying Later passages and questions. On a Later passage, flag the first question, then put your LOTD for every question on the passage. Make a note on your whiteboard of the first question in the passage so you can easily jump back to the passage.

When working a Now passage, you may still encounter a Later question. For these stand-alone Later questions, flag the question but don't put in your LOTD. When you get to the end of a passage, check the bar at the bottom of the screen to make sure you have answered every question up to that point.

Science Basic Approach

There are a few small changes to the Science approach when taking the ACT Online Test.

1. **Work the Figures**
   You can't highlight the figures. Experiment with taking quick notes about the variables, units, and trends on your whiteboard and determine whether it helps you find the needed information quickly.

2. **Work the Questions**
   Highlight the words and phrases from the figures in the question to help guide you to the relevant information.

3. **Work the Answers**
   Use the Answer Eliminator tool to work POE on answer choices with multiple parts.

Let's look at an example.

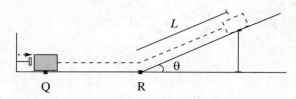

A block is placed on a frictionless horizontal surface at point Q. The block is pushed with a plunger and given initial velocity v along the horizontal surface. At point R, the block slides up a ramp with coefficient of friction f to a maximum distance L along the ramp. The distance between points Q and R is 1.0 m.

Figure 1

Figure 2, below, shows how L varies with v for different f on a ramp with $\theta = 20°$. Figure 3 (on the following page) shows how L varies with v for different θ on a ramp with $f = 0.1$.

Key	
Marker	f
□	0.15
○	0.30
△	0.60
×	0.90

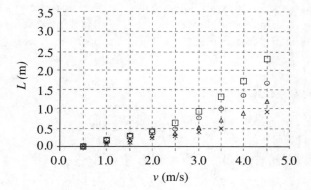

Figure 2

Scrolling Passages
Most passages in Science will require scrolling down to see all the figures. Look for a scroll bar for every passage!

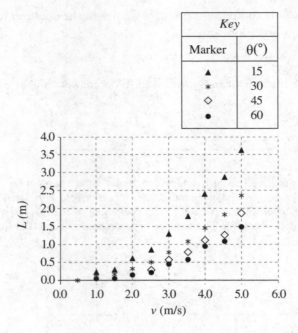

Key	
Marker	$\theta(°)$
▲	15
∗	30
◇	45
●	60

Figure 3

If $f = 0.90$ for the sliding block and $v = 5.5$ m/s, L will most likely be closest to which of the following?

- **A.** 0.3 m
- **B.** 0.7 m
- **C.** 1.5 m
- **D.** 3.0 m

Here's How to Crack It

Start by Working the Figures. Figure 1 shows the points Q and R and variables L and θ, but there are no numbers or trends. Figure 2 shows a direct relationship between L (m) and v (m/s); mark this on your whiteboard. Furthermore, the legend gives values of f; as f increases, L decreases. Mark these relationships on your whiteboard. Figure 3 also shows a direct relationship between L (m) and v (m/s); the legend, however, gives θ (°). As θ increases, L decreases. Put these on your whiteboard as well. Note that Figures 2 and 3 show both L and v; Figure 2 has f, whereas Figure 3 has θ.

Your whiteboard should look like the following:

Figure 2: L (m) ↑ v (m/s) ↑ and f ↑ L ↓

Figure 3: L (m) ↑ v (m/s) ↑ and θ ↑ L ↓

The question refers to the variables f, v, and L; highlight those variables. Figure 2 has all three variables. The highest value of v given in the figure is 4.5, so start there and use the trend to make a prediction about a v of 5.5. At $v = 4.5$ and $f = 0.90$, L is approximately 0.9. The trend is increasing, so a v of 5.5 must result in an L value of greater than 0.9; eliminate (A) and (B).

An L value of 3.0 would be higher than any value already in Figure 2, and extending the trend for the line created by the $f = 0.90$ marks would not result in L increasing to 3.0 by the time v reaches 5.5; eliminate (D). Although you can't physically extend the line because it's on a computer screen, it may be a good idea to use your finger to trace where you would draw on the screen. The correct answer is (C).

You'll still approach the passage that's all or mostly text as if it is a Reading passage. Unlike in Reading, you will want to Map the Questions during the Preview step, as there will not be a group of questions about each passage like there is in the Dual Reading passage. Instead, the questions will not be asked in any particular order, so use your whiteboard to map out which scientist(s) or experiment(s) each question refers to. As with the other sections, at the five-minute warning, flag your question, put in your LOTD on any unanswered question, then keep working until time runs out.

WRITING

As you have probably guessed, you'll be typing the Writing test on the ACT Online Test. But before we get to writing the essay, there are a few minor points to note about the format of this test on the computer.

First, you won't be able to highlight when Working the Prompt or Perspectives, so be sure to write notes on your whiteboard. Second, ACT has given the prompt and perspectives on one screen, then repeated them on the screen that contains a text box. Feel free to do your work on the screen within the text box. If you're used to making your essay outlines on a computer, you can use the text box to do so here, as long as you remember to delete any notes before the section comes to an end.

When writing the essay, all the same points apply to both the pencil-and-paper and online tests (have a clear thesis, make and organize your arguments in a way that is easy to follow, etc.). When you have 5 minutes left, quickly type up a conclusion paragraph (if you haven't already), then go back and finish up your body paragraph ideas. It's more important to have a conclusion than it is to have perfect body paragraphs. Finally, spend a minute or two at the end to quickly fix any obvious typos or grammatical issues.

When you practice the Writing test at home, type your essay in a word processing program instead of writing it by hand. Be sure to turn off spell check, as the ACT does not provide it, so you don't want to rely on it.

That's it! Everything you've learned for the pencil-and-paper ACT can be applied to the ACT Online Test with a few small tweaks. You've got this!

Part II
Science

Chapter 3
The ACT
Science Test

THE ACT SCIENCE TEST

For many students, the Science test is the most difficult. Whether the subject matter alone intimidates or the time crunch stresses, the Science test can be difficult to finish. In this chapter, you'll learn how to order the passages and apply a basic approach that makes the most of the time you have.

FUN FACTS ABOUT THE SCIENCE TEST

The Science test consists of 40 questions and 6 passages that you must answer in 35 minutes.

This is not a test of science content, but of science reasoning. ACT describes the necessary skills required for the natural sciences as "interpretation, analysis, evaluation, reasoning, and problem solving."

Trends and Relationships

We think all those skills are best understood as identifying trends and relationships. Whether you are asked to look up a value or synthesize information, it all comes down to the patterns and connections shown by variables, figures, experiments, and scientists. Look for trends *within* a figure, and look for relationships *between* figures.

Outside Knowledge

For the topics of the passages, ACT will pull from biology, chemistry, physics, and the Earth/space sciences, such as geology, astronomy, and meteorology. Most of the questions are answered by the passages and figures provided, but you should also expect two to three questions requiring outside knowledge.

The Passages

On each ACT, the order of the passages will vary, but the distribution of passage types is always the same.

Passages with Figures

At least five of the six passages will have data represented in figures—usually tables or graphs—but there are also diagrams of various kinds and the odd pie chart or other graphic. There will also be some text, but as you'll see when you get to the Basic Approach, on all but the Science Reading passage, the data in the figures is the most important part. These passages have six or seven questions each.

Science Reading Passage

One of the six passages is what ACT calls "Conflicting Viewpoints"; it has seven questions, and it's fundamentally different from the other passages in one important respect. This passage will sometimes have a figure of some kind, but the most important part of the passage is in the text—hence our name for it, the Science Reading passage. There will be several different hypotheses about an issue in this passage, and in order to answer the questions, you'll have to read the hypotheses.

PERSONAL ORDER OF DIFFICULTY (POOD)

There are many things about the Science test that make it difficult. For starters, it's last, and chances are you're already exhausted by the time you get to it. Taking it as a single-section test might be a way to combat that fatigue, but many will still find it challenging: science-phobes can be intimidated by the subject matter, while science geeks can be thwarted by the time crunch. One simple thing you can do to make it a little easier is to forget about ACT's order. On every ACT, work the passages in an order that makes sense for you.

NOW PASSAGES

Every time you take the ACT, for practice and for real, pick the order of the passages that makes sense for you. The best passages to do Now are those with the most transparent relationships. When you pick your Now passages, choose from the ones that have figures. By nature, the Science Reading passage is different, and even superior readers find it takes longer to work than the most straightforward of the passages with figures. What makes a good Now passage? There are five things to consider.

1. Small Tables and Graphs

A good Now passage can have tables, graphs, or both. Good Now tables should be no more than 3–4 rows or columns, and graphs should have no more than 3–4 curves.

2. Easy-to-Spot Consistent Trends

Look for graphs with all the curves heading in the same direction: all up, all down, or all flat. Look for tables with numbers in a consistent direction: up, down, or flat.

3. Numbers, not Words or Symbols

Consistent trends are easier to spot when the figure features numbers, not words or symbols.

4. Short Answers

Look for as many questions as possible with short answers, specifically answers with numbers and short relationship words like "increase" or "decrease."

5. Your Science POOD

Don't forget to factor in your familiarity and comfort with the topic when spotting good Now passages. For example, if you've just studied DNA, a passage on DNA will strike you as easier, regardless of how the figures look.

Now Versus Easy

We are deliberately calling these Now passages rather than Easy passages. That's because even a passage with simple figures will have one or two tough questions. But no need to panic—the toughest questions are easier to crack when you get the central trends and relationships. On passages with incomprehensible figures, the easiest questions will take you longer because you will keep asking yourself, "What is this saying again?" You'll always work good Now passages more quickly, and good time management is what the ACT is all about.

PACING

With just 35 minutes to read as many as 7 passages and answer 40 questions, you have an average of just under six minutes for every passage. But should you spend exactly equal time on every passage? Of course not. If you make smart choices of good Now passages, you should be able to work them in less time, leaving yourself more time for the tougher passages. Think about the pacing chart we discussed in Chapter 1. Think about how many points you will likely need to hit your goal.

Be Ruthless and Flexible

Every Now passage will have at least one tough question, just as every Later passage will have at least one or two easy questions. Use Chapters 5–7 to practice, but even on the Now passages, know when to guess on a tough question and move onto the next passage. Don't let one tough question drag you down.

Need More Practice?
1,523 ACT Practice Questions provides 6 tests' worth of Science passages.

PROCESS OF ELIMINATION (POE)

The most direct Science questions will ask you to look up a value or a relationship. The most complex will ask you to synthesize information or draw a conclusion. The more difficult the question, the less it will help to just stare at the figure waiting for divine guidance to help you magically *see* the answer. As is often the case on the ACT, spotting the wrong answers can be much easier than magically divining the right answers. In our 3-step Basic Approach, we'll discuss in greater detail how to use POE.

THE BASIC APPROACH

The most efficient way to boost your Science score is to pick your order and apply our 3-step Basic Approach to passages with figures. Follow our smart, effective strategy to earn as many points as you can.

> **Science Reading**
> The Science Reading passage is fundamentally different from the passages with figures and requires a different approach.

Step 1: Work the Figures

Take 10–30 seconds to review your figures. What are the variables? What are the units? In what direction do the variables move?

Graphs present trends visually. For tables, you need to make it visual. Mark the trends for each variable with an arrow. Here are three tables from a good Now passage with the trends marked.

STEP 1

Passage II

Table 1	
Angle between axis of first and second filters (degrees)	Intensity of emerging beam (W/m^2)
0	4.00
15	3.73
30	2.99
45	2.01
60	1.00
75	0.27
90	0.00

↑   ↓

Table 2	
Angle between axis of first and second filters (degrees)	Intensity of emerging beam (W/m^2)
0	8.00
15	7.46
30	6.01
45	3.99
60	2.00
75	0.54
90	0.00

↑   ↓

Table 3	
Angle between axis of first and second filters (degrees)	Intensity of emerging beam (W/m²)
0	6.01
15	5.60
30	4.49
45	2.99
60	1.50
75	0.41
90	0.00

↑ ↓

STEP 2 » Step 2: Work the Questions

For each question, look up the value or relationship on the figure(s) as directed. Use your POOD to mark tougher questions as Later questions. Read the passage text if and only when you can't answer a question from the figures.

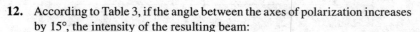

Try an example.

12. According to Table 3, if the angle between the axes of polarization increases by 15°, the intensity of the resulting beam:

    F. halves.
    G. doubles.
    H. increases, but not by any constant factor.
    J. decreases, but not by any constant factor.

Here's how you might use the POOD strategy on ACT Science questions.

Here's How to Crack It

Because you've already marked the trends, you know that as the angle increases, the intensity decreases. Eliminate (G) and (H). Next, look at how the numbers change. From 0 to 15 degrees, the intensity decreases by only 0.41, which is not half of 6.01. Eliminate (F) and choose (J).

Passages with figures will include actual text. Read the passage intros and experiment descriptions *only* when you can't answer a question from a figure.

Try another example.

○

---

10. How does the setup of Experiment 1 differ from that of Experiment 2 ?

    F. In Experiment 1, the original beam was polarized, but in Experiment 2, it was unpolarized.

    G. In Experiment 1, the original beam was unpolarized, but in Experiment 2, it was polarized.

    H. In Experiment 1, the scientists tested a wider range of angles than they did in Experiment 2.

    J. In Experiment 1, the original beam of light was more intense than the one in Experiment 2.

Here's How to Crack It

The range of angles in both Table 1 and Table 2 is the same, so you can eliminate (H). It's hard to tell from the tables what the "original" intensity of the beam of light was, and the tables give no information about polarization, so now is the time to read the experiment descriptions.

Experiment 1

    The scientists used a laser emitting unpolarized light. The light was directed toward a polarization filter with an axis of polarization pointing straight up, and then through another whose axis of polarization varied. The scientists chose to describe the axis of the second filter by examining the angle between its axis and the axis of the first filter. The intensity of the original beam was 8 W/m^2 (watts per square meter). Their results are shown in Table 1.

Experiment 2

    The scientists repeated the experimental setup of Experiment 1 but used a laser emitting polarized light with an axis of polarization pointing straight up. The intensity of the original beam was still 8 W/m^2. The results are shown in Table 2.

Since both experiments started with an intensity of 8 W/m^2, eliminate (J). The light in Experiment 1 was unpolarized, while the light in Experiment 2 was polarized. Choice (G) correctly describes this set-up.

○

Step 3: Work the Answers

In Question 12, the central task involved looking up a relationship you'd already marked. You used POE to eliminate two answers, but from the beginning, you were in command of the question. On Question 10, good POE eliminated (H) and (J). Once you have it narrowed down to (F) and (G), you could either choose (G) because it's supported by the passage, or eliminate (F) because it isn't supported and then choose (G) because it's the only one left.

On more difficult questions, POE will always be the best bet. You might be asked to synthesize information from several figures, evaluate a hypothesis, or draw a conclusion, and it will always be easier to eliminate answer choices that contradict the figures and/or passage.

Try another example.

11. The scientists hypothesize that the color of the original beam of light will affect the intensity of the emerging beam. The frequency of a beam of light determines its color. Which of the following would be the best way to test this hypothesis?

 A. Repeating the experiments using more than two polarizing filters
 B. Repeating the experiments on different planets
 C. Repeating the experiments using beams of both high and low frequencies
 D. Repeating the experiments using different intensities for the original beam

Remember POE
If you're stuck, don't forget about POE. It can get you out of a tight spot!

Here's How to Crack It

Use POE. Whenever a question asks about how to test something, eliminate answers that have nothing to do with the goal. The question identifies color as an important variable on intensity and identifies frequency as the determinant of color. Eliminate any choice that doesn't address color or frequency. Only (C) is left standing.

Repeat

Make your way through the rest of the questions, repeating steps 2 and 3. Look up answers in the figures, and read only when you can't answer a question based on the figures. For questions that don't involve numbers and increase/decrease relationships, POE is the way to go.

Let's try the Basic Approach on a sample Now passage.

Passage I

Electromagnets are used in a variety of industrial processes and often consist of a large *solenoid*, a helical coil of wire, that produces a uniform *magnetic field strength* when a current passes through it (see Figure 1).

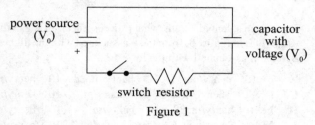

power source
(V_0)

capacitor
with
voltage (V_0)

switch resistor

Figure 1

The magnetic field of a solenoid is a factor of its resistance to changes in current, a property called *inductance* (L). The *relative permeability*, μ, is a property of the material within the solenoid coils which may magnify the magnetic field strength.

Figure 2 shows how magnetic field strength varies with the number of coils (N) at different currents (I) when the length and cross-sectional area of the solenoid is held constant.

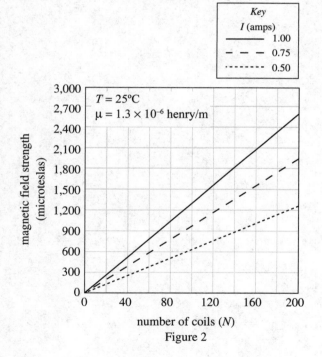

Key

I (amps)
——— 1.00
– – – 0.75
········· 0.50

$T = 25°C$
$\mu = 1.3 \times 10^{-6}$ henry/m

magnetic field strength (microteslas)

number of coils (N)

Figure 2

Figure 3 shows, for specific values of A (cross-sectional area of the solenoid) and N, how L varies with solenoid length at 25°C.

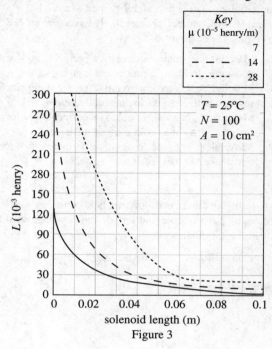

Key
μ (10^{-5} henry/m)
——— 7
– – – 14
········· 28

$T = 25°C$
$N = 100$
$A = 10$ cm²

L (10^{-3} henry)

solenoid length (m)

Figure 3

1. For the conditions specified in Figure 2 and $I = 0.75$ amps, the solenoid will attract iron metal particles most strongly when the number of coils is closest to which of the following?

   A. 0 coils
   B. 40 coils
   C. 120 coils
   D. 200 coils

2. According to Figure 2, does magnetic field strength vary with current?

   F. Yes; as current decreases, magnetic field strength increases.
   G. Yes; as current increases, magnetic field strength increases.
   H. No; as current decreases, magnetic field strength increases.
   J. No; as current remains the same, magnetic field strength increases.

3. Suppose that Material X and Material Y are two common materials used to make solenoid coils and that Material X has a higher relative permeability than Material Y. Based on Figure 3, which material most likely has a greater resistance to changes in current?

   A. Material X; because as relative permeability increases, resistance to changes in current increases.

   B. Material X; because as relative permeability increases, resistance to changes in current decreases.

   C. Material Y; because as relative permeability increases, resistance to changes in current increases.

   D. Material Y; because as relative permeability increases, resistance to changes in current decreases.

4. Assuming all other conditions are held constant, which of the following pairs of solenoid length and μ values would have the highest inductance?

	length (m)	μ (henry/m)
F.	0.02	5×10^{-5}
G.	0.03	5×10^{-5}
H.	0.02	9×10^{-5}
J.	0.03	9×10^{-5}

5. According to Figure 3, for $\mu = 14 \times 10^{-5}$ henry/m, as the length of the solenoid increases, L:

   A. increases only.

   B. decreases only.

   C. varies, but with no consistent trend.

   D. remains the same.

6. For a given solenoid length, what is the correct ranking of the values of μ in Figure 3, from the μ associated with the highest L to the μ associated with the lowest L?

   F. 7×10^{-5} henry/m, 14×10^{-5} henry/m, 28×10^{-5} henry/m

   G. 14×10^{-5} henry/m, 28×10^{-5} henry/m, 7×10^{-5} henry/m

   H. 7×10^{-5} henry/m, 28×10^{-5} henry/m, 14×10^{-5} henry/m

   J. 28×10^{-5} henry/m, 14×10^{-5} henry/m, 7×10^{-5} henry/m

7. Based on Figure 2, a solenoid containing 100 coils with a magnetic field strength of 300 would most likely have been produced by a current:

   A. less than 0.50 amps.

   B. between 0.50 and 0.75 amps.

   C. between 0.75 and 1.00 amps.

   D. greater than 1.00 amps.

Take a minute to consider what makes this a now passage:

1. Small Tables and Graphs ☑
2. Easy-to-Spot Consistent Trends ☑
3. Numbers, not Words or Symbols ☑
4. Short Answers ☑

Now that you've established that you want to work this passage Now, let's dive into the Basic Approach.

Step 1: **Work the Figures**

Take 10–30 seconds to examine the figures. Figure 1 doesn't show any trends or variables, so focus most of your energy on Figures 2 and 3.

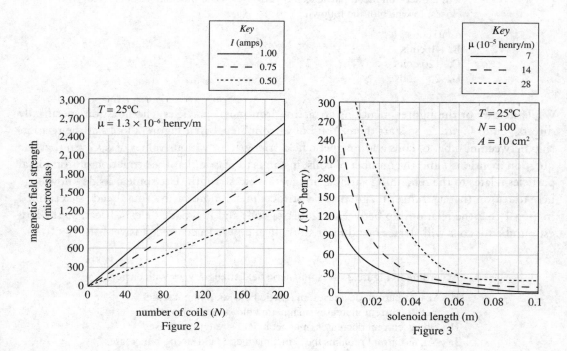

Figure 2

Figure 3

Key information to take note of in Figure 2:

- The *x*-axis shows the number of coils (*N*) and the *y*-axis shows the magnetic field strength (in microteslas).
- The graph shows a direct relationship (as one increases, so does the other) between *N* and magnetic field strength for all three lines.
- The three different lines represent different values of *I* in amps.

Key information to take note of in Figure 3:

- The x-axis shows the solenoid length (in m) and the y-axis shows L (in 10^{-3} henry).
- The graph shows an inverse relationship (as one increases, the other decreases) between solenoid length and L for all three lines.
- The three different lines represent different values of μ in 10^{-5} henry/m. Don't worry if you don't know what 10^{-3} henry/m or 10^{-5} henry/m means; for now it's enough to just know that those are the units the graph uses.

Step 2: Work the Questions and
Step 3: Work the Answers

1. For the conditions specified in Figure 2 and $I = 0.75$ amps, the solenoid will attract iron metal particles most strongly when the number of coils is closest to which of the following?

    A. 0 coils
    B. 40 coils
    C. 120 coils
    D. 200 coils

While neither of the figures mentions attracting iron metal particles, the question specifically directs you to Figure 2, so start there. You know from Step 1 that Figure 2 looks at the relationship between number of coils and magnetic field strength for various values of I. Given that the question mentions I and the number of coils, it stands to reason that the attraction of iron metal particles relates to the remaining variable: magnetic field strength. Use some outside knowledge here to reason that a stronger magnetic field attracts metal more easily. You already determined in Step 1 that the relationship between number of coils and magnetic field is direct, so the largest number of coils will attract metal most strongly at any I. The correct answer is (D).

2. According to Figure 2, does magnetic field strength vary with current?

    F. Yes; as current decreases, magnetic field strength increases.
    G. Yes; as current increases, magnetic field strength increases.
    H. No; as current decreases, magnetic field strength increases.
    J. No; as current remains the same, magnetic field strength increases.

Current isn't mentioned by name in Figure 2, but a quick glance at the passage text introducing Figure 2 identifies I as current. Since the three lines that represent different currents have different magnetic field strengths at every number of coils except $N = 0$, the magnetic field strength *does* vary with current. Eliminate (H) and (J). The solid line, which represents $I = 1.00$ amps has the highest magnetic field strength at each number of coils. The lowest current, $I = 0.50$ amps, has the lowest magnetic field strength. Therefore, as current increases, the magnetic field strength increases, which is (G).

Question 3 is a good time to implement your POOD strategy. This question is longer and wordier than many of the others, so save it for Later when you are more familiar with the passage. Question 4 can wait as well since it involves synthesizing information from two different trends. Let's move on to Question 5, which is short, has short answers, and only involves a single relationship.

5. According to Figure 3, for $\mu = 14 \times 10^{-5}$ henry/m, as the length of the solenoid increases, L:

    A. increases only.
    B. decreases only.
    C. varies, but with no consistent trend.
    D. remains the same.

In Step 1, you already determined that for all three values of μ, the value of L decreases as the length of the solenoid increases. The answer is (B).

6. For a given solenoid length, what is the correct ranking of the values of μ in Figure 3, from the μ associated with the highest L to the μ associated with the lowest L ?

    F. 7×10^{-5} henry/m, 14×10^{-5} henry/m, 28×10^{-5} henry/m
    G. 14×10^{-5} henry/m, 28×10^{-5} henry/m, 7×10^{-5} henry/m
    H. 7×10^{-5} henry/m, 28×10^{-5} henry/m, 14×10^{-5} henry/m
    J. 28×10^{-5} henry/m, 14×10^{-5} henry/m, 7×10^{-5} henry/m

You can pick any solenoid length greater than zero in Figure 3 to spot the trend. At any solenoid length, the dotted line that represents $\mu = 28 \times 10^{-5}$ henry/m is above the other two lines, indicating that $\mu = 28 \times 10^{-5}$ henry/m has the highest L value. Eliminate (F), (G), and (H) because they do not list 28×10^{-5} henry/m first. Only (J) is left.

7. Based on Figure 2, a solenoid containing 100 coils with a magnetic field strength of 300 would most likely have been produced by a current:

    A. less than 0.50 amps.
    B. between 0.50 and 0.75 amps.
    C. between 0.75 and 1.00 amps.
    D. greater than 1.00 amps.

Find 100 coils on the x-axis in Figure 2. At this point, the lowest magnetic field strength of the three lines shown is approximately 500 microteslas at $I = 0.50$ amps. Since you already determined in Question 2 that magnetic field strength increases with increasing current, a magnetic field strength of 300 microteslas would correspond to a current of less than 0.50 amps, which matches (A).

It's time to use what you've learned on all the Now questions to tackle the two questions you saved for Later. Try Question 4 first:

4. Assuming all other conditions are held constant, which of the following pairs of solenoid length and μ values would have the highest inductance?

	length (m)	μ (henry/m)
F.	0.02	5×10^{-5}
G.	0.03	5×10^{-5}
H.	0.02	9×10^{-5}
J.	0.03	9×10^{-5}

The question asks for the highest *inductance*, which is not a term that appears in the figures. This is where a small amount of reading is required. Look through the passage text for the word *inductance*. The second paragraph says *the magnetic field of a solenoid is a factor of its resistance to changes in current, a property called inductance (L)*. In Step 1, you've already identified that as solenoid length increases, L decreases. Since the question asks for the *highest* inductance, the solenoid length should be the smallest option. Eliminate (G) and (J). You've also identified in Question 6 that the highest μ (28×10^{-5} henry/m) is associated with the highest L (inductance). Eliminate (F) because it has a lower μ . The correct answer is (H).

Finally, look back at Question 3:

3. Suppose that Material X and Material Y are two common materials used to make solenoid coils and that Material X has a higher relative permeability than Material Y. Based on Figure 3, which material most likely has a greater resistance to changes in current?

A. Material X; because as relative permeability increases, resistance to changes in current increases.
B. Material X; because as relative permeability increases, resistance to changes in current decreases.
C. Material Y; because as relative permeability increases, resistance to changes in current increases.
D. Material Y; because as relative permeability increases, resistance to changes in current decreases.

POE is a great option for this question. Start by eliminating any answers that are illogical. Given that Material X has a higher relative permeability, if resistance to changes in current increases as relative permeability increases, then Material Y cannot have a greater resistance to changes in current. Eliminate (C). Likewise, if resistance to changes in current increases as relative permeability decreases, Material X cannot have a greater resistance to changes in current. Eliminate (B). In Question 4, you identified that resistance to changes in current is inductance, (L). Look back at the passage text for a reference to *relative permeability*. In the second paragraph the passage states: *The relative permeability, μ, is a property of the material within the solenoid coils....* Therefore, the question is asking about the relationship between μ and L. You've already determined in Questions 4 and 6 that the highest μ leads to the highest L, so as relative permeability increases, resistance to changes in current also increases. Eliminate (D). The correct answer is (A).

LATER PASSAGES

The Basic Approach works on all passages with figures, not just the Now passages featuring consistent trends in tables and graphs.

Step 1: Work the Figures

Some ACT passages will feature an illustration, a diagram, or tables and graphs with no consistent trends. Take 10–15 seconds to review the figure. When there are no consistent trends, a figure doesn't reveal the main point as readily. You'll learn the main point as you work the questions and answers. Don't spend too much time looking for patterns or trends—if you don't see any, move on to Step 2.

Step 2: Work the Questions

Even on Later passages, several questions will ask you to look something up on the figure. The more confusing the figure, however, the more likely you are to waste valuable time trying to figure everything out from staring at the figure, waiting for a flash of inspiration to hit. Use your POOD to seek out the most straightforward questions in a passage to tackle first. Many questions will ask you to look something up on the figures. For more complicated questions, move to Step 3 and use POE.

Step 3: Work the Answers

The wordier the answers, the more you should use POE. Start by eliminating answer choices that contradict the figures. If necessary, use key words from the question and/or answer choices to find relevant information in the text of the passage. Above all, remember not to get stuck on the hard questions—you may be better off moving to the easier questions on the next passage!

PRACTICE

Try the Basic Approach on your own. Start with the Now passages in Chapter 5 before moving on to the Later Passages in Chapter 6.

Chapter 4
Science Reading
Strategy

SCIENCE READING

The Science Reading passage contains questions about two or more viewpoints, theories, or hypotheses regarding the same scientific topic. The ACT calls them "Conflicting Viewpoints," but we call them Science Reading because while they sometimes have figures, the majority of the information necessary to answer the questions comes from the passage text. There is no way around reading on the Science Reading passage!

Now or Later?

These passages may be Now, Later, or Never passages for you, depending on your POOD. If you're a strong reader or there are some particularly tricky Later passages in the test, you might do the Science Reading passage between the Now passages and the Later passages. Otherwise, do it Later or Never.

Recognizing the Science Reading Passage

Since this passage requires a different approach, it's important that you know how to recognize it. Here are the key things that all Science Reading passages have in common:

- A lot of text: approximately half of the Science Reading passages will have some type of figure, but ALL will have a significant amount of text.
- 2–4 different viewpoints: the viewpoints (sometimes called theories or hypotheses) are usually presented as Students 1–4 or Scientists 1–4, and each viewpoint is separated under its own italicized heading.
- 7 questions: these questions will be a mix of viewpoint specific questions and comparing viewpoints questions.

Science Reading Basic Approach

Apply our 4-step Science Reading Basic Approach to earn as many points as you can. Let's work through it with a sample Science Reading passage.

Step 1: Preview

First, read the introduction to see what scientific topic the viewpoints are addressing. Unlike many of the other Science passages, you cannot skip the introduction! Generally, the longer the introduction is, the more important it is.

A group of students added 100 mg of Salt A to an Erlenmeyer flask containing 100 mL of water at 20°C. The mixture was heated over a Bunsen burner, and a thermometer was placed in the flask to acquire temperature readings (Figure 1).

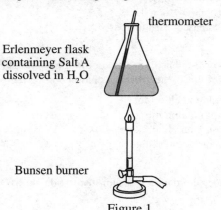

Figure 1

Table 1			
Salt	Ions produced	Molar mass (g/mol)	ΔH°_{diss} (kJ/mol)
Sodium chloride	2	58.4	+3.9
Calcium chloride	3	111.0	−81.2
Ammonium nitrate	2	80.1	+25.7
Potassium hydroxide	2	56.11	−57.6
Magnesium sulfate	2	120.38	−91.0

The mixture was heated, and temperature readings were acquired every 30 sec until the solution reached a full boil and the solid had completely dissolved. The boiling temperature for the solution was measured to be 104°C. The procedure was repeated with Salt B, which resulted in a boiling temperature of 110°C.

The teacher asked 3 of the students in the group to explain why the solutions had different boiling temperatures.

The number of ions produced, molar mass, and enthalpy change dissolution (ΔH°_{diss}) of some common salts are shown in Table 1.

Table 1 shows some properties of some common salts. There aren't any obvious trends to note in Table 1, so don't spend too much time trying to make sense of it yet. Before you move on though, determine what topic the students are discussing. The students are discussing different explanations for *why the solutions had different boiling points.*

Next, go straight to the questions and identify which viewpoint you'll need to read in order to answer the question. Any question that just covers Student 1, should be labeled "1," any passage that just covers Student 2 should be labeled "2," and any question that just covers Student 3 should be labeled "3." For questions that cover all 3, write "all."

all 1. Suppose that Salt A had been potassium hydroxide and Salt B had been magnesium sulfate. The results of the experiment would have supported the explanation(s) provided by which student(s)?

   A. Student 2 only
   B. Student 3 only
   C. Students 1 and 3 only
   D. Students 2 and 3 only

2 2. Suppose that the students also tested ammonium nitrate in the experiment and found it to have resulted in a boiling temperature in solution of 107°C. Student 2 would claim that ammonium nitrate:

   F. has a greater molar mass than Salt A, but a smaller molar mass than Salt B.
   G. has a greater molar mass than Salt B, but a smaller molar mass than Salt A.
   H. has a greater enthalpy change of dissolution than Salt A, but a smaller enthalpy change of dissolution than Salt B.
   J. has a greater enthalpy change of dissolution than Salt B, but a smaller enthalpy change of dissolution than Salt A.

2 3. Which of the following graphs of the relative number of particles produced is most consistent with Student 2's explanation?

   A.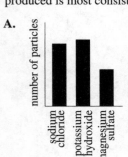
   B.

   C.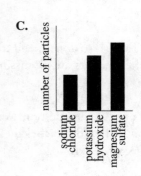
   D.

all 4. Over the course of the experiment, the readings on the thermometer:

   F. increased only.
   G. decreased only.
   H. increased, then decreased.
   J. decreased, then increased.

3 5. Based on Student 3's explanation, which of the salts in Table 1 would result in the greatest solution boiling temperature?

   A. Calcium chloride
   B. Ammonium nitrate
   C. Potassium hydroxide
   D. Magnesium sulfate

all 6. Consider the data for cesium hydroxide shown in the table below:

Ions produced	Molar mass (g/mol)	$\Delta H°_{diss}$ (kJ/mol)
2	149.91	−71.6

Which student(s), if any, would predict that cesium hydroxide would produce a solution with a lower boiling temperature than calcium chloride?

   F. Student 1 only
   G. Students 2 and 3 only
   H. Students 1, 2, and 3
   J. None of the students

2 7. Is the claim "If equal amounts of salt are dissolved, sodium chloride will result in a greater boiling point than ammonium nitrate" consistent with Student 2's explanation?

   A. No, because sodium chloride has a smaller molar mass than ammonium nitrate.
   B. No, because sodium chloride has a more negative enthalpy change of dissolution.
   C. Yes, because sodium chloride has a smaller molar mass than ammonium nitrate.
   D. Yes, because sodium chloride has a more negative enthalpy change of dissolution.

Step 2: **One Side at a Time**

Read one viewpoint and answer all questions on that viewpoint only. Sometimes there are not many stand-alone viewpoint specific questions, while sometimes over half of the questions are viewpoint specific. Usually you will start with Viewpoint 1, but in this case, 3 of the 7 questions refer to Student 2 only, while none of them refer to Student 1 only. In situations in which one viewpoint is relevant to more questions than the others, it's good to start there.

Student 2

The solution containing Salt B had a higher boiling point because it had a lower *molar mass* (the mass of 6.02×10^{23} particles). Consider equal amounts of two salts with different molar masses. The salt with the greater molar mass will require more mass to result in the same number of particles. Since more heat energy is required to boil water with more interactions, the solution with more salt particles will boil at a higher temperature. Thus, if equal amounts of two salts with different molar masses are added, the salt with the lower molar mass will result in more particles and a greater solution boiling point than a salt with a greater molar mass.

Recall that the topic is why the solutions boiled at different temperatures. Student 2's response can be summarized as the following: a smaller molar mass leads to a higher boiling point. Try Question 2:

2. Suppose that the students also tested ammonium nitrate in the experiment and found it to have resulted in a boiling temperature in solution of 107°C. Student 2 would claim that ammonium nitrate:

    F. has a greater molar mass than Salt A, but a smaller molar mass than Salt B.
    G. has a greater molar mass than Salt B, but a smaller molar mass than Salt A.
    H. has a greater enthalpy change of dissolution than Salt A, but a smaller enthalpy change of dissolution than Salt B.
    J. has a greater enthalpy change of dissolution than Salt B, but a smaller enthalpy change of dissolution than Salt A.

Use POE. Eliminate (H) and (J) because Student 2 never mentions *enthalpy change of dissolution*. Choice (F) means that Salt B has the greatest molar mass of the three solutions, but Student 2 states specifically that Salt B had a *smaller molar mass* than Salt A, so eliminate (F). Since the boiling point for ammonium nitrate is in between the boiling points mentioned in the introduction for Salt A and Salt B, Student 2 would claim the molar mass of ammonium nitrate was greater than that of Salt B, but less than that of Salt A. The correct answer is (G).

3. Which of the following graphs of the relative number of particles produced is most consistent with Student 2's explanation?

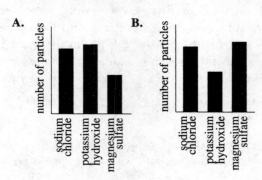

Refer back to Student 2's discussion and look for the term *particles*. Student 2 says *if equal amounts of two salts with different molar masses are added, the salt with the smaller molar mass will result in more particles*. Student 2 does not mention any of the 3 salts, but Table 1 does. Look to Table 1 to compare the molar masses of the three salts. Potassium hydroxide has the smallest molar mass, at 56.11 g/mol, so Student 2 would expect potassium hydroxide to have the most particles produced. Eliminate (B) and (C) because they show magnesium sulfate with the highest number of particles. Eliminate (D) because potassium hydroxide and magnesium sulfate should not be equal since they do not have the same molar mass. Only (A) is consistent with Student 2's discussion.

7. Is the claim "If equal amounts of salt are dissolved, sodium chloride will result in a greater boiling point than ammonium nitrate" consistent with Student 2's explanation?

   A. No, because sodium chloride has a smaller molar mass than ammonium nitrate.

   B. No, because sodium chloride has a more negative enthalpy change of dissolution.

   C. Yes, because sodium chloride has a smaller molar mass than ammonium nitrate.

   D. Yes, because sodium chloride has a more negative enthalpy change of dissolution.

Rather than tackling the Yes or No first, focus on the reasons and use POE. Since Student 2 did not discuss enthalpy change of dissolution, eliminate (B) and (D). Recall that you've already established that Student 2 believes that a smaller molar mass leads to a higher boiling point. Both (A) and (C) state that sodium chloride has a smaller molar mass, so Student 2 would believe that sodium chloride will have a higher boiling point. This is consistent with the claim, so eliminate (A) and choose (C).

Now that you've finished all of the Student 2 specific questions, it's time to move on to Step 3.

Step 3: The Other Side(s)

Read the next viewpoint and do all the questions that pertain to that viewpoint only. On passages with more than two viewpoints, you will have to repeat this step. Regardless of how many viewpoints there are, read one viewpoint at a time and work any stand-alone questions that pertain to it before moving on to the next viewpoint.

Since Student 3 has a stand-alone question, let's do Student 3 next.

Student 3

The solution containing Salt B had a higher boiling point because Salt B releases more heat upon dissolving than Salt A. The *enthalpy change of dissolution* (ΔH°_{diss}) is a measure of the net amount of heat energy absorbed in the process of dissolving a salt. Salts that absorb more energy to dissolve will have more positive ΔH°_{diss} values and will make the solution cooler. Salts that absorb less energy than they release will have more negative ΔH°_{diss} values and will make the solution warmer. If equal amounts of two salts with different ΔH°_{diss} values are dissolved in solution, the solution containing the salt with the more negative ΔH°_{diss} value will release more heat and thus result in a greater boiling point.

Student 3's viewpoint on why the boiling points differed can be summarized as the following: solutions with a more negative enthalpy change of dissolution (ΔH°_{diss}) will release more heat and thus result in a greater boiling point. Try Question 5:

5. Based on Student 3's explanation, which of the salts in Table 1 would result in the greatest solution boiling temperature?

    A. Calcium chloride
    B. Ammonium nitrate
    C. Potassium hydroxide
    D. Magnesium sulfate

Since Student 3 says that the solutions with more negative ΔH°_{diss} values have greater boiling points, refer to Table 1 to find the solution with the most negative ΔH°_{diss} value. In Table 1, magnesium sulfate has the most negative ΔH°_{diss} value at –91 kJ/mol, so Student 3 would expect magnesium sulfate to have the greatest boiling point temperature. The correct answer is (D).

Next, repeat Step 3 with the final viewpoint: Student 1.

Student 1

The solution containing Salt B had a higher boiling point because Salt B produces more ions in solution than Salt A. As the solid dissolves, the salt ionizes and interacts with water molecules. This causes more interactions between the ions and water, thus requiring more energy for water molecules to break these interactions and become a gas (boiling). Since salts become ions in solution, salts that produce more ions will have more interactions with water than salts producing fewer ions. Thus, if two salts of equal amounts are added to water, the solution containing the salt that produces more ions will boil at the higher temperature.

There are no stand-alone questions about Student 1, but it's still good to take note of Student 1's position before you move on to Step 4. Student 1's viewpoint can be summarized as the following: solutions with more ions will boil at higher temperatures.

Now that you have a good idea of what the students believe and how they differ, it's time to move on to Step 4.

Step 4: Compare and Contrast

Always save all of the compare and contrast questions for last. You'll have a much easier time keeping track of who said what, how they agree, and how they disagree at this point. Use POE as much as possible.

Try Question 4 first because it is short and has short answers:

> **4.** Over the course of the experiment, the readings on the thermometer:
>
> **F.** increased only.
> **G.** decreased only.
> **H.** increased, then decreased.
> **J.** decreased, then increased.

None of the students discussed a thermometer, so refer back to the introduction. Figure 1 shows a thermometer, and the description below it states that *the mixture was heated, and temperature readings were acquired every 30 sec until the solution reached a full boil and the solid had completely dissolved.* Since the mixture is only heated, it can be inferred that its temperature increased only. There's no indication that the substance is ever cooled, so (F) is the only answer supported by information from the passage.

Next, try Question 1:

> **1.** Suppose that Salt A had been potassium hydroxide and Salt B had been magnesium sulfate. The results of the experiment would have supported the explanation(s) provided by which student(s)?
>
> **A.** Student 2 only
> **B.** Student 3 only
> **C.** Students 1 and 3 only
> **D.** Students 2 and 3 only

According to the introduction, Salt A had a boiling point of 104°C and Salt B had a boiling point of 110°C. If Salt A is potassium hydroxide and Salt B is magnesium sulfate, you need to determine which student(s)' explanations would predict that magnesium sulfate would have a higher boiling point than potassium hydroxide. Use POE. Since Student 3 is in most of the answers, start with Student 3. You already determined in Question 5 that Student 3 would expect magnesium sulfate to have the highest boiling point due to the fact that it has the most negative ΔH°_{diss} value. Therefore, Student 3's theory is supported by the results of the experiment. Eliminate (A). Student 2 believes a smaller molar mass leads to a higher boiling point, so look at Table 1 to compare the molar masses of magnesium sulfate and potassium hydroxide. According to Table 1, the molar mass of magnesium sulfate (120.38 g/mol) is greater than that of potassium hydroxide (56.11 g/mol), so Student 2 would expect potassium hydroxide to have a higher boiling point. This does not agree with the results of the experiment, so eliminate (D). Finally, Student 1 believes that solutions with more ions boil at higher temperatures. According to Table 1, both solutions produce 2 ions, so Student 1 would expect them to boil at the same temperature. Eliminate (C) as this does not match the results of the experiment. Only Student 3's explanation matches the results of the experiment, so the answer is (B).

Finally, finish with Question 6:

6. Consider the data for cesium hydroxide shown in the table below:

Ions produced	Molar mass (g/mol)	ΔH°_{diss} (kJ/mol)
2	149.91	−71.6

Which student(s), if any, would predict that cesium hydroxide would produce a solution with a lower boiling temperature than calcium chloride?

F. Student 1 only
G. Students 2 and 3 only
H. Students 1, 2, and 3
J. None of the students

Compare the new values given in the question to those for calcium chloride given in Table 1 and use POE. Cesium hydroxide produces 2 ions, while calcium chloride produces 3. Since Student 1 believes that solutions with more ions have higher boiling points, Student 1 would agree with the prediction that cesium hydroxide, with fewer ions, would have a lower boiling point than calcium chloride. Eliminate (G) and (J). Cesium hydroxide has a molar mass 149.91 g/mol, while calcium chloride has a molar mass of 111.0 g/mol. Student 2 believes that solutions with smaller molar masses have higher boiling points. Therefore, Student 2 would agree with the prediction that cesium hydroxide, with a greater molar mass, would have a lower boiling temperature. Eliminate (F). The only option left is (H).

PRACTICE

You can apply this same basic approach to the Science Reading passage regardless of whether there are 2, 3, or 4 different viewpoints. Try it yourself with the practice passages in Chapter 7, then try the complete tests in Part III. Make sure to go through your answers and consider how you can improve after each practice test before attempting the next!

Chapter 5
Now Passages

Passage I

Reduction by carbon process, thermite process, and reduction by heating alone are different ways of converting a metal oxide to pure metal. Reactions 1–3 are examples of these processes using zinc oxide, manganese dioxide, and mercuric oxide, respectively.

Reaction 1: $ZnO + C \rightarrow Zn + CO$

Reaction 2: $3MnO_2 + 4Al \rightarrow 3Mn + 2Al_2O_3$

Reaction 3: $2HgO \xrightarrow{\text{heating}} 2Hg + O_2$

In each case, the resulting sample is composed of the metal and another product, which is filtered out to leave only the pure metal.

Figures 1–3 below show how *percent pure metal* (% PM) varied as a function of time in Reactions 1–3, respectively, both in the absence and the presence of a magnetic field.

$$\% \text{ PM} = \frac{\text{mass of pure metal}}{\text{mass of metal oxide } + \text{ mass of pure metal}} \times 100$$

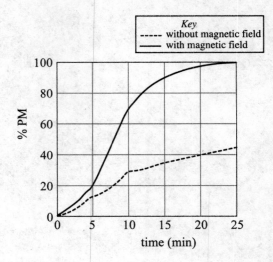

Figure 2

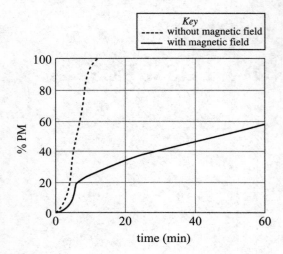

Figure 1

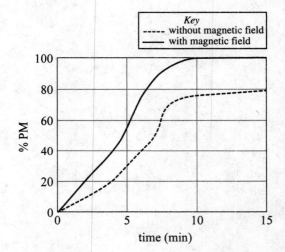

Figure 3

1. According to Figure 1, during Reaction 1 with a magnetic field, the % PM observed at 20 min was approximately:

   A. 20%.
   B. 25%.
   C. 35%.
   D. 40%.

2. Suppose that during Reaction 3 with a magnetic field, the magnetic field had been removed at time = 5 min. Three minutes later, at time = 8 min, the % PM would most likely have been:

   F. less than 20%.
   G. between 20% and 40%.
   H. between 40% and 60%.
   J. greater than 60%.

3. According to Figure 2, in Reaction 2, how did the absence of a magnetic field affect the yield of pure metal at time = 20 min? The yield obtained without a magnetic field was about:

   A. $\frac{2}{5}$ the yield obtained with a magnetic field.

   B. $\frac{4}{5}$ the yield obtained with a magnetic field.

   C. $2\frac{1}{2}$ times that of the yield obtained with a magnetic field.

   D. 3 times the yield obtained with a magnetic field.

4. A chemist claimed that separating pure metal using a magnetic field is always faster than without a magnetic field. Do Figures 1–3 support this claim?

   F. No; in Reaction 1 the % PM reached 0% sooner without a magnetic field than with a magnetic field.
   G. No; in Reaction 1 the % PM reached 100% sooner without a magnetic field than with a magnetic field.
   H. Yes; the % PM consistently reached 0% sooner with a magnetic field for all three reactions than without.
   J. Yes; the % PM consistently reached 100% sooner with a magnetic field for all three reactions than without.

5. If Reaction 3 had been graphed as *percent of metal oxide* (% MO) as time increases instead of % PM:

$$\% \text{ MO} = \frac{\text{mass of metal oxide}}{\text{mass of metal oxide} + \text{mass of pure metal}} \times 100$$

   Which of the following graphs best represents how Figure 3 would have appeared?

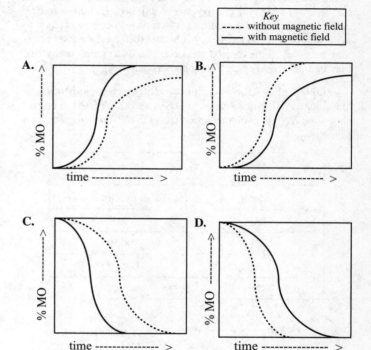

6. Suppose Reaction 2 and Reaction 3 were started at the same time in the presence of a magnetic field. Which metal, manganese or mercury, would reach 50% PM first, and how much faster would it be?

   F. The manganese will reach 50% PM approximately 3.5 minutes before the mercury.
   G. The mercury will reach 50% PM approximately 3.5 minutes before the manganese.
   H. The manganese will reach 50% PM approximately 8 minutes before the mercury.
   J. The mercury will reach 50% PM approximately 8 minutes before the manganese.

Passage II

When light strikes a metal surface, the energy of the photons is transferred to the metal surface and frees electrons from the metal in a process called the *photoelectric effect*. The energy required to free an electron differs depending on the type of metal and is called the *work function* of the metal. The energy contained within a photon can be determined by that photon's frequency. The *threshold frequency* for a metal, or f_T, is the minimum frequency at which the photon energy will be sufficient to free an electron. This is the frequency at which photon energy is equal to work function. If the frequency is higher than f_T, the extra energy may be given to the ejected electron. The maximum energy that may be transferred at each frequency is called K_{max}.

Table 1 shows the work functions in electron volts (eV) for aluminum, (Al), zinc (Zn), nickel (Ni), and silver (Ag). Figure 1 shows the K_{max} of each metal in relation to the frequency for each of the metals.

Table 1	
Metal	Work function (eV)
Al	4.08
Zn	4.30
Ag	4.73
Ni	5.01

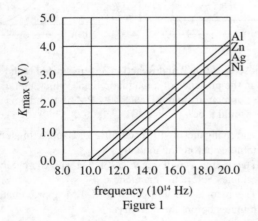

frequency (10^{14} Hz)
Figure 1

1. For a photon to free an electron from Zn, the photon's work function must be at least:

   A. 4.23 eV.
   B. 4.30 eV.
   C. 4.61 eV.
   D. 5.31 eV.

2. Based on Figure 1, which of the following correctly ranks Al, Ni, and Ag in order of increasing K_{max} at 15.0×10^{14} Hz ?

   F. Al, Ag, Ni
   G. Al, Ni, Ag
   H. Ni, Ag, Al
   J. Ni, Al, Ag

3. Based on Table 1 and Figure 1, as frequency increases, K_{max}:

   A. decreases.
   B. increases.
   C. increases, then decreases.
   D. decreases, then increases.

4. Based on Figure 1, for electrons ejected from Al by photons with frequency = 26.0×10^{14} Hz, K_{max} would be:

   F. less than 4.0 eV.
   G. between 4.0 eV and 4.5 eV.
   H. between 4.5 eV and 5.0 eV.
   J. greater than 5.0 eV.

5. Photons having frequencies of 12.0×10^{14} Hz and 18.0×10^{14} Hz strike a new metal, Metal Q, resulting in freed electrons with the following K_{max}:

Photon frequency (10^{14} Hz)	K_{max} (eV)
12.0	0.5 eV
18.0	3.0 eV

   Based on Table 1 and Figure 1, the work function of Metal Q is most likely closest to which of the following?

   A. 4.01 eV
   B. 4.20 eV
   C. 4.28 eV
   D. 4.51 eV

6. Based on Figure 1, the threshold frequency of Ag is approximately:

   F. 3.5×10^{14} Hz.
   G. 11.5×10^{14} Hz.
   H. 16.0×10^{14} Hz.
   J. 20.0×10^{14} Hz.

Passage III

Scientists studied the effects of Drug X on various strains of bacteria in the *Staphylococcus* genus. Table 1 shows the bacteria that were tested and the ED_{50} (the dosage necessary to achieve a therapeutic effect for 50% of the population that is given the medication) of each bacterial strain.

Table 1		
Bacterium	Species	ED_{50} of Drug X (mg/L)
A	*Staphylococcus aureus*	15.3
B	*Staphylococcus carnosus*	30.6
C	*Staphylococcus gallinarum*	22.7
D	*Staphylococcus vitulinus*	91.3
E	*Staphylococcus warneri*	62.6

Six flasks containing 500 mL of nutrient broth were prepared, each with 10,000 cells of *Staphylococcus aureus*. Drug X was then added to five of the flasks in different concentrations, and all six flasks were incubated at 37°C for 24 hours. This procedure was then repeated for the four other bacterial strains. Figure 1 shows the percentage of cells killed for each bacterial strain at each concentration of Drug X.

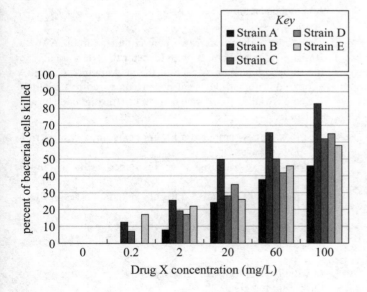

Figure 1

1. According to Figure 1, as the concentration of Drug X increased, the percent of bacterial cells killed from Strain C:

   A. increased, then remained the same.
   B. decreased, then remained the same.
   C. increased only.
   D. decreased only.

2. Based on Table 1, which strain of bacterium requires the highest concentration of Drug X to achieve a therapeutic effect for 50% of the population that is given the medication?

   F. Strain A
   G. Strain B
   H. Strain D
   J. Strain E

3. Based on Figure 1, if cells from Strain B had been treated with Drug X at a concentration of 200 mg/L, the percent of bacterial cells killed would most likely have been:

   A. less than 75%.
   B. between 75% and 80%.
   C. between 80% and 85%.
   D. greater than 85%.

4. According to Table 1, the concentration of Drug X necessary to achieve a therapeutic effect for 50% of the population infected with Strain E was approximately 4 times the concentration of Drug X necessary to achieve a therapeutic effect for 50% of the population infected with:

   F. Strain A.
   G. Strain B.
   H. Strain C.
   J. Strain D.

5. According to Figure 1, which of the following actions leads to the largest increase in the number of Strain E bacterial cells killed by Drug X ?

   A. Increasing the concentration of Drug X from 0 mg/L to 0.2 mg/L
   B. Increasing the concentration of Drug X from 2 mg/L to 20 mg/L
   C. Increasing the concentration of Drug X from 20 mg/L to 60 mg/L
   D. Increasing the concentration of Drug X from 60 mg/L to 100 mg/L

6. A researcher hypothesized that the strain with the lowest therapeutic dose will have more cells killed than any of the other strains at all dosages of Drug X under 30 mg/L. Is this hypothesis supported by the data in Table 1 and Figure 1 ?

   F. Yes; Strain A has the least percentage of bacteria killed at dosages of 0.2, 2, and 20 mg/L.
   G. Yes; Strain B has the least percentage of bacteria killed at dosages of 2 and 20 mg/L.
   H. No; Strain A has the greatest percentage of bacteria killed at dosages of 0.2, 2, and 20 mg/L.
   J. No; Strain B has the greatest percentage of bacteria killed at dosages of 2 and 20 mg/L.

Passage IV

A *resistor* is an object that creates electrical resistance in a circuit.

R is the electrical resistance, in *ohms* (Ω), which describes the tendency of a resistor to oppose electric conduction. Conductance, *G*, in siemens (S), is the inverse of *R*: it describes the tendency of a resistor to allow electric conduction. When a voltage, *V*, in volts (V), is run across a circuit, *R* will affect the resulting current, *I*, measured in amperes (A).

Students tested several different resistors. For each trial, the students applied a series of voltages across a circuit that contained a resistor and measured the resulting current. The students then calculated the power, *P*, in watts (W), delivered through the circuit. *P* is a measure of the rate at which current flows across a circuit.

Study 1

In Trials 1–5, the circuit contained a blue resistor with $R = 0.005\ \Omega$. The results are shown in Table 1. Each trial had a different voltage (*V*) across the circuit.

Table 1			
Trial	V (V)	I (A)	P (W)
1	0.02	4	0.08
2	0.04	8	0.32
3	0.06	12	0.72
4	0.08	16	1.28
5	0.09	18	1.62

Study 2

In Trials 6–10, the circuit contained a red resistor with $R = 0.015\ \Omega$. As in Study 1, each trial had a different voltage (*V*) across the circuit.

Table 2			
Trial	V (V)	I (A)	P (W)
6	0.02	1.3	0.03
7	0.04	2.7	0.11
8	0.06	4	0.24
9	0.08	5.3	0.43
10	0.09	6	0.54

Study 3

In Trials 11–15, the circuit contained a green resistor with $R = 0.040\ \Omega$. As in the prior studies, each trial had a different voltage (*V*) across the circuit.

Table 3			
Trial	V (V)	I (A)	P (W)
11	0.02	0.5	0.01
12	0.04	1	0.04
13	0.06	1.5	0.09
14	0.08	2	0.16
15	0.09	2.2	0.20

1. If an additional trial had been conducted in Study 1 with $V = 0.03$ V, the value of *P* for this additional trial would most likely have been:

   A. less than 0.08 watts.
   B. between 0.08 watts and 0.32 watts.
   C. between 0.32 watts and 0.72 watts.
   D. greater than 1.62 watts.

2. In each study, as the voltage across each circuit increased, the electrical power:

   F. remained the same.
   G. varied, but with no general trend.
   H. decreased only.
   J. increased only.

3. The students then tested two new circuits, Circuit A (with Resistor A) and Circuit B (with Resistor B). The students ran the same voltage across each of the new circuits. Circuit A exhibited a higher electrical power compared to Circuit B. Based on Studies 1–3, which resistor has the higher electrical resistance?

   A. Resistor A, because a higher resistance results in a lower power.
   B. Resistor A, because a lower resistance results in a lower power.
   C. Resistor B, because a higher resistance results in a lower power.
   D. Resistor B, because a lower resistance results in a lower power.

4. In which of the following trials was the *conductance* (*G*) of the circuit the greatest?

   F. Trial 1
   G. Trial 6
   H. Trial 11
   J. Trials 1, 6, and 11 all have the same conductance.

5. Prior to the studies, 4 students made predictions about which of the 3 resistors, if any, would have the lowest P for a given V. Student L predicted that it would be the blue resistor. Student M predicted that it would be the red resistor. Student N predicted that it would be the green resistor, and Student O predicted that all three resistors would have the same P for a given V. Which prediction is correct?

   A. Student L
   B. Student M
   C. Student N
   D. Student O

6. A student concluded that, for a constant resistance, increasing the value of V by a factor of 3 increases the value of P by a factor of 9. Which pair of trials best supports this conclusion?

   F. 1 and 8
   G. 2 and 4
   H. 6 and 13
   J. 11 and 13

7. A fourth resistor, the purple resistor, has a current of 3 A at a voltage of 0.06 V. The resistance of the purple resistor is most likely:

   A. less than 0.005 ohms.
   B. between 0.005 and 0.015 ohms.
   C. between 0.015 and 0.040 ohms.
   D. greater than 0.040 ohms.

Passage V

In 3 studies, students investigated the thermal expansion of rectangular metal rods various lengths and materials (see Figure 1).

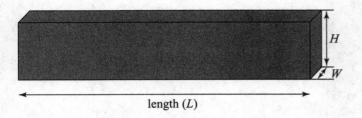

Figure 1

Using the water bath shown in Figure 2, the students heated the rods to different temperatures.

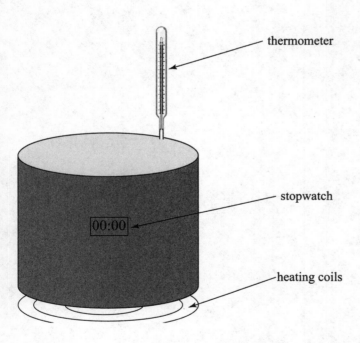

Figure 2

In each trial, the rod was transferred to a water bath preheated to a particular temperature and then allowed to incubate for a set amount of time. During the incubation process, water temperature was kept constant while the metal rods underwent thermal expansion.

After completion of the incubation, the metal rod was removed, and the length, width, and height of the metal rod were promptly measured. After being measured, the metal rod returned to room temperature and reverted to its original dimensions.

The intrinsic thermal expansion of the metal rod was represented by the *volumetric expansion constant, β.*

Study 1

In Trials 1–4, students determined the change in volume, ΔV, for rods of different lengths, L (see Table 1). In every trial, the time of incubation was 30 minutes and the temperature was 80°C.

Table 1		
Trial	L (mm)	ΔV (mm^3)
1	50	1.5
2	100	3.1
3	150	4.5
4	200	5.9

Study 2

In Trials 5–8, students determined ΔV for rods of the same L composed of Metals W–Z, respectively. Each metal had a different value of β (see Table 2). In every trial, L = 100 mm, the time of incubation was 30 minutes, and the temperature was 80°C.

Table 2			
Trial	Metal	β (°C^{-1})	ΔV (mm^3)
5	W	0.8	1.7
6	X	1.4	3.1
7	Y	2.2	4.9
8	Z	4.6	10.2

Study 3

In Trials 9–12, students determined ΔV for rods at different temperatures (see Table 3). In every trial, L = 100 mm, and the incubation time was 30 minutes.

Table 3		
Trial	Temperature (C°)	ΔV (mm^3)
9	40	5.1
10	60	7.7
11	80	10.2
12	100	12.8

1. If density is defined as mass divided by volume, which of the following is true concerning the change in density of the metal beam after incubation in the water bath?

    A. Density increases because the volume increases.
    B. Density decreases because the volume decreases.
    C. Density increases because the mass increases.
    D. Density decreases because the volume increases.

2. If, in Study 3, a trial had been conducted in which the incubation temperature was 70°C, ΔV would most likely have been closest to which of the following?

    F. 6.5 mm^3
    G. 7.2 mm^3
    H. 8.9 mm^3
    J. 10.4 mm^3

3. If the thermal energy contained within the metal rod is proportional to the product of the incubation time and the initial length, in which of the following trials does the rod contain the greatest amount of thermal energy following incubation?

    A. Trial 2
    B. Trial 4
    C. Trial 10
    D. Trial 12

4. The results of Study 1 are best represented by which of the following graphs?

    F.
    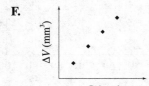
    G.
    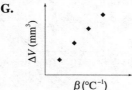
    H.
    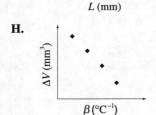
    J.
    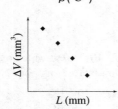

5. The beam tested in Study 3 was most likely composed of which of the metals tested in Study 2 ?

    A. Metal W
    B. Metal X
    C. Metal Y
    D. Metal Z

6. Based on the results of Studies 1 and 2, for a given temperature, which of the following combinations of L and β would yield the greatest thermal expansion?

	L (mm)	β (°C^{-1})
F.	100	2.2
G.	100	4.6
H.	200	2.2
J.	200	4.6

7. In a new study, Study 4, the conditions of Study 2 were replicated except that the bars used in Study 4 were 20% wider than those used in Study 2. Based on the information in Study 1 and Study 2, how would the values of β and ΔV in Trials 13–16 of Study 4 compare to those in Trials 5–8, respectively?

    A. In Trials 13–16, the values of β would be greater than those in Trials 5–8, and the values of ΔV would be the same as those in Trials 5–8.
    B. In Trials 13–16, the values of β would be the same as those in Trials 5–8, and the values of ΔV would be greater than those in Trials 5–8.
    C. In Trials 13–16, the values of β and ΔV would be the same as those in Trials 5–8.
    D. In Trials 13–16, the values of β and ΔV would be greater than those in Trials 5–8.

Passage VI

Ethylene glycol is the main ingredient in antifreeze and has the chemical structure shown below:

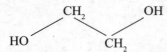

Figures 1–3 show how solutions of antifreeze vary as the concentration of ethylene glycol changes. Concentration is given as the percent ethylene glycol by volume in water (% EG) at atmospheric pressure (101.3 kPa). Figure 1 shows how the melting point (the temperature at which a solid would begin melting) of antifreeze varies with % EG. Figure 2 shows how the boiling point of antifreeze varies with % EG. Figure 3 shows how the density at 25°C varies with % EG.

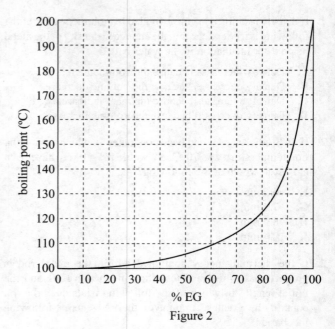

Figure 2

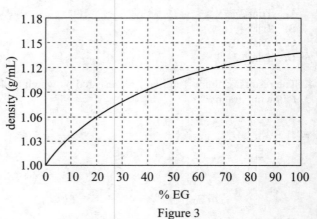

Figure 3

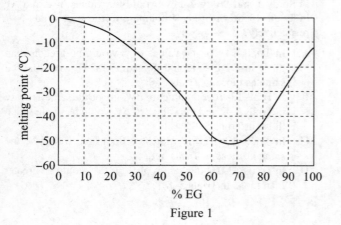

Figure 1

1. At 101.3 kPa, which of the following solutions will have the *lowest* freezing point?

A.   0% EG
B.   33% EG
C.   68% EG
D.   100% EG

2. According to Figure 1, the temperature at which solid anti-freeze begins to melt in a 60% EG solution at 101.3 kPa is closest to which of the following?

F. −60°C
G. −48°C
H. −12°C
J. 0°C

3. Based on Figure 2, which of the following solutions has a boiling point equal to pure water at 101.3 kPa ?

A. 0% EG
B. 13% EG
C. 68% EG
D. 100% EG

4. At 25°C, as the % EG increases from 0% to 100%, the mass per unit volume:

F. increases only.
G. decreases only.
H. increases, then decreases.
J. decreases, then increases.

5. According to Figures 2 and 3, a solution of antifreeze that has a density of 1.09 g/mL at 25°C will have a boiling point closest to which of the following?

A. 100°C
B. 104°C
C. 111°C
D. 122°C

6. Based on the information in the passage, what is the chemical formula for ethylene glycol?

F. $C_2H_6O_2$
G. $C_6H_6O_2$
H. $C_2H_4O_2$
J. C_2H_2O

Passage VII

In 1789, Mt. Mantu erupted off the coast of Brunei, releasing a cloud of ash that lowered global temperatures for 15 years. When a volcano erupts, it releases a cloud of ash, dust, and debris into the atmosphere thousands of times the volume of the volcano. In addition, at the time of the eruption, the volcano produces a mud and ash flow along the sides of the volcano. The ash flow around Mt. Mantu covered an area 30 times larger than the original size of the volcano. Figure 1 shows the volume of the ash clouds released by volcanoes of differing diameters during the last 200 million years.

Figure 2 shows the average amount of time elapsed between consecutive major eruptions of various volcanoes of similar sizes, for a range of volcano sizes. Figure 3 shows the number of major volcanic eruptions of various volcanic ash flow diameters over the past 1,000 years for three different mountain ranges.

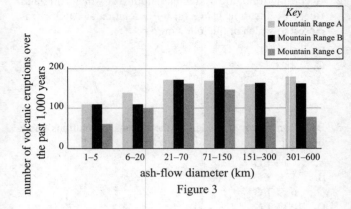

Figure 3

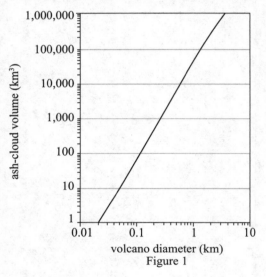

Figure 1

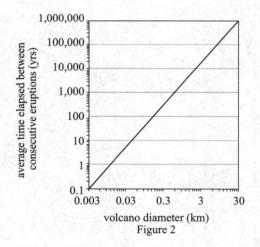

Figure 2

1. If 100 km³ of ash was released by Mt. Mantu, according to Figure 1, Mt. Mantu's diameter was most likely closest to which of the following?

   A. 0.01 km
   B. 0.02 km
   C. 0.1 km
   D. 1 km

2. According to Figure 2, as the volcano diameter increases, the average amount of time between consecutive eruptions:

   F. increases only.
   G. decreases only.
   H. varies, but with no general trend.
   J. remains the same.

3. According to Figure 3, for any given range of volcanic ash flows, the number of eruptions within the past 1,000 years in Mountain Range C is:

   A. less than the number in either Mountain Range A or Mountain Range B.
   B. less than the number in Mountain Range A, but greater than the number in Mountain Range B.
   C. greater than the number in either Mountain Range A or Mountain Range B.
   D. greater than the number in Mountain Range A, but less than the number in Mountain Range B.

4. Suppose a volcano similar to Mt. Mantu created an ash flow that was 30 km in diameter. Based on Figure 1 and other information provided, that volcano would most likely have released a volume of ash closest to which of the following?

   F.   5,000 km^3
   G.   10,000 km^3
   H.   50,000 km^3
   J.   150,000 km^3

5. Assume that a volcano with a diameter of 30 km erupted 500,000 years ago. If the time that elapses between eruptions is equal to the average amount of time given in Figure 2, the volcano should erupt approximately:

   A.   250,000 years from now.
   B.   500,000 years from now.
   C.   1,000,000 years from now.
   D.   1,500,000 years from now.

6. Mt. Vesuvius has a crater at the summit of the volcano that is over 6 km wide. A geologist reports that Mt. Vesuvius has experienced 8 major eruptions in the past 17,000 years. Is the eruption history of Mt. Vesuvius consistent with the information in Figure 2 ?

   F.   Yes; Mt. Vesuvius erupts at a rate similar to the rate depicted in Figure 2 for a volcano of similar size.
   G.   Yes; Mt. Vesuvius erupts more frequently than the rate depicted in Figure 2 for a volcano of similar size.
   H.   No; Mt. Vesuvius erupts less frequently than the rate depicted in Figure 2 for a volcano of similar size.
   J.   No; Mt. Vesuvius erupts more frequently than the rate depicted in Figure 2 for a volcano of a similar size.

Passage VIII

Scientists studied how to heat water with a light bulb using the circuit shown in Figure 1.

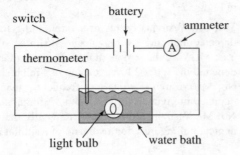

Figure 1

In this circuit, a light bulb is in the middle of a water bath containing 1 kg of water at 10.00°C. Light bulbs contain a wire called a *filament* which is part of the circuit. When electricity flows through the filament, it gets very hot due to resistance, *R*, in the filament, producing light. This heats the water in the water bath, which is measured by the thermometer in the water bath.

When the switch is closed, electricity flows through zero-resistance wires from the battery, through the *ammeter*, which measures the current of the electricity of the circuit. From the ammeter, electricity flows through the filament in the light bulb, which heats the water. The scientists allowed the circuit to run for 10 minutes (600 seconds) before measuring the temperature of the water bath.

Study 1

The scientists studied the effects of different lengths of filament made of tungsten on the temperature of 1 kg of 10.00°C water after the circuit ran for 10 minutes. The cross-sectional area of all of the filaments was 0.10 mm². The battery used in the circuit was a 9-volt battery.

Table 1		
Length (meters)	Current (amps)	Final water temperature (°C)
0.50	33.33	53.06
0.75	21.95	38.35
1.00	16.67	31.53
1.25	13.24	27.10

Study 2

The scientists studied the effects of different cross-sectional areas of filament made of tungsten on the temperature of 1 kg of 10.00°C water after the circuit ran for 10 minutes. The length of all of the filaments was 1.0 m. The battery used in the circuit was a 9-volt battery.

Table 2		
Cross-sectional area (mm²)	Current (amps)	Final water temperature (°C)
0.05	8.33	20.77
0.10	16.67	31.53
0.15	25.00	42.30
0.20	33.33	53.06

Study 3

The scientists studied the effects of battery voltage on the temperature of 1 kg of 10.00°C water after the circuit ran for 10 minutes. All filaments were made of tungsten with a length of 1.0 m and a cross-sectional area of 0.10 mm².

Table 3		
Battery voltage (volts)	Current (amps)	Final water temperature (°C)
3	5.56	11.39
6	11.11	19.57
9	16.67	31.53
12	22.22	48.28

Study 4

The scientists studied the effects of different filament metals on the temperature of 1 kg of 10.00°C water after the circuit ran for 10 minutes. All filaments had a length of 1.0 m. The battery used in the circuit was a 9-volt battery.

Table 4		
Metal	Current (amps)	Final water temperature (°C)
Magnesium	20.36	36.30
Nickel	12.88	26.63
Platinum	8.49	20.97
Tungsten	16.67	31.53

1. Which of the following correctly lists the filament metals in Study 4 in order of increasing water temperature change?

   A. Nickel, tungsten, platinum, magnesium
   B. Tungsten, platinum, nickel, magnesium
   C. Platinum, nickel, tungsten, magnesium
   D. Magnesium, tungsten, nickel, platinum

2. Based on the results of Studies 2 and 4, the cross-sectional area of the test filament in Study 4 was most likely closest to which of the following?

F. 0.05 mm^2
G. 0.10 mm^2
H. 0.15 mm^2
J. 0.20 mm^2

3. Based on the results of Study 1 and Study 3, which of the following battery voltages and filament lengths will increase the temperature of the water bath the most in this circuit if the filament is a tungsten wire with a cross-sectional area of 0.10 mm^2 and the circuit runs for 10 minutes?

	battery voltage (V)	length (m)
A.	5	0.10
B.	7	0.10
C.	5	0.25
D.	7	0.25

4. Suppose that the voltage of the battery used in Study 2 had been 3 volts rather than 9 volts. Based on the results of Study 3, if the cross-sectional area of the wire were 0.15 mm^2 in Study 2, the final water temperature would be closest to which of the following?

F. 10°C
G. 14°C
H. 28°C
J. 42°C

5. Given the position of the ammeter in the circuit shown in Figure 1, which of the following assumptions about current in the circuit were the scientists most likely making?

A. Almost none of the current went through the switch.
B. Almost none of the current went through the test filament.
C. Nearly all of the current went through the test filament.
D. Nearly all of the current went through the battery.

6. The results of Study 1 are best represented by which of the following figures?

F.
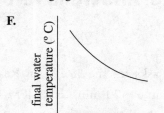

G.
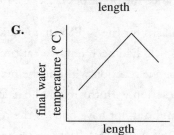

H.
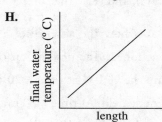

J.
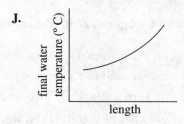

NOW PASSAGES: ANSWERS AND EXPLANATIONS

Passage I

1. **C** The question asks for the % PM in Reaction 1 with a magnetic field after 20 minutes. Look at Figure 1. At time = 20 min, the % PM is between 20% and 40%. Therefore, (A) and (D) can be eliminated. Since the point lies closer to 40 than 20, (B) can be eliminated. The correct answer is (C).

2. **J** The question asks for the % PM that would have been observed at time = 8 minutes for Reaction 3 if the magnetic field had been removed at time = 5 min. Figure 3 corresponds to Reaction 3. Notice that the % PM for the reaction without the magnetic field is approximately 75% at 8 minutes, and the % PM for the reaction with the magnetic field is over 90%. A reaction that had a magnetic field for part of the time and did not have one for the remainder of the time would fall in between 75% and 90%. Eliminate (F), (G), and (H). The correct answer is (J).

3. **A** The question asks how the absence of a magnetic field affected the yield of pure metal at time = 20 min in Reaction 2. The description of the figures states that % PM represents the *percent pure metal*. Compare the % PM at time = 20 min for the reaction with a magnetic field and the reaction without a magnetic field. At time = 20 min, % PM with a magnetic field was almost 100% and % PM without a magnetic field was 40%. That means that % PM without a magnetic field was 40%, or $\frac{2}{5}$ of the % PM with a magnetic field. The correct answer is (A).

4. **G** The question asks if Figures 1–3 support the claim that separating pure metal using a magnetic field is always faster than without a magnetic field. Figures 1–3 do not all express the same relationship between % PM with a magnetic field and % PM without a magnetic field. Eliminate (H) and (J). Both (F) and (G) refer to Figure 1, and since the % PM increases as time increases, eliminate (F). The correct answer is (G).

5. **C** The question asks about % MO as opposed to % PM. If % PM increases in Reaction 3, then the metal oxide is being used up as the pure metal forms. Therefore, the graphs for % MO should decrease as time increases, eliminating (A) and (B). For Reaction 3, % PM reaches 100% faster with a magnetic field than without. Therefore, the metal oxide will get used up faster for the reaction with a magnetic field, eliminating (D). The correct answer is (C).

6. **G** The question asks whether manganese or mercury would reach 50% PM first in the presence of a magnetic field. The introduction states that Reaction 2 is manganese dioxide and Reaction 3 is mercuric oxide, and Figures 2 and 3 refer to Reactions 2 and 3, respectively. Therefore, Figure 2 represents the percent pure metal of manganese and Figure 3 represents the percent pure metal of mercury. In Figure 2, with the presence of a magnetic field, the curve reaches 50% PM at approximately 8 minutes. In Figure 3, with the presence of a magnetic field, the curve reaches 50% PM at approximately 4.5 minutes. Therefore, the mercury reaches 50% PM approximately 3.5 minutes faster than the manganese. The correct answer is (G).

Passage II

1. **B**   The question asks for the minimum photon work function required for a photon to free an electron from Zn. From Table 1, the work function for Zn is listed as 4.30 eV. The text in the second paragraph indicates that the work function of a metal is *the energy required to free an electron.* Therefore, (B) is the correct answer.

2. **H**   The question asks which of the following correctly ranks Al, Ni, and Ag in order of increased K_{max} at 15.0×10^{14} Hz. Examine Figure 1. Figure 1 shows that at all frequencies, Ni has the lowest K_{max}, so eliminate (F) and (G). Al has the highest K_{max}, so eliminate (J). Thus, (H) is the correct answer.

3. **B**   The question asks what happens to K_{max} as frequency increases. Figure 1 shows a direct relationship between K_{max} and frequency for all 4 metals. As frequency increases, the K_{max} value increases. The correct answer is (B).

4. **J**   The question asks, based on Figure 1, what the K_{max} would be for electrons ejected with a frequency of 26.0×10^{14} Hz. Look at the line for Al in Figure 1 and notice that a frequency of 26.0×10^{14} Hz is not plotted on the *x*-axis. The largest point is 20.0×10^{14} Hz, and the corresponding K_{max} is about 4.2 eV. Based on the trend of the graph, K_{max} will increase with increasing frequency. Use this information to eliminate (F) and (G). How much will K_{max} increase from 20.0×10^{14} to 26.0×10^{14}? Look at the K_{max} for 14.0×10^{14} as a comparison. The K_{max} value here is approximately 1.8 eV, which means K_{max} increased about 2.4 eV from a 6.0×10^{14} increase in frequency. Therefore, the K_{max} at 26.0×10^{14} will be quite large, larger than 5.0 eV. The correct answer is (J).

5. **D**   The question asks what the function of Metal Q would most likely be based on the information in the given table. Use the given data for Metal Q and apply it to Figure 1. If Metal Q's K_{max} is 0.5 eV and 3.0 eV at frequencies of 12.0×10^{14} Hz and 18.0×10^{14} Hz, respectively, you can see that these points lie between Zn and Ag. Table 1 shows the work functions of Zn and Ag as 4.30 eV and 4.73 eV, respectively. Therefore, Metal Q's work function should be between 4.30 eV and 4.73 eV, as in (D).

6. **G**   The question asks for the approximate threshold frequency of Ag based on Figure 1. According to the passage, the threshold frequency is *the minimum frequency at which the photon energy will be sufficient to free an electron. If the frequency is higher than the threshold energy, the extra energy may be given to the ejected electron...The maximum energy that may be transferred at each frequency is the K_{max}.* Therefore, the K_{max} is zero until the frequency rises above the threshold frequency. Figure 1 shows that the K_{max} for Ag is zero until approximately 11.5×10^{14} Hz. As the frequency increases above 11.5×10^{14} Hz, the K_{max} begins to rise, indicating that the threshold frequency has been surpassed. The correct answer is (G).

Passage III

1. **C**   The question asks what happened to the percent of Strain C bacterial cells killed as the concentration of Drug X increased. Look at Figure 1. As the concentration of Drug X increases, the percent of bacterial cells of Strain C also increases. Therefore, (C) is the correct answer.

2. **H**   The question asks which strain of bacterium requires the highest concentration of Drug X to achieve a therapeutic effect for 50% of the population given the medication. According to the passage text, the ED_{50} is *the dosage necessary to receive a therapeutic effect for 50% of the population that is given the medication.* From Table 1, compare the values of ED_{50}. Strain D has the maximum value, so (H) is the correct answer.

3. **D**   The question asks, based on Figure 1, what percent of bacterial cells from Strain B would most likely have been killed by Drug X at a concentration of 200 mg/L. In Figure 1, the percent of bacterial cells killed increases as the concentration of Drug X increases. Thus, according to the data, a concentration of 200 mg/L would result in a greater percentage of bacterial cells killed than a concentration of 100 mg/L would. Since the percentage killed at a concentration of 100 mg/L is approximately 83%, eliminate (A), (B), and (C). The correct answer is (D).

4. **F**   The question asks for which strain the concentration of Drug X required to achieve a therapeutic effect in 50% of the population infected with Strain E is 4 times higher than the concentration necessary to achieve a therapeutic effect for 50% of the population infected with the strain in question. From the data in Table 1, Strain E has an ED_{50} of 62.6. Look for a strain with an ED_{50} that is approximately one-fourth of 62.6. Strain A has an ED_{50} of 15.3, which when multiplied by 4 is approximately 60. Thus, the correct answer is (F).

5. **C**   The question asks which action leads to the largest increase in the number of Strain E bacterial cells killed by Drug X. Examine the bars for Strain E in Figure 1. Increasing the drug concentration from 0 mg/L to 0.2 mg/L increases the percent of bacterial cells killed from 0 to approximately 17. Increasing the drug concentration from 0.2 mg/L to 2 mg/L only increases the percent of bacterial cells by a few percent, so eliminate (B). Increasing the drug concentration from 2 mg/L to 60 mg/L increases the percent of cells killed from 22 to 46, which is more than the amount in (A); eliminate (A). Increasing the drug concentration from 60 mg/L to 100 mg/L increases the percent of cells killed from 46 to 58, which is less than in (C), so eliminate (D). The correct answer is (C).

6. **J**   The question asks if the data in Table 1 and Figure 1 support a researcher's hypothesis that the strain with the lowest therapeutic dose will have more cells killed than any other strains at all dosages of Drug X under 30 mg/L. Take this question one step at a time. Refer to Table 1 first. The strain with the lowest therapeutic dose (ED_{50}) is Strain A, with a therapeutic dose of 15.3 mg/L. Use some POE. Since Strain A has the lowest therapeutic dose, the researcher's hypothesis is that Strain A would also have the highest percentage of bacteria killed at dosages of 0.2, 2, and 20 mg/L. You can eliminate (F) and (H) because the reasons for *Yes* and *No* reverse this relationship. Note that the ED_{50} in Table 1 is the dose at which 50% of people *achieve a therapeutic effect.* It does not mean that 50% of the bacteria

were killed. Refer to Figure 1 in order to answer the second part of this question. At a concentration of 2 mg/L of Drug X, Strain B has the highest percentage of bacterial cells killed (at approximately 25%). Eliminate (G). The correct answer is (J).

Passage IV

1. **B** The question asks for the most likely value of P that would result from an additional trial in Study 1 with $V = 0.03$ V. Table 1 shows that as voltage increases, power increases. For $V = 0.03$ V, the voltage is between the values for Trials 1 and 2, so the expected value for P should lie between the results for Trial 1 (0.08 W) and Trial 2 (0.32 W). Therefore, (B) is the correct answer.

2. **J** The question asks what happened to the electrical power as the voltage increased in each study. Tables 1, 2, and 3 all show that P increases when V increases. Choice (J) reflects this trend.

3. **C** The question asks whether Circuit A or Circuit B has a higher electrical resistance given that Circuit A exhibited a higher electrical power than Circuit B. Look at Tables 1–3 to compare trials with different resistances and the same voltage. Take Trials 2, 7, and 12, for example, which all have the same voltage. Trial 12 has the highest resistance, and Trial 2 has the lowest. Trial 12, however, has the lowest power, and Trial 2 has the highest. Therefore, as resistance increases, power decreases, and so (C) is the correct answer.

4. **F** The question asks which trial had the greatest conductance of the circuit. Conductance (G) is defined in the passage as the inverse of resistance (R). All three studies have different resistances, so all Trials 1, 6, and 11 cannot have the same conductance. Eliminate (J). Study 1 has the lowest resistance of the three studies, so the greatest conductance must be in a trial from Study 1. Only (F) represents a trial from Study 1. The correct answer is (F).

5. **C** The question asks which of the given student's predictions about the resistor with the lowest P was correct. Since the different circuits had different power outputs at a given voltage, (D) is incorrect. Compare three trials, one from each study, that have the same voltage. Trials 1, 6, and 11 show that the power output is lowest for a given voltage in Study 3. Study 3 contained a green resistor, which matches Student N's prediction. The correct answer is (C).

6. **J** The question asks which pair of trials best supports the conclusion that increasing the value of V by a factor of 3 increases the value of P by a factor of 9 for a constant resistance. Eliminate (F) and (H) because the trials are in different studies, so the value of R is not constant. Choice (G) is incorrect because the value of V in Trial 4 is double that in Trial 2, rather than increased by a factor of 3. Choice (J) shows the correct relationship.

7. **C** The question asks for the resistance of a purple resistor that has a current of 3 A at a voltage of 0.06 V. Notice that there are three resistors used in Studies 1–3. Since this question is asking about the resistance of a fourth resistor, it's important to note the resistance of each of the first three. The resistors in Studies 1–3 have resistances of 0.005 Ω, 0.015 Ω, and 0.040 Ω. As the resistance increases from

Study 1 to Study 3, the values for I (current) at each voltage decrease. At $V = 0.06$, the current in Study 2 is 4 A, and the current in Study 3 is 1.5 A. Since the current of the fourth resistor falls between these two values, the resistance must fall between 0.015 Ω and 0.040 Ω as well, which matches (C).

Passage V

1. **D** The question asks which of the following statements concerning the change in density of the metal beam in the water bath is true. According to the passage, during thermal expansion of the metal rod, the only variable that changes is the volume, and it is always increasing since the metal rod is expanding. Use this information to eliminate (B) and (C). Since density is defined as mass divided by volume, when the thermal expansion causes an increase in volume, the density decreases. The correct answer is (D).

2. **H** The question asks what the ΔV would most likely have been in an additional trial in Study 3 with an incubation temperature of 70°C. The data in Table 3 shows that ΔV for 60°C is 7.7 mm^3 and ΔV for 80°C is 10.2 mm^3. Since 70°C is between these two values, the corresponding value of ΔV should be between 7.7 mm^3 and 10.2 mm^3. The correct answer is (H).

3. **B** The question asks for the trial in which the rod contains the greatest amount of thermal energy. The question states that thermal energy is *proportional to the product of incubation time and initial length*. In each study, incubation time is held constant. Use POE, and look for the trial with the greatest initial length. The correct answer is (B).

4. **F** The question asks which graph best represents the results of Study 1. According to Table 1, the two variables are the length of the metal rod (L) and the change in volume of the metal rod (ΔV). Notice that as L increases, ΔV increases. Choices (G) and (H) display a relationship between β and ΔV, which is part of Study 2, not Study 1. Choice (J) incorrectly displays an inverse relationship between L and ΔV. The correct answer is (F).

5. **D** The question asks which metal the beam tested in Study 3 was most likely composed of. The incubation temperature in Study 2 was held constant at 80°C. Compare the value of ΔV in Table 3 at 80°C to the values in Table 2. In Study 3, ΔV was 10.2 mm^3 at 80°C, which corresponds to Metal Z in Table 2. The correct answer is (D).

6. **J** The question asks which of the following combinations of L and β would yield the greatest thermal expansion. Refer to Table 1 first. Table 1 shows that the greatest thermal expansion (increase in ΔV) occurs with larger values of L. Eliminate (F) and (G). Now look at Table 2. In Table 2, the greatest thermal expansion occurs with larger values of β. Eliminate (H). The correct answer is (J).

7. **B** The question asks how the values of β and ΔV in a new study with wider bars would compare to the values of β and ΔV in Study 2. The question says *Based on the information in Study 1 and Study 2*, so this is a good clue that the information in Study 1 may be helpful. Study 1 shows that as the length of the bar increases, the ΔV increases. Since this is a rectangular rod whose volume is $l \times w \times h$, increasing the width will affect volume in the same way as increasing the length will. Therefore, increasing the

width of a bar will increase the ΔV. Eliminate (A) and (C). The text of Study 2 also states that *Each metal had a different value of β*. In Study 4, the metals are the same as those in Study 2, so the values of β would remain the same as those in Trials 5–8. Eliminate (D). The correct answer is (B).

Passage VI

1. **C**   The question asks which solution will have the *lowest* freezing point. *Freezing point* does not appear on any of the figures, so you'll need a bit of outside knowledge here. Think about it this way: the freezing point is the point at which a substance turns from a liquid into a solid. The melting point is the point at which a substance turns from a solid into a liquid. Therefore, freezing point and melting point are one and the same. Use Figure 1. According to the passage, all readings are taken at atmospheric pressure 101.3 kPa, so you can disregard that part of the question. The melting point of the solution seems to be lowest at slightly under 70% EG. The correct answer is (C).

2. **G**   The question asks for the temperature at which solid anti-freeze begins to melt in a 60% EG solution at 101.3 kPa. Use Figure 1. According to the passage, all readings are taken at atmospheric pressure 101.3 kPa, so you can disregard that part of the question. According to Figure 1, at 60% EG, the melting point is roughly –48°C. The correct answer is (G).

3. **A**   The question asks which of the following solutions has a boiling point equal to pure water at 101.3 kPa. The substance that will behave most like pure water and boil at the same temperature would be pure water itself. Choice (A), 0% EG, would mean a solution of no ethylene glycol and all water. Increasing the % EG, as in (B), (C), and (D), and therefore decreasing the percentage of water, would make the solution behave less like water. The correct answer is (A).

4. **F**   The question asks what happens to the mass per unit volume as the % EG increases from 0% to 100%. A little outside knowledge is helpful here: *density* and *mass per unit volume* are one and the same. Even without the outside knowledge, examining the units in the figures can help you understand where to look for the answer. In Figure 3, the vertical axis is in g/mL. Since a gram is a measurement of mass and a mL is a measurement of volume, the density (g/mL) is mass per unit volume. According to the passage, all density readings are taken at a temperature of 25°C, so you can disregard that temperature and just look at Figure 3. According to this graph, as % EG increases, the density steadily increases as well. The correct answer is (F).

5. **B**   The question asks for the approximate boiling point of a solution of antifreeze with a density of 1.09 g/mL at 25°C. According to Figure 3, a substance with a density of 1.09 g/mL has 40% EG. According to Figure 2, a substance with 40% EG has a boiling point of approximately 104°C. The correct answer is (B).

6. **F**   The question asks for the chemical formula for ethylene glycol. Refer to the diagram of its chemical structure. There are two carbon atoms: one in each CH_2. Eliminate (G). Next, there are 6 hydrogen atoms: one in each OH, and 2 in each CH_2. Eliminate (H) and (J). The only remaining answer is (F).

Passage VII

1. **C**   The question asks for the most likely diameter of Mt. Mantu given that Mt. Mantu released 100 km^3 of ash. According to Figure 1, when the volcano releases 100 km^3 of ash, its diameter is approximately 0.1 km, which is (C).

2. **F**   The question asks, according to Figure 2, what happens to the average amount of time between consecutive eruptions as the volcano diameter increases. Figure 2 shows a direct relationship. As *average time elapsed* increases, *volcano diameter* also increases. Only (F) represents this trend.

3. **A**   The question requires you to compare the number of eruptions within the past 1,000 years in Mountain Range C with those in Mountain Ranges A and B. Use POE. Pick any point on the graph. For 1–5 km ash-flows, for example, the bar showing the number of volcanic eruptions in Mountain Range C is lower than the bars for both of the other mountain ranges. Eliminate (B), (C), and (D). Only (A) accurately describes this trend.

4. **H**   The question asks how much ash would most likely be released from a volcano similar to Mt. Mantu that created an ash flow of 30 km in diameter. The passage states that Figure 1 *shows the volume of the ash clouds released by volcanoes of differing diameters*. It also states that the *ash flow around Mt. Mantu covered an area 30 times larger than the original size of the volcano*. Therefore, if the ash flow in the question is 30 km, the original size of the volcano must be 30 times smaller, or 1 km. According to Figure 1, a volcano with a diameter of 1 km will have an ash-cloud volume greater than 10,000 and less than 100,00 km^3. Only (H) falls in this range.

5. **B**   The question asks, based on Figure 2, when a volcano with a diameter of 30 km should erupt next given that it erupted 500,000 years ago. According to Figure 2, a volcano with a diameter of 30 km should have approximately 1,000,000 years between eruptions. Therefore, since this volcano erupted 500,000 years ago, it will not erupt for another 1,000,000 − 500,000 = 500,000 years. The correct answer is (B).

6. **J**   The question asks if the eruption history given for Mt. Vesuvius is consistent with the information in Figure 2. According to Figure 2, a volcano with a diameter of 6 km would have an average of over 10,000 years between major eruptions. If the crater on Mt. Vesuvius is over 6 km, then the time between eruptions should be more than 10,000 years. In other words, the volcano should erupt less than once every 10,000 years according to Figure 2. The question states that Mt. Vesuvius has erupted 8 times in 17,000 years, so this is far more frequently than the information in Figure 2 would suggest. The correct answer is (J).

Passage VIII

1. **C**   The question asks which answer lists the filament metals in Study 4 in order of increasing water temperature change. The results of Study 4 are in Table 4. According to Table 4, the final water temperature with a platinum filament was 20.97°C, which is the smallest increase in water temperature. Eliminate answer choices that do not list platinum first. Eliminate (A), (B), and (D). The correct answer is (C).

2. **G**   The question asks what the cross-sectional area of the test filament was in Study 4, based on the results of Studies 2 and 4. Find the link between the two studies. In Study 4 the metal was varied, but in Study 2 it was not. Scan the Study 2 description to determine that this study used tungsten filaments. In Table 4, the current in the tungsten filament was 16.67 amps and the final water temperature was 31.53°C. Look in Table 2 to find the data that matches this information. When the cross-sectional area was 0.10 mm^2, the current was 16.67 amps and the final water temperature was 31.53°C. The correct answer is (G).

3. **B**   The question asks, based on the results of Study 1 and Study 3, which of the battery voltages and filament lengths would increase the temperature of water the most if a tungsten wire filament with a cross-sectional area of 0.10 mm^2 was used and the circuit ran for 10 minutes. Look at the information in Table 1 and Table 3 to learn about the relationships among battery voltage, filament length, and water temperature. In Table 1, the scientists used a tungsten wire with a cross-sectional area of 0.10 mm^2. The final water temperature was higher when the length of the filament was shorter. Eliminate (C) and (D). Now look at Table 3. In Table 3, the scientists used a tungsten wire with a cross-sectional area of 0.10 mm^2, and the final water temperature was higher when the voltage of the battery was higher. Eliminate (A) because 5 V is lower than the 7 V in (B). The correct answer is (B).

4. **G**   The question asks, based on the results of Study 3, what would have happened to the final temperature of the water bath if the voltage of the battery used in Study 2 had been 3 volts instead of 9 volts. Based on the information in Table 3, when the battery voltage changed from 9 to 3 volts, the temperature changed from 31.53°C to 11.39°C. 11 is approximately 1/3 of 32. In Table 2, with a 9-volt battery, when the cross-sectional area of the wire was 0.15 mm^2, the final water temperature was 42.30°C. Based on the results of Study 2, when the voltage dropped from 9 to 3 volts, the resulting temperature would be approximately 1/3 of the 42, which is 14. The correct answer is (G).

5. **C**   The question asks which assumption the scientists made about current in the circuit, given the position of the ammeter in Figure 1. The description of the figure states that *when the switch is closed, electricity flows through zero resistance wires from the battery, through the ammeter, which measures the current of the electricity of the circuit. From the ammeter, electricity flows through the filament in the light bulb, which heats the water.* The current goes through the ammeter before it goes through the filament. Eliminate (A), as the switch allows the current to operate. If no current went through the switch, the electricity would not flow through the filament. Eliminate (B), as the passage states that the electricity flows through the filament. Eliminate (D), as the passage says the electricity flows from the battery, not through the battery. The correct answer is (C).

6. **F** The question asks which figure best represents the results of Study 1. The results of Study 1 are in Table 1. In all the answer choices, the *x*-axis is *length* and the *y*-axis is *final water temperature* (°C). In Table 1, as the length increases, the final temperature always decreases. Only (F) shows this relationship. The correct answer is (F).

Chapter 6
Later Passages

Passage I

In an experimental device known as a cloud chamber, energetic protons and neutrons pass through a vapor of condensed alcohol, causing the ionization (acquired charge) of some of the alcohol molecules. The ionized alcohol molecules begin as condensation nuclei around which the alcohol vapor continues to condense until a high-energy mist is formed. When the mist has acquired enough charge, energetic particles passing through the vapor form tracks visible to the naked eye. These tracks can be accelerated by the application of a magnetic force, under which positively and negatively charged ions will travel in opposite directions.

Two studies using cloud chambers were done at a research center in a temperate climate, using supercooled gaseous ethanol as a medium. The cloud chamber temperature ranged from 0°C to –150°C.

Study 1

Four types of anions (A–D) were used. Anions of each type, when released into the cloud chamber, emit groups of electrons into the chamber with a specific distribution of charges (see Table 1).

Table 1				
Anion type	Percent of groups of electrons having charges (coulombs):			
	0.1–0.5	0.6–1.0	1.1–1.5	1.6–2.0
A	70	20	8	2
B	75	10	8	7
C	80	8	7	5
D	85	7	5	3
Note: 1 coulomb is the charge of 6.24×10^{18} electrons.				

A device containing all 4 types of anions was placed next to the cloud chamber. A computer in the device determined when to release anions, which type of anion to release, and how many anions to release to generate 10, 100, 1,000, or 10,000 condensation nuclei per cm^3 within the chamber. The average number of tracks produced by each type of anion and at each concentration of condensation nuclei is shown in Figure 1.

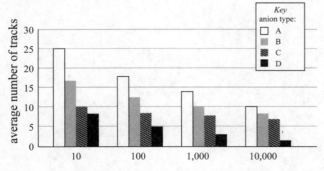

Figure 1

Study 2

The magnetic force required to make each track accelerate away from a straight line was recorded over an hour following the release of the four types of anions into two types of cloud chambers: one with ethanol vapor and one with water vapor. The averaged results for both types of cloud chambers are shown in Figure 2.

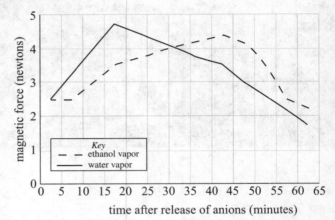

Figure 2

1. According to the results of Study 1, as the condensation nuclei concentration increased, the average number of tracks generated:

   A. increased for all 4 types of anions.
   B. increased for anion types A and B but decreased for anion types C and D.
   C. decreased for all 4 types of anions.
   D. decreased for anion types A and B but increased for anion types C and D.

2. Based on the passage, what is the correct order of tracks, high-energy mist, and condensation nuclei, according to the stage of development, from earliest to latest?

   F. High-energy mist, tracks, condensation nuclei
   G. Condensation nuclei, high-energy mist, tracks
   H. Tracks, high-energy mist, condensation nuclei
   J. Tracks, condensation nuclei, high-energy mist

3. According to the results of Study 2, how did the magnetic force required in the cloud chamber with ethanol vapor differ from the magnetic force required in the cloud chamber with water vapor, with respect to their maximum strength?

A. It took more time for the magnetic force in the ethanol vapor to reach a maximum strength, and it reached a greater maximum strength.

B. It took less time for the magnetic force in the ethanol vapor to reach a maximum strength, and it reached a greater maximum strength.

C. It took more time for the magnetic force in the ethanol vapor to reach a maximum strength, and it reached a lesser maximum strength.

D. It took less time for the magnetic force in the ethanol vapor to reach a maximum strength, and it reached a lesser maximum strength.

4. The design of Study 1 differed from the design of Study 2 in that Study 1, the:

F. tracks of condensation nuclei were analyzed, whereas in Study 2, the concentration of condensation nuclei was analyzed.

G. strength of magnetic fields was measured, whereas in Study 2, the concentration of condensation nuclei was analyzed.

H. tracks of condensation nuclei were analyzed, whereas in Study 2, the strength of magnetic fields was analyzed.

J. strength of magnetic fields was analyzed, whereas in Study 2, tracks of condensation nuclei were analyzed.

5. Which of the following statements gives the most likely reason that data from the cloud chamber were not recorded below a temperature of –150°C? Below –150°C, there would be present:

A. only water vapor.
B. only alcohol vapor.
C. ice crystals but little water vapor.
D. solidified alcohol but little alcohol vapor.

6. Which of the following statements about the concentration of condensation nuclei in the 4 types of anions is supported by Table 1 ?

F. For all 4 types of anions, the majority of particles belonged to the largest charge category.

G. For all 4 types of anions, the majority of particles belong to the smallest charge category.

H. For anion types A and B, most anions belong to the largest charge category, whereas for anion types C and D, most anions belong to the smallest charge category.

J. For anion types A and B, most anions belong to the smallest charge category, whereas for anion types C and D, most anions belong to the largest charge category.

Passage II

Escherichia coli (E. coli) are commonly used in laboratories for the expression, replication, and purification of introduced circular pieces of DNA called *plasmids*. Engineered plasmids encode a gene of interest and often genes that confer resistances to select antibiotics. Antibiotic resistance may be analyzed using the *disk diffusion method*. During the disk diffusion method, bacteria from a single *colony*, or a cluster of genetically identical cells, are incubated in liquid growth media and spread on agar plates (see Figure 1). Small paper disks containing a known concentration of antibiotic are set on the agar plates, and the bacteria are allowed to grow at optimal temperatures. Laboratory strains of *E. coli* lacking plasmids containing genes of resistance to select antibiotics will be unable to grow near the disk containing that antibiotic. Only bacteria that have received the introduced plasmid containing an antibiotic resistance gene should be able to grow in the presence of the antibiotic-containing disk.

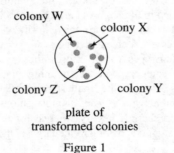

colony W

colony X

colony Z

colony Y

plate of
transformed colonies

Figure 1

Experiment 1

A biotech company has engineered new laboratory strains (A–E) of *E. coli* and is testing whether each strain could grow in the presence of a variety of common antibiotics—ampicillin (Amp), kanamycin (Kan), penicillin (Pen), and tetracycline (Tet). Each of the strains was incubated in a clear nutrient media containing either extra sugar (glucose) or an antibiotic at 37°C for 24 hours. After 24 hours, the growth media was examined for *turbidity* or cloudiness, a signal of bacterial growth (see Table 1).

Strain	Nutrient media				
	Glu	Amp	Kan	Pen	Tet
A	+	−	+	−	−
B	+	−	−	+	−
C	+	−	−	+	+
D	+	+	+	−	−
E	+	−	+	+	−

Table 1

Note: + indicates presence of turbidity;
− indicates no change in appearance

Experiment 2

The scientists at the biotech company tested Strain A for growth after *transformation*, a process of introducing engineered plasmids with antibiotic-resistance containing plasmids. Four different transformed colonies (W, X, Y, and Z) and untransformed Strain A were incubated in liquid growth media and spread on agar plates. To identify which colonies had received which resistance genes, disks containing one of each of the common antibiotics were then placed on the agar plate, and the bacteria were permitted to grow at 37°C (see Figure 2).

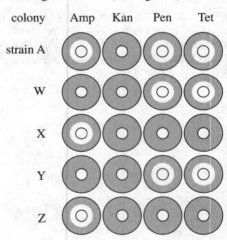

Figure 2

1. Suppose *E. coli* Strain D had been incubated on plates containing kanamycin and tetracycline (Kan + Tet) disks and growth near both disks was observed. Do the data in Table 1 support this observation?

   A. Yes; the results shown in Table 1 indicate that Strain D can grow in the presence of both Kan and Tet.
   B. Yes; the results shown in Table 1 indicate that Strain D cannot grow in the presence of Kan.
   C. No; the results shown in Table 1 indicate that Strain D can grow in the presence of both Kan and Tet.
   D. No; the results shown in Table 1 indicate that Strain D cannot grow in the presence of Tet.

2. Which of the labeled colonies shown in Figure 2 is most likely to have received a plasmid conferring resistance to tetracycline?

   F. Colonies W and X
   G. Colonies W and Y
   H. Colonies X and Y
   J. Colonies X and Z

3. According to Table 1, how many strains tested in Experiment 1 were able to grow in nutrient media containing penicillin?

   A. 0
   B. 1
   C. 2
   D. 3

4. Based on Table 1 and Figure 2, which colonies, if any, likely received a plasmid with resistance genes to ampicillin and kanamycin?

   F. Colony W only
   G. Colony X only
   H. Colonies W and Y
   J. Colonies X and Z

5. Before beginning the experiments, the scientists sprayed the lab area down with a disinfectant. The most likely reason that the disinfectant was used was to avoid contaminating:

   A. the nutrient growth media with strains that were lab generated.
   B. the agar plates with strains that were lab generated.
   C. both the nutrient growth media and agar plates with strains that were lab generated.
   D. both the nutrient growth media and agar plates with strains that were not lab generated.

6. Which of the colonies shown in Figure 2 did NOT grow in the presence of ampicillin?

   F. Colony W
   G. Colony X
   H. Colony Y
   J. None of the strains

7. One of the laboratory technicians was hospitalized for an *E. coli* infection. The infection did not respond to penicillin or tetracycline, but improved after treatment with ampicillin. The technician was most likely infected with:

   A. Strain A.
   B. Strain B.
   C. Strain C.
   D. Strain D.

Passage III

The pesticides *propargyl bromide* (PBr) and *1,3-dichloropropene* (1,3-D) are removed from the soil by a variety of factors, including uptake by plants, adsorption by soil, and breakdown by microorganisms, such as those found in manure. Also, PBr can degrade into *propargyl alcohol.*

Three pairs of pesticide-free soil samples were collected for a study: heavily manure-amended (H1, H2), slightly manure-amended (S1, S2), and unamended (U1, U2), as described in Table 1. On day 1, PBr was added to H1, S1, and U1 and 1,3-D was added to H2, S2, and U2 to produce an initial pesticide concentration of 500 mg/L in each soil sample. PBr, propargyl alcohol, and 1,3-D concentrations in the soil were measured at intervals over the next 12 weeks (see Figures 1–3).

Table 1	
Soil	Description of soil
Heavily manure-amended (H1, H2)	Abundant composted steer manure throughout the soil
Slightly manure-amended (S1, S2)	Limited composted steer manure throughout the soil
Unamended (U1, U2)	No composted steer manure throughout the soil

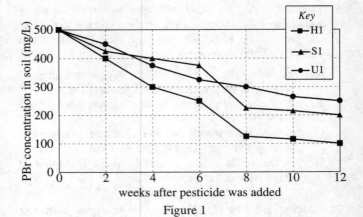

Figure 1

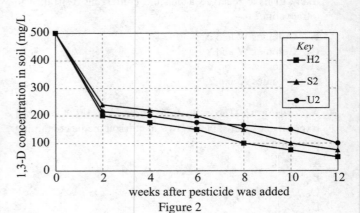

Figure 2

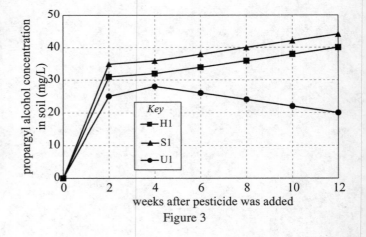

Figure 3

1. Assume that the environmental factors (ultraviolet radiation, wind drift, temperature, and moisture) for each soil sample remained constant over the 12 weeks of the study. According to Figure 2, 12 weeks after 1,3-D was added, what percent of the original 1,3-D concentration remained in the soil in U2 ?

   A. Less than 10%
   B. Between 10% and 30%
   C. Between 30% and 50%
   D. Greater than 50%

2. According to Figure 1, 5 weeks after PBr was added, the concentration in the soil in S1 compared to its concentration in H1 was about:

   F. 112 mg/L lower.
   G. 112 mg/L higher.
   H. 275 mg/L lower.
   J. 275 mg/L higher.

3. According to Figures 1 and 3, as the PBr concentration in S1 decreased, the propargyl alcohol concentration:

   A. decreased only.
   B. decreased, then increased.
   C. increased only.
   D. increased, then decreased.

4. Is the statement "Over the 12 weeks of the study, PBr concentration was most reduced in the unamended soil sample" supported by the data in Figure 1 ?

   F. Yes; 12 weeks after PBr was added, its concentration was least in U1.
   G. Yes; 12 weeks after PBr was added, its concentration was least in H1.
   H. No; 12 weeks after PBr was added, its concentration was least in U1.
   J. No; 12 weeks after PBr was added, its concentration was least in H1.

5. As shown in Figure 2, every time the 1,3-D concentrations in the soil in H2, S2, and U2 were measured during the study, the concentrations in S2 and H2 were found to be very similar to the concentration in U2. The most likely explanation for this is that in S2 and H2:

   A. adsorption onto soil particles and plant uptake played a more significant role in removing 1,3-D than did breakdown to form PBr.
   B. adsorption onto soil particles and plant uptake played a less significant role in removing 1,3-D than did breakdown to form PBr.
   C. bacterial decomposition played a more significant role in removing 1,3-D than did adsorption onto soil particles and plant uptake.
   D. bacterial decomposition played a less significant role in removing 1,3-D than did adsorption onto soil particles and plant uptake.

6. After two weeks, in which soil was the concentration of PBr reduced the least and in which soil was the concentration of 1,3-D reduced the least?

	PBr	1,3-D
F.	U1	S2
G.	H1	H2
H.	U1	U2
J.	S1	U2

7. A farmer asserted that the propargyl alcohol concentration in all soils containing composted steer manure increases every week during the first twelve weeks after treatment with PBr. Do the data in Table 1 and Figure 3 support this assertion?

   A. Yes; the propargyl alcohol concentration increased every week for H1, S1, and U1.
   B. Yes; the propargyl alcohol concentration increased every week for both H1 and S1.
   C. No; the propargyl alcohol concentration does not increase every week for U1.
   D. No; the propargyl alcohol concentration does not increase every week for both H1 and S1.

Passage IV

Honeybees often rely on their strong sense of smell to find nectar and pollen. Several scientists performed three experiments to test the hypothesis that western honeybees (*Apis mellifera*) are more strongly attracted to some scents than others.

Experiment 1

Common sunflowers (*Helianthus annuus*) do not produce much natural fragrance. Three drops of essential oil in one of five scents (chamomile, jasmine, lavender, rosemary, and sage) were added to each of twenty *H. annuus* flowers that had recently bloomed such that there were four flowers with each scent. All of the sunflowers were placed equally spaced in a glass container. An *A. mellifera* bee was then placed in the glass container and observed for 2 hours. Scientists recorded the number of times the bee landed on a flower of each scent. The same procedure was repeated for an additional 49 *A. mellifera* bees. The average number of visits to each flower scent over the 2 hours is shown in Figure 1.

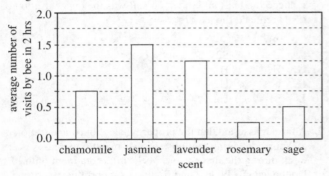

Figure 1

Experiment 2

The procedure for Experiment 1 was repeated with the same set of 50 *A. mellifera* bees and the same 20 *H. annuus* flowers two weeks later as the *H. annuus* neared the end of their blooming period. Each flower received three more drops of the same essential oil that was applied to it in Experiment 1. The average number of visits to each flower scent over the 2 hours is shown in Figure 2.

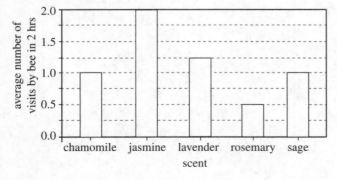

Figure 2

Experiment 3

The procedure for Experiment 1 was repeated except with 20 recently bloomed prairie sunflowers (*Helianthus pauciflorus*) instead of *H. annuus* flowers. The average number of visits to each flower scent over the 2 hours is shown in Figure 3.

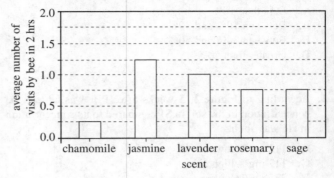

Figure 3

1. Suppose that an additional experiment was performed in which the scientists repeated Experiment 2 except that they recorded the scent of the flowers visited by 25 bees in 2 hrs. Assuming the 25 bees in the new experiment behaved in the same way as the bees in Experiment 2, would the total number of recorded visits to flowers more likely have been greater than or less than the total number of visits to flowers in Experiment 2 ?

   A. Greater, because the number of bees visiting the flowers would have been four times as great.
   B. Greater, because the number of bees visiting the flowers would have been two times as great.
   C. Less, because the number of bees visiting the flowers would have been one-fourth as great.
   D. Less, because the number of bees visiting the flowers would have been one-half as great.

2. Was the scientists' hypothesis supported by the results of the experiments?

   F. No; in each experiment, on average, the bees landed on the same number of flowers with each scent in 2 hrs.
   G. No; in each experiment, on average, the bees landed on more jasmine-scented flowers than flowers with any other scent in 2 hrs.
   H. Yes; in each experiment, on average, the bees landed on the same number of flowers with each scent in 2 hrs.
   J. Yes; in each experiment, on average, the bees landed on more jasmine-scented flowers than flowers with any other scent in 2 hrs.

3. How many total sunflowers were needed to complete Experiments 1–3 ?

   A. 20
   B. 30
   C. 40
   D. 60

4. Which of the following experiments could be used to determine if a different species of pollinator would have the same scent preferences for *H. annuus* near the end of their blooming period?

   F. Repeat Experiment 2 with *A. mellifera* as the pollinator.
   G. Repeat Experiment 2 with a species of pollinator other than *A. mellifera*.
   H. Repeat Experiment 3 with *A. mellifera* as the pollinator.
   J. Repeat Experiment 3 with a species of pollinator other than *A. mellifera*.

5. Which of the following calculations was most likely used to calculate each of the values in Figure 3 ?

   A. $\dfrac{\text{Number of visits to prairie sunflowers scented with a particular scent}}{\text{Number of bees released}}$

   B. $\dfrac{\text{Number of visits to common sunflowers scented with a particular scent}}{\text{Number of bees released}}$

   C. $\dfrac{\text{Total number of visits to prairie sunflowers}}{\text{Number of bees released}}$

   D. $\dfrac{\text{Total number of visits to common sunflowers}}{\text{Number of bees released}}$

6. Which of the following statements regarding the sunflowers used in Experiments 2 and 3 is consistent with the information provided in the passage?

   F. The sunflowers used in Experiment 2 are members of the same genus as those used in Experiment 3, but they are not members of the same species.
   G. The sunflowers used in Experiment 2 are members of the same species as those used in Experiment 3, but they are not members of the same genus.
   H. The sunflowers used in both Experiments 2 and 3 are members of the same genus and species.
   J. The sunflowers used in Experiment 2 are neither members of the same genus nor species as those used in Experiment 3.

7. Which of the following statements is most consistent with the results of Experiments 1 and 2 ? As the *H. annuus* sunflowers neared the end of their blooming period, they attracted, on average:

   A. fewer bee visits in 2 hrs than they did when they had recently bloomed.
   B. more bee visits in 2 hrs than they did when they had recently bloomed.
   C. fewer bee visits in 2 hrs than did the recently bloomed prairie sunflower.
   D. the same number of bee visits in 2 hrs than did the recently bloomed prairie sunflower.

Passage V

Saccharomyces cerevisiae (a yeast used in baking) contains the enzyme *catalase*. Catalase performs the important function of catalyzing the decomposition of toxic hydrogen peroxide (H_2O_2) into water (H_2O) and oxygen (O_2) by the following reaction:

$$2H_2O_2 \xrightarrow{\text{catalase}} 2H_2O + O_2$$

Lactobacillus acidophilus (a bacteria used in yogurt production) does not contain the catalase enzyme so it can only decompose H_2O_2 slowly.

Scientists tried to transfer *S. cerevisiae's* catalase gene into *L. acidophilus*.

Experiment 1

Four versions of *S. cerevisiae's* catalase gene (cat1–cat4) were cloned and incorporated into a neutral vector (a neutral biological organism which carries a gene from one organism to another). A vector without a catalase gene was also created.

Six genetically identical samples of *L. acidophilus* (S1–S6) were grown and suspended in 1.0 cm³ H_2O at 22°C. S1–S4 were each respectively exposed to the vectors containing one of the four versions of *S. cerevisiae's* catalase. S5 was exposed to the vector containing no *S. cerevisiae* catalase gene. S6 was exposed to distilled water (see Table 1). A 100 mL sample of a 25% concentration of H_2O_2 at 22°C was added to each flask.

Each solution was then shaken for 2 minutes. Table 1 shows, after 2 minutes, the percentage of the original H_2O_2 remaining, the percentage of the H_2O_2 that was decomposed, and the mass of the O_2 produced by each sample.

Table 1				
Sample	Catalase exposure	H_2O_2 remaining (%)	H_2O_2 decomposed (%)	O_2 produced (g)
S1	cat1 + vector	53.7	46.3	7.89
S2	cat2 + vector	38.7	61.3	10.44
S3	cat3 + vector	67.1	32.9	5.61
S4	cat4 + vector	62.4	37.6	6.41
S5	vector	99.7	0.3	0.05
S6	distilled water	99.7	0.3	0.05

Experiment 2

Four genetically different samples of *L. acidophilus* were grown (S7–S10). Each sample was exposed to a vector containing cat2. A 100 mL sample of a 25% concentration of H_2O_2 at 22°C was added to each flask.

Each solution was then shaken for 2 minutes. Table 2 shows, after 2 minutes, the percentage of the original H_2O_2 remaining, the percentage of the H_2O_2 that was decomposed, and the mass of the O_2 produced by each sample.

Table 2				
Sample	Catalase exposure	H_2O_2 remaining (%)	H_2O_2 decomposed (%)	O_2 produced (g)
S7	cat2 + vector	36.1	63.9	10.89
S8	cat2 + vector	38.7	61.3	10.44
S9	cat2 + vector	99.7	0.3	0.05
S10	cat2 + vector	39.9	60.1	10.24

1. One of the *L. acidophilus* samples in Experiment 2 was genetically identical to the *L. acidophilus* used in Experiment 1. Based on the results of Experiments 1 and 2, this strain was most likely:

    A. S7.
    B. S8.
    C. S9.
    D. S10.

2. Which of the following best explains why the scientists wanted to transfer a catalase gene from one organism to another?

    F. To increase the amount of H_2O_2 that *S. cerevisiae* could decompose in 2 minutes
    G. To decrease the amount of H_2O_2 that *S. cerevisiae* could decompose in 2 minutes
    H. To increase the amount of H_2O_2 that *L. acidophilus* could decompose in 2 minutes
    J. To decrease the amount of H_2O_2 that *L. acidophilus* could decompose in 2 minutes

3. The scientists believed that 1 of the 4 cloned genes in Experiment 1 produced a catalase enzyme that was less efficient than the enzyme produced by the three other genes. Based on the results, this gene was most likely:

    A. cat1.
    B. cat2.
    C. cat3.
    D. cat4.

4. To determine whether the vector alone could cause H_2O_2 to be decomposed, one should compare the results between which two samples?

    F. S2 and S3
    G. S2 and S4
    H. S4 and S5
    J. S5 and S6

5. At the end of Experiment 2, which of the samples had decomposed the greatest percentage of H_2O_2?

    A. S7
    B. S8
    C. S9
    D. S10

6. Based on the results of Experiment 2, the scientists concluded that the transfer of cat2 to one sample was unsuccessful. The unsuccessful transfer most like occurred in:

    F. S7.
    G. S8.
    H. S9.
    J. S10.

Passage VI

Students conducted experiments to study the relationship between temperature and pressure in gases.

The set-up of the experiment consisted of an air-tight system composed of a 100 cm³ Buchner flask sealed with a stopper containing a thermometer. The hose connector arm of the flask was attached to a 30 cm³ gas syringe with the stopper set at 10 cm³, making the total volume the gas occupied 110 cm³. A diagram of the apparatus is below.

The flask was filled with 100 mL nitrous oxide gas at 23°C.

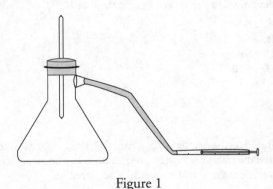

Figure 1

Experiment 1

The experimental system was placed in a warm water bath. When the thermometer read 24°C, the gas syringe had opened to 15 cm³. When the thermometer read 25°C, the gas syringe had opened to 20 cm³.

Experiment 2

The experimental system was placed in a cool water bath. When the thermometer read 21°C, the gas syringe had closed to 5 cm³. When the thermometer read 19°C, the gas syringe had closed to 0 cm³.

Experiment 3

Two mixtures of nitrous oxide gas and chlorine gas were prepared and each put into an experimental system the same as that used in Experiments 1 and 2. Mixture I had a larger concentration of nitrous oxide gas than did Mixture II. The two experimental systems were placed in 27°C water baths. When the systems had been heated to the temperature of the water bath and the thermometers read 27°C, the gas syringe for Mixture I had opened to 30 cm³ and the gas syringe for Mixture II had opened to 27 cm³.

Next, both experimental systems were placed in a –90°C water bath. When both systems had been cooled to the temperature of the water bath and the thermometers read –90°C, the gas syringes for both systems had closed to 0 cm³ and liquid appeared in the flasks.

1. Based on the results of Experiments 1 and 2, 200 mL of nitrous oxide in a system with which of the following temperatures would have the *largest* volume?

    A. 0°C
    B. 20°C
    C. 40°C
    D. 80°C

2. Which of the following changes to Experiment 3 would have provided the most information about the effect of decreasing temperature on the volume of a mixture of nitrous oxide gas and chlorine gas?

    F. Using a larger flask
    G. Using a smaller flask
    H. Using a water bath with a temperature of –100°C to cool the system
    J. Using a water bath with a temperature of –50°C to cool the system

3. Suppose the gas syringe in Experiment 2 had been replaced with a balloon as shown below.

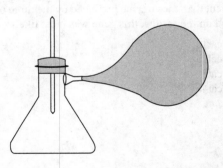

If the new system were placed in a warm water bath and the temperature of the system increased to 30°C, what effect, if any, would there be on the balloon?

    A. The balloon would increase in volume, because the volume of the gas increases as temperature increases.
    B. The balloon would decrease in volume, because the volume of the gas increases as temperature increases.
    C. The balloon would increase in volume, because the volume of the gas decreases as temperature increases.
    D. The balloon would stay the same size, because the volume of the gas is not affected by temperature.

4. Suppose equal volumes of Mixtures I and II from Experiment 3 were combined and placed in the experimental set-up in a 27°C water bath. The gas syringe would most likely open to:

    F. less than 20 cm³.
    G. between 20 cm³ and 27 cm³.
    H. between 27 cm³ and 30 cm³.
    J. greater 30 cm³.

5. Assume that the total mass of the gases in Mixture I is equal to the total mass of the gases in Mixture II. Based on the results of Experiment 3, which gas, chlorine gas or nitrous oxide, has a lower density at 27°C ?

   A. Chlorine gas; because the volume of Mixture I is higher than the volume of Mixture II at 27°C.
   B. Nitrous oxide; because the volume of Mixture I is higher than the volume of Mixture II at 27°C.
   C. Chlorine gas; because the volume of Mixture I is lower than the volume of Mixture II at 27°C.
   D. Nitrous oxide; because the volume of Mixture I is lower than the volume of Mixture II at 27°C.

6. As the temperature of the gas was changed in Experiment 1, which of the other properties of the nitrous oxide gas changed?

   I. Volume
   II. Density
   III. Weight

   F. I only
   G. II only
   H. I and II only
   J. I, II, and III

7. Which of the following graphs best shows how volume of the nitrous oxide gas changed with temperature in Experiment 1 ?

   A.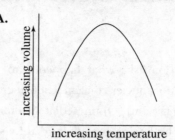

   B.

   C.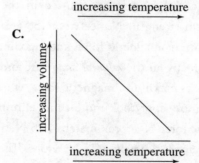

   D.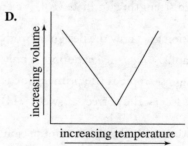

LATER PASSAGES: ANSWERS AND EXPLANATIONS

Passage I

1. **C**   The question asks what happened to the average number of tracks generated in Study 1 as the condensation nuclei concentration increased. In Figure 1, all four anions follow the same trend, so eliminate (B) and (D) immediately. From left to right in the graph, the concentration of condensation nuclei is increasing for all four anions, and as this value increases, the average number of tracks decreases for all four anions. Only (C) accurately reflects this trend.

2. **G**   The question asks for the correct order of tracks, high-energy mist, and condensation nuclei from earliest stage of development to latest. Read if and only when a question can't be answered from the figures. The introduction provides the order of development, correctly described in (G).

3. **C**   The question asks how the magnetic force required in the cloud chamber with ethanol vapor differed from the magnetic force required in the cloud chamber with water vapor, with respect to their maximum strength. Notice from the answer choices that this question has two components: time to maximum magnetic force and maximum magnetic force itself. Notice also that all the answer choices focus on the *ethanol vapor*. According to Figure 2, the ethanol vapor took about 40 minutes to reach its maximum magnetic force, whereas the water vapor took only about 15 minutes. Therefore, the ethanol vapor took more time; eliminate (B) and (D). The ethanol vapor reached a maximum magnetic force of approximately 4.25 Newtons, while the water vapor reached a maximum magnetic force of approximately 4.75 Newtons. Therefore, the ethanol vapor's magnetic force reached a lesser maximum strength; eliminate (A). The correct answer is (C).

4. **H**   The question asks how the design of Study 1 differed from the design of Study 2. Note the axes on each of the graphs. *Magnetic force* appears only in Study 2, which eliminates (G) and (J) immediately. Then, since magnetic force is the primary focus of Study 2, eliminate (F) because it contains no mention of magnetic force. The correct answer is (H).

5. **D**   The question asks why data from the cloud chamber were not recorded below −150°. This requires a bit of logical thinking and some outside knowledge. Only Study 2 is concerned with *water vapor*, whereas the general introduction discusses *alcohol vapor*. Therefore, it can be inferred that the entire experiment deals with *alcohol vapor*, making changes in water vapor only partially relevant, eliminating (A) and (C). Then, between the two answer choices, which is more likely to be the case at temperatures *below* −150°C? Alcohol in this temperature range is colder and therefore more likely to be solid than vapor. Only (D) reflects this information correctly.

6. **G**   The question asks which of the statements about the concentration of condensation nuclei in the 4 types of anions is supported by Table 1. According to Table 1, 70–85% of all four types of anions fit in to the 0.1–0.5 category, or the *smallest charge category*. There are no exceptions in Table 1, so the only answer choice that can work is (G).

Passage II

1. **D** The question asks if the data in Table 1 would support an observation of growth near discs containing kanamycin and tetracycline in a sample of *E. coli* Strain D. Use POE. If you're not sure whether to answer *Yes* or *No*, check the reasons. Based on Table 1, the + sign indicates turbidity. According to the description of Experiment 1, turbidity is a sign of bacterial growth. Therefore, Table 1 indicates that Strain D can grow in the presence of Glu, Amp, and Kan. Eliminate (B), which states that Strain D cannot grow in the presence of Kan. Also, according to Table 1, Strain D cannot grow in the presence of Pen or Tet. Eliminate (A) and (C), which suggest that Strain D can grow in the presence of Tet. Only (D) remains.

2. **J** The question asks which of the labeled colonies shown in Figure 2 is most likely to have received a plasmid conferring resistance to tetracycline. The question refers to Figure 2, but the presence of Strain A at the top of the figure links back to Figure 1. A + sign in Figure 1 indicates turbidity, which is a signal of bacterial growth. According to Figure 1, Strain A can grow only when cultured in the antibiotic-free control medium (Glu) or in the presence of Kan. It cannot grow in the presence of Amp, Pen, or Tet. Therefore, it can be inferred that the larger white regions shown in the Strain A plates with Amp, Pen, and Tet indicate a lack of growth around the antibiotic disk (the small white circle). The colonies that have received a *plasmid conferring resistance to tetracycline* should show growth (shaded regions) around the antibiotic disk. Colonies X and Z are able to grow around the tetracycline disk and are therefore resistant to tetracycline. The correct answer is (J).

3. **D** The question asks how many strains tested in Experiment 1 were able to grow in nutrient media containing penicillin, according to Table 1. The passage states that turbidity is a sign of bacterial growth and it is indicated by a +. According to Table 1, Strains B, C, and E were able to grow in the presence of penicillin, or Pen. Choice (D) gives the correct number.

4. **H** The question asks which colonies, if any, based on Table 1 and Figure 2, likely received a plasmid with resistance genes to ampicillin and kanamycin. A + sign in Figure 1 indicates turbidity, which is a signal of bacterial growth. According to Table 1, Strain A can grow in Glu and Kan media. It cannot grow in the presence of Amp, Pen, or Tet. It can be inferred that the larger white regions shown in the Strain A plates with Amp, Pen, and Tet indicate a lack of growth around the antibiotic disk (the small white circle). Therefore, the colonies that have received a *plasmid with resistance genes to ampicillin and kanamycin* should show shaded growth around the antibiotic disk in the Amp and Kan columns. Colonies W and Y have this shaded growth, making (H) the best answer.

5. **D** The question asks for the most likely reason disinfectant was used before beginning the experiments to avoid contaminating. Use POE and common sense. Notice (A), (B), and (C) all contain mention of substances that are *lab generated*. Only (D) contains mention of strains that are *not lab generated*. Think about it this way: scientists are trying to control the environment of their experiment, so they don't want things from outside (things that are *not lab generated*) to contaminate the things in the experiment. The correct answer is (D).

6. **G** The question asks which of the colonies shown in Figure 2 did NOT grow in the presence of ampicillin. A + sign in Figure 1 indicates turbidity, which is a signal of bacterial growth. According to Table 1, Strain A can grow in Glu and Kan media. It cannot grow in the presence of Amp, Pen, or Tet. Therefore, it can be inferred that the larger white regions shown in the Strain A plates with Amp, Pen, and Tet indicate a lack of growth around the antibiotic disk (the small white circle). A colony that did NOT grow in the presence of ampicillin should show a larger white region in the Amp column. Of the choices given, only colony X has a larger white region, making (G) the best answer.

7. **C** The question asks which strain is a technician most likely infected with if his infection responded to ampicillin but not to penicillin or tetracycline. If the infection did not respond to penicillin or tetracycline, then the strain was able to grow in the presence of those antibiotics. According to Table 1, only Strain C can grow in the presence of both penicillin and tetracycline, so the correct answer is (C).

Passage III

1. **B** The question asks what percent of the original 1,3-D concentration remained in the soil in U2 12 weeks after it was applied. Examine Figure 2. At the end of 12 weeks, the PBr concentration for U2 has decreased from 500 mg/L to 100 mg/L. 100 out of 500 is 20%. The correct answer is (B).

2. **G** The question asks how the concentration of PBr in S1 compared to that in H1 5 weeks after application. In Figure 1, find the difference in PBr concentration between S1 and H1 after 5 weeks. At the 5-week mark, the concentration of PBr in S1 was about 375 mg/L. Meanwhile, the concentration of H1 was about 275 mg/L. Since S1 is higher than H1, eliminate (F) and (H). The difference between S1 and H1 is about 100 mg/L. Therefore, the best answer is (G).

3. **C** The question asks how the propargyl alcohol concentration changed as the PBr concentration in S1 decreased. According to Figure 1, as the number of weeks increases, the concentration of PBr decreases for all three soil samples. In Figure 3, as the number of weeks increases, the propargyl alcohol concentration in S1 also increases. The correct answer is (C).

4. **J** The question asks if the statement *Over the 12 weeks of the study, PBr concentration was most reduced in the unamended soil sample* is supported by the data in Figure 1. Look at Figure 1. The unamended soil sample refers to U1, which has the highest concentration of PBr at the end of the 12 weeks. The highest concentration means the least reduction in concentration, so the statement is not supported. Eliminate (F) and (G). Now examine the supporting statements in (H) and (J). Choice (H) incorrectly states that PBr concentration was the least in U1. Eliminate (H). Since PBr concentration was the least in H1, the correct answer is (J).

5. **D** This question asks for an explanation for the similarity in concentration between H2, S2, and U2 in Figure 2. Use POE. Eliminate (A) and (B) because they mentioned PBr, which was not used in any of the three soil samples in question. Since all three soil samples differed greatly in steer manure content, according to the passage, the bacterial count should also vary. If bacterial decomposition played a significant role in removing 1,3-D, then the concentrations of the three soil samples should not be so similar. Eliminate (C). The correct answer is (D).

6. **F**   The question asks which soils the pesticide concentrations *reduced the least* after two weeks. Since the pesticide concentrations start at 500 mg/L for all three soils, this is the same as asking for the soils in which the concentrations of PBr and 1,3-D are the highest after 2 weeks. Figure 1 shows the concentration of PBr. After two weeks, the U1 soil has the highest concentration. Eliminate (G) and (J). Figure 2 shows the concentrations of 1,3-D. After two weeks, S2 has the highest concentration, so eliminate (H). The correct answer is (F).

7. **B**   The question asks if a farmer's assertion that *propargyl alcohol concentration in all soils containing composted steer manure increases every week during the first twelve weeks after treatment with PBr* is supported by the data in Table 1 and Figure 3. Use POE. Table 1 indicates that there is no composted steer manure in U1, so only the trends for S1 and H1 are relevant. Eliminate (C). Figure 3 shows that the concentration of propargyl alcohol increases each week for S1 and H1, so the assertion is supported. Eliminate (D). Eliminate (A) because this incorrectly states that the concentration increases every week in U1 as well. The correct answer is (B).

Passage IV

1. **D**   The question asks how the number of recorded visits would change if Experiment 2 were repeated with 25 bees. Read the description of Experiment 2 to find the number of honeybees used originally; the experiment originally used one bee and then an *additional 49…bees* for a total of 50 bees. Since fewer bees were used in the additional experiment, the number of recorded visits would be less; eliminate (A) and (B). Compare (C) and (D). The number of bees in the additional experiment is half of the original amount; eliminate (C) because it says *one-fourth as great*. The correct answer is (D).

2. **J**   The question asks if the scientists' hypothesis was supported by the experiments. Compare the answer choices and use POE. Based on the graphs from the three experiments, the bees landed more often on jasmine-scented flowers. Since the flowers were not visited the same amount, eliminate (F) and (H). Skim the text to find the scientists' hypothesis. The introduction says that the hypothesis was that *western honeybees (Apis mellifera) are more strongly attracted to some scents than others*. This hypothesis is supported because the bees visited the jasmine-scented flowers more often than flowers with other scents. Eliminate (G). The correct answer is (J).

3. **C**   The question asks how many total sunflowers were needed to complete the three experiments. Read the description of the experiments to find the number of sunflowers used. In Experiment 1, 20 sunflowers were used. In Experiment 2, the passage says that *the same 20 H. annuus flowers* were used, so the total is still 20 sunflowers for two experiments. In Experiment 3, *20 recently bloomed prairie sunflowers* were used. Therefore, the total number of sunflowers used in the three experiments is 20 + 20 = 40. The correct answer is (C).

4. **G**   The question asks which experiment could be done to determine if a *different species of pollinator* would have the same scent preferences for *H. annuus near the end of their blooming period*. Compare the answer choices and use POE. Since the choices refer to Experiments 2 and 3, read the descriptions of

those experiments to find the one that used flowers near the end of their blooming period. Experiment 2 used flowers that *neared the end of their blooming period*, and Experiment 3 used *recently bloomed* flowers. Eliminate (H) and (J) because those say to repeat Experiment 3. Since *A. mellifera* was the pollinator used in Experiment 2, *A. mellifera* should not be tested again to test the scent preferences of a *different* species of pollinator. Eliminate (F). The correct answer is (G).

5. **A**   The question asks which calculation was used for Figure 3. Figure 3 shows the results of Experiment 3, so read the description of that experiment. Experiment 3 used prairie sunflowers. Eliminate (B) and (D) because those refer to *common sunflowers*. Figure 3 shows the average number of visits to flowers with particular scents, so eliminate (C) which refers to the *total number of visits*. The correct answer is (A).

6. **F**   The question asks which statement is accurate regarding the sunflowers used in Experiments 2 and 3. Compare the answer choices and use POE. The answer choices are about the genus and species of the flowers. Find the information about the sunflowers in the descriptions of the experiments. Experiment 2 used the same common sunflowers as Experiment 1; the scientific name is *Helianthus annuus*. Experiment 3 used prairie sunflowers; the scientific name is *Helianthus pauciflorus*. Since there are two different types of sunflowers used, eliminate (H), which says the flowers used were *members of the same genus and species*. Outside knowledge is needed here to know that scientific names are written as *Genus species* in that order. Therefore, the sunflowers are members of the same genus but different species. The correct answer is (F).

7. **B**   The question asks which statement is consistent with the results of Experiments 1 and 2. The statement compares the number of visits to *H. annuus* at the end of their blooming period to recently bloomed flowers. Since prairie sunflowers were only used in Experiment 3 and the question is about Experiments 1 and 2, eliminate (C) and (D) because they refer to prairie sunflowers. Compare the number of visits in Figure 1, which shows visits to the recently bloomed sunflowers, to the number of visits in Figure 2, which shows visits to the sunflowers at the end of the blooming period. For each scent, there are more visits recorded in Figure 2 than Figure 1. Therefore, there is a greater number of visits to sunflowers at the end of their blooming period than to recently bloomed flowers. The correct answer is (B).

Passage V

1. **B**   The question asks which of the *L. acidophilus* samples in Experiment 2 was mostly likely genetically identical to the *L. acidophilus* used in Experiment 1. Look at the answers to see what information from Table 2 most closely matches information found in Table 1. Notice that S7–S10 all have been exposed to cat2 + vector, which means that the correct answer must match S2. All the columns of Sample 8 match all the columns of Sample 2. The correct answer is (B).

2. **H**   The question asks why the scientists wanted to transfer a catalase gene from one organism to another. The term *catalase gene* is not mentioned in the tables, so look at the passage. In the introduction, the passage states that Lactobacillus acidophilus...*does not contain the catalase enzyme so it can only decompose H_2O_2 slowly. Scientists tried to transfer* S. cerevisiae's *catalase gene into* L. acidophilus. Since

the scientists wanted to transfer the catalase gene into *L. acidophilus*, eliminate (F) and (G) because they mention the incorrect organism. Compare the remaining answers, which only differ regarding an increase or decrease in the amount of decomposition of H_2O_2. According to the quote, *L. acidophilus* without the catalase enzyme can only decompose H_2O_2 slowly, so the scientists would want to increase the amount. Eliminate (J). The correct answer is (H).

3. **C** The question asks which of the cloned genes in Experiment 1 produced a catalase enzyme that was less efficient than the enzyme produced by the three other genes. According to the passage, *catalase performs the important function of catalyzing the decomposition of toxic hydrogen peroxide (H_2O_2) into water (H_2O) and oxygen (O_2)*. The least efficient catalase enzyme would be the enzyme that decomposes the smallest percentage of H_2O_2. According to Table 1, Sample 3 decomposed 32.9% of H_2O_2, which is the smallest percentage. The correct answer is (C).

4. **J** The question asks which results should be compared to determine whether the vector alone could cause H_2O_2 to be decomposed the comparison sample must contain the vector alone and a control that does not contain the vector at all. Sample 5 is the sample that includes only the vector. Eliminate (F) and (G), as they do not include Sample 5. The control is distilled water, which is Sample 6. The correct answer is (J).

5. **A** The question asks which of the samples had decomposed the greatest percentage of H_2O_2 by the end of Experiment 2. The results of Experiment 2 are in Table 2. Look at the column labeled H_2O_2 *decomposed* to determine the greatest percentage. In Sample 7, 63.9% of H_2O_2 was decomposed, which is the larger than the percent in any other sample. The correct answer is (A).

6. **H** The question asks which sample in Experiment 2 most likely had an unsuccessful transfer of cat2. According to the passage, *catalase performs the important function of catalyzing the decomposition of toxic hydrogen peroxide (H_2O_2) into water (H_2O) and oxygen (O_2)*. Check the samples in Table 2 to see which one had the smallest amount of H_2O_2 decomposed. In Sample 9, only 0.3% of the H_2O_2 decomposed. The H_2O_2 in this sample was mainly not decomposed, so it is likely that the transfer of cat2 was unsuccessful. The correct answer is (H).

Passage VI

1. **D** The question asks which temperature would result in the largest volume for 200 mL of nitrous oxide, based on the results of Experiments 1 and 2. In both experiments, the nitrous oxide is in an air-tight Buchner flask. *The hose connector arm of the flask was attached to a 30 cm^3 gas syringe with the stopper set at 10 cm^3, making the total volume the gas occupied 110 cm^3*. In Experiment 1, when the temperature of the warm water bath is increased from 24 to 25°C, the gas syringe opens from 15 to 20 cm^3. The temperature increase is associated with a volume increase. In Experiment 2, when the temperature of the warm water bath is decreased from 21 to 19°C, the gas syringe closes from 5 to 0 cm^3. The temperature decrease is associated with a volume decrease. The largest volume, therefore, would be associated with the highest temperature. 80°C is the highest temperature listed in the answers. The correct answer is (D).

2. **J**   The question asks which change to Experiment 3 would provide the most information about the effect of decreasing temperature on a mixture of gases. Eliminate (F) and (G), as they don't mention temperature. Choice (H) mentions decreasing temperature, but when the scientists cooled the mixtures to −90°C in Experiment 3, the gas syringe had completely closed to zero, so no additional information could be collected if the system was cooled to a lower temperature of −100°C. Choice (J) mentions decreasing temperature to −50°C. Data from this temperature could provide more information on the temperature change. The correct answer is (J).

3. **A**   The question asks what would happen if a new system that uses a balloon instead of a syringe were used in Experiment 2 and the temperature was then increased to 30°C. Look for mentions of the relationship between the volume of the syringe and the temperature of the water bath. In Experiment 2, the mixture decreased in volume when the temperature decreased from 21°C to 19°C. Therefore, the relationship is direct and volume would increase if the temperature increased. Eliminate (B), as it mentions a decrease in volume and (D) because it says the volume would not change. Eliminate (C) because it describes an inverse relationship between temperature and volume. The correct answer is (A).

4. **H**   The question asks what the gas syringe would most likely open to if equal volumes of Mixtures I and II from Experiment 3 were combined and placed in the experimental set-up in a 27°C water bath. *When the systems were at 27°C, the gas syringe for Mixture I had opened to 30 cm³ and the gas syringe for Mixture II had opened to 27 cm³*. A mixture of the two gases would lead to an amount in between 27 and 30 cm³. The correct answer is (H).

5. **B**   The question asks whether chlorine gas or nitrous oxide has a lower density at 27°C, assuming that the total mass of the gases in Mixture I is equal to the total mass of the gases in Mixture II. Use POE. According to Experiment 3, *the gas syringe for Mixture I had opened to 30 cm³ and the gas syringe for Mixture II had opened to 27 cm³*. Therefore, Mixture I had a larger volume than Mixture II. Eliminate (C) and (D) because these say the volume of Mixture 1 was lower. You need a little outside knowledge to finish this question: density is mass divided by volume. Therefore, since Mixture I had a larger volume, it must have had a smaller density than Mixture II. The passage states that *Mixture I had a larger concentration of nitrous oxide gas than did Mixture II*, so nitrous oxide must have a lower density than chlorine gas. The correct answer is (B).

6. **H**   The question asks which other properties of the nitrous oxide changed as the temperature of the gas was changed in Experiment 1. In Experiment 1, when the temperature of the warm water bath is increased from 24 to 25°C, the volume increased. Eliminate (G), as it does not include volume. Density is mass divided by volume, so it would also change as the volume changed. Eliminate (F), as it does not include density. The experiment does not provide any information on the weight of the nitrous oxide gas. Eliminate (J). The correct answer is (H).

7. **B**   The question asks which graph best shows how the volume of the nitrous oxide gas changed with temperature in Experiment 1. In Experiment 1, as the temperature increased from the initial 23°C to 24°C to 25°C, the syringe opened from 10 cm³ to 15 cm³ to 20 cm³. As the temperature increased, the volume only increased. Only (B) reflects this trend. The correct answer is (B).

Chapter 7
Science Reading
Passages

Passage I

Scarlet larkspur, a type of wildflower found in the western United States, usually blooms in early summer. The number of flower blooms varies from year to year due to several factors, including precipitation and the presence of certain smoke-derived organic compounds (such as butenolides). Before conducting a study, four scientists discuss their theories about how precipitation and forest fires affect the prevalence of scarlet larkspur.

Scientist 1

Scarlet larkspur grows best in habitats where forest fires are common. The compounds in the smoke of a forest fire spur germination of scarlet larkspur seeds. As a result, the number of scarlet larkspur blooms will be greater on hillsides that experienced a fire in the previous summer than on hillsides that did not. Precipitation does not affect the growth of scarlet larkspur.

Scientist 2

Scarlet larkspur grows best in habitats with dry soil. Drought conditions prevent competition by inhibiting the germination of seeds from competing wildflower species. As a result of decreased competition, scarlet larkspur will produce more blooms on hillsides that have experienced below average rainfall during the spring. Forest fires do not affect the growth of scarlet larkspur.

Scientist 3

Scarlet larkspur is a versatile plant capable of flourishing under a variety of conditions. The level of competition faced by scarlet larkspur is similar at all precipitation levels, and the smoke from forest fires does not affect seed germination rates. Therefore, neither precipitation nor recent forest fires will affect the number of scarlet larkspur blooms found on a hillside.

Scientist 4

Scarlet larkspur grows well in habitats with dry soil, and it also grows well in habitats that have experienced a recent forest fire. Dry soil limits competition from other wildflower species, and compounds in smoke spur the germination of scarlet larkspur seeds. The greatest number of scarlet larkspur blooms will be found on hillsides that have experienced below average spring rainfall and a forest fire in the previous summer.

Study

The scientists selected a variety of hillsides throughout the western United States and categorized them into four groups based on their spring precipitation totals and the presence or absence of a forest fire the *previous* summer. None of the locations experienced forest fires in the fall, winter, or spring. The scientists calculated the average number of scarlet larkspur blooms per 100 m² at the beginning of the summer under each set of conditions. The results are shown in Table 1.

Table 1		
Below average rainfall?	Blooms without forest fire	Blooms with forest fire
Yes	593	984
No	456	768

1. A researcher found that releasing a synthetic butenolide aerosol into a nursery increased the number of scarlet larkspur seeds that germinated. This finding is consistent with the theories of which of the scientists?

   A. Scientist 1 only
   B. Scientists 1 and 4 only
   C. Scientist 3 only
   D. Scientists 3 and 4 only

2. Based on Scientist 4's hypothesis, a scarlet larkspur seed would be *least* likely to bloom into a scarlet larkspur flower on a hillside with:

   F. a recent forest fire and plentiful spring rain.
   G. a recent forest fire and minimal spring rain.
   H. no recent fires and plentiful spring rain.
   J. no recent fires and minimal spring rain.

3. Compare the average number of scarlet larkspur blooms for the hillsides without a recent forest fire and below average rainfall to the average number of blooms on the hillsides without a recent forest fire and average or above average rainfall. Are the results of the study consistent with the theory of Scientist 2 ?

   A. Yes; there were more scarlet larkspur blooms on the hillsides that experienced below average rainfall.
   B. Yes; there were fewer scarlet larkspur blooms on the hillsides that experienced below average rainfall.
   C. No; there were more scarlet larkspur blooms on the hillsides that experienced below average rainfall.
   D. No; there were fewer scarlet larkspur blooms on the hillsides that experienced below average rainfall.

4. Prior to conducting the study, which scientist would most likely have predicted that the average number of scarlet larkspur blooms per 100 m² would be approximately the same for all of the hillsides studied?

   F. Scientist 1
   G. Scientist 2
   H. Scientist 3
   J. Scientist 4

5. In another study, a researcher selected 10 hillsides that were exposed to forest fire smoke over the course of a year. The researcher then recorded the total number of days that each hillside was exposed to smoke and estimated the percentage of the hillside that was covered in scarlet larkspur blooms the following summer. The results are shown in the figure below.

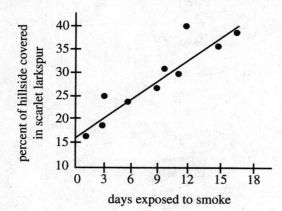

The results shown in the figure above are consistent with the theory or theories of which of the scientists?

A. Scientist 1 only
B. Scientist 2 only
C. Scientists 1 and 4 only
D. Scientists 2 and 4 only

6. The results of the study shown in Table 1 are most consistent with the theory of which scientist?

F. Scientist 1
G. Scientist 2
H. Scientist 3
J. Scientist 4

7. All of the following questions can be directly answered by the results of the study shown in Table 1 EXCEPT:

A. Can scarlet larkspur seeds germinate without the presence a forest fire within the past 12 months?
B. Does a decrease in precipitation decrease the competition that the scarlet larkspur faces from other flowering species?
C. Do summer forest fires coincide with an increase in the number of scarlet larkspur blooms the following summer?
D. Does the average number of scarlet larkspur blooms per 100 m² differ between hillsides with below average spring rainfall and hillsides with average or above average spring rainfall?

Passage II

Phytoplankton are a natural part of aquatic ecosystems, but a *harmful algal bloom* (HAB) occurs when a phytoplankton species grows out of control, endangering water quality, wildlife, and human health. Two graduate students present their theories about the development of HABs.

Student 1

Heavy rains can lead to a significant increase in agricultural runoff, sending large amounts of nitrogen and phosphorous into a lake. In a healthy lake, the majority of both of these nutrients are trapped in an unusable form in the sediment. The growth of phytoplankton is curbed by the lack of available nitrogen. However, a lake experiencing an HAB has approximately 90% of its nitrogen in useable form (70% from agricultural runoff and another 20% from microbial activity).

Due to the excess nitrogen, the algae grows until it overwhelms much of the other plant life. While the runoff initially increases dissolved oxygen levels, the decomposition of these dead plants eventually leads to decreasing dissolved oxygen levels. Once the oxygen drops below a critical threshold, dead zones will sometimes form that extend from the surface to depths of almost 30 m. Algal blooms spread rapidly, but they also quickly consume the excess nitrogen. After the nitrogen levels return to normal, the HAB will dissipate within a couple of weeks.

Student 2

Nutrients such as nitrogen and phosphorous are concentrated in the sediment at the bottom of lakes. When dissolved oxygen levels drop due to decreased water movement (such as during droughts or periods of decreased wind activity), a series of biochemical processes causes phosphorous to be released into the water. During an HAB, up to 60% of the phosphorous in the lake is in readily available form in the water instead of in the sediment. The prevalence of phosphorous fuels the growth of phytoplankton.

HABs form on or near the surface, but they release toxic gases that kill so much aquatic life that dead zones can extend up to 90 m below the surface. The decomposing organic matter further decreases the oxygen levels, spurring the release of even more nutrients. Once an HAB begins, it tends to worsen over time. Without human intervention, an HAB is likely to spread until it consumes an entire lake.

1. Which of the following pie charts is most consistent with Student 1's description of the distribution of nitrogen in a lake experiencing an HAB ?

A.

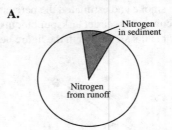

B.

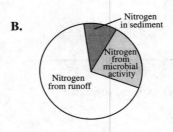

C.

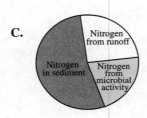

D.

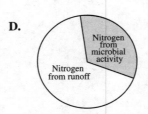

2. Which of the students, if either, state(s) that decreasing dissolved oxygen levels leads to the release of nutrients from the sediments?

   F. Neither Student 1 nor Student 2
   G. Student 1 only
   H. Student 2 only
   J. Both Student 1 and Student 2

3. *Ephemeroptera* (mayfly larvae) and *Tubificidae* (sludge worms) are indicator species used to identify changes in certain water quality characteristics. *Ephemeroptera* usually outnumber *Tubificidae* when dissolved oxygen levels are sufficient, but they cannot survive when oxygen levels drop below normal range. In contrast, *Tubificidae* flourish in low dissolved oxygen environments. Based on the passage, which of the two indicator species would each student expect to be more prevalent in a lake at the start of an HAB ?

	Student 1	Student 2
A.	*Ephemeroptera*	*Tubificidae*
B.	*Ephemeroptera*	*Ephemeroptera*
C.	*Tubificidae*	*Ephemeroptera*
D.	*Tubificidae*	*Tubificidae*

4. A study reveals that the majority of harmful algal blooms in a region occur annually in the beginning of summer and usually clear up by mid-fall without any intervention. The results of this study would better support the theory of which student?

   F. Student 1; Student 1 claims that HABs clear up naturally after the bloom consumes the excess nitrogen.
   G. Student 1; Student 1 claims that HABs usually require human intervention to dissipate.
   H. Student 2; Student 2 claims that HABs clear up naturally after the bloom consumes the excess nitrogen.
   J. Student 2; Student 2 claims that HABs usually require human intervention to dissipate.

5. The *photic zone* of a lake is the upper layer of water in which enough sunlight permeates to permit photosynthesis. The photic zone of a particular lake extends from the surface to a depth of approximately 50 m. Which of the students, if either, would most likely believe that the dead zone created by an HAB could extend *below* the photic zone of this lake?

   A. Neither Student 1 nor Student 2
   B. Student 1 only
   C. Student 2 only
   D. Both Student 1 and Student 2

6. A third student claims that lake sediment contains phosphorous in a form that is not readily available to aquatic life. Which of the students, if either, would likely agree with this claim?

   F. Neither Student 1 nor Student 2
   G. Student 1 only
   H. Student 2 only
   J. Both Student 1 and Student 2

7. A *limiting factor* is a naturally occurring element, the relative scarcity of which limits the growth of certain plants or animals in an ecosystem. Which of the following correctly pairs a student with the element that student most likely believes is the limiting factor with regard to phytoplankton growth?

   A. Student 1: dissolved oxygen
   B. Student 1: nitrogen
   C. Student 2: dissolved oxygen
   D. Student 2: nitrogen

Passage III

Four scientists studied flamingos at three wetlands in Spain and observed some adults with dark pink coloring and some adults with light pink coloring. Each scientist proposed a theory for this observation.

Scientist 1

All flamingos are born with gray feathers that are retained for 2–3 years. Whether the flamingo will have dark pink or light pink coloring as an adult is determined by Gene P, which has two alleles (*P* and *p*) and 3 possible genotypes (*PP*, *Pp*, and *pp*). A flamingo with the Gene P genotype *pp* produces light pink coloring in its feathers. A flamingo with either the Gene P genotype *PP* or *Pp* produces dark pink coloring in its feathers. The diet and the behavior of the flamingo has no effect on the development of pink coloring in its feathers.

Scientist 2

All flamingos are born with gray feathers that are retained for 2–3 years. Whether the flamingo will have dark pink or light pink coloring as an adult is determined by Gene P, which has two alleles (*P* and *p*) and 3 possible genotypes (*PP*, *Pp*, and *pp*). A flamingo with either the Gene P genotype *PP* or *Pp* produces light pink coloring in its feathers. A flamingo with the Gene P genotype *pp* produces dark pink coloring in its feathers. The diet and the behavior of the flamingo has no effect on the development of pink coloring in its feathers.

Scientist 3

All flamingos are born with gray feathers that are retained for 2–3 years. If the flamingo has a steady diet high in *carotenoids*, it will have dark pink coloring as an adult. Carotenoids, such as canthaxanthin, are photosynthetic compounds that dissolve in fats and are deposited in growing feathers, turning them dark pink. A lack of carotenoids in a flamingo's diet will result in new feather growth that is light pink, and the existing color will be lost through molting. All flamingos studied are genetically the same, so genetics do not influence flamingo color.

Scientist 4

All flamingos are born with gray feathers that are retained for 2–3 years. Adult flamingos produce an oil high in carotenoids from a gland near their tails, which they dab onto their feathers with their beaks. Flamingos that have reached breeding age (3-6 years old) and have not yet found a mate engage in this behavior more frequently during mating season, causing their feathers to turn dark pink, whereas flamingos not searching for a mate engage in the behavior less frequently and have light pink feathers. Once a dark pink flamingo has secured a mate or mating season ends, the flamingo will decrease the behavior and the feathers will return to a light pink color. All flamingos studied are genetically the same and eat the same diet, so neither genetics nor diet influence flamingo color.

1. Which scientist would be the most likely to agree that the availability of aquatic plants and algae in a habitat affects the color of the flamingos that live there?

   A. Scientist 1
   B. Scientist 2
   C. Scientist 3
   D. Scientist 4

2. Suppose it were discovered that flamingos with darker pink coloring are more attractive to potential mates. Would this discovery better support the theory of Scientist 3 or Scientist 4?

   F. Scientist 3, because Scientist 3 indicated that flamingoes trying to attract a mate are dark pink.
   G. Scientist 3, because Scientist 3 indicated that flamingoes trying to attract a mate are light pink.
   H. Scientist 4, because Scientist 4 indicated that flamingoes trying to attract a mate are dark pink.
   J. Scientist 4, because Scientist 4 indicated that flamingoes trying to attract a mate are light pink.

3. All 4 of the scientists' theories are consistent with which of the following statements?

   A. Neither light pink nor dark pink flamingos have experienced a change in feather color over the course of their lifetimes.
   B. Only light pink flamingos have experienced a change in feather color over the course of their lifetimes.
   C. Only dark pink flamingos have experienced a change in feather color over the course of their lifetimes.
   D. Both light pink and dark pink flamingos have experienced a change in feather color over the course of their lifetimes.

4. Which of the scientists, if any, would be likely to agree that the conclusion of the mating season will cause a light pink flamingo to become dark pink?

   F. None of the scientists
   G. Scientists 1 and 2 only
   H. Scientists 1 and 3 only
   J. Scientist 3 only

5. Suppose 50 mated pairs of light pink flamingos in a population bred and hatched one egg per pair in a mating season. The parent flamingos and their offspring lived under the same conditions at the wetland and engaged in the same behaviors. Upon maturity, 39 of the offspring had light pink coloring and 11 had dark pink coloring. These results best support the theory of which scientist?

   A. Scientist 1
   B. Scientist 2
   C. Scientist 3
   D. Scientist 4

6. Based on Scientist 1's theory, if a light pink flamingo and a dark pink flamingo mated over several mating seasons and produced both light pink and dark pink offspring, the Gene P genotype of the parent with the:

   F. light pink coloring must be *Pp*.
   G. light pink coloring must be *PP*.
   H. dark pink coloring must be *Pp*.
   J. dark pink coloring must be *PP*.

7. Which of the scientists would be likely to agree that flamingos given high doses of synthetic canthaxanthin could have either light pink or dark pink coloring?

   A. Scientists 1 and 2 only
   B. Scientists 1, 2, and 4 only
   C. Scientists 2, 3, and 4 only
   D. Scientists 1, 2, 3, and 4

SCIENCE READING PASSAGES: ANSWERS AND EXPLANATIONS

Passage I

1. **B** The question asks which theories are consistent with the finding that synthetic butenolide increases the germination of scarlet larkspur seeds. The introduction says that *butenolides* are smoke-derived compounds released during forest fires. Both Scientist 1 and Scientist 4 state that compounds in smoke spur the germination of scarlet larkspur seeds. Therefore, the finding that synthetic butenolide increases the germination of scarlet larkspur seeds is consistent with the theories of Scientists 1 and 4, which is (B).

2. **H** The question asks, based on Scientist 4's hypothesis, under which conditions a scarlet larkspur seed would be *least* likely to bloom. Scientist 4 states that *Scarlet larkspur grows well in habitats with dry soil, and it also grows well in habitats that have experienced a recent forest fire.* Therefore, a seed would be *least* likely to bloom when the soil is moist and there has not been a recent forest fire. The correct answer is (H).

3. **A** The question asks if the results of the study are consistent with the theory of Scientist 2. Use POE. Table 1 shows that, for hillsides without a recent forest fire, there were more blooms (593) on the hillsides with below average rainfall than on the hillsides with more rainfall (456). Eliminate (B) and (D). Scientist 2 states that *Scarlet larkspur will produce more blooms on hillsides that have experienced below average rainfall during the spring.* This agrees with the finding. The correct answer is (A).

4. **H** The question asks, before the study was performed, which scientist would have been most likely to predict that all of the hillsides studied would have a similar number of scarlet larkspur blooms. The hillsides differ in rainfall and in the presence or absence of forest fires the previous summer. The only scientist that will expect all the hillsides to have approximately the same number of scarlet larkspur blooms is the scientist who thinks that neither of these two factors affects the number of scarlet larkspur blooms. Scientist 3 does not think blooms are affected by precipitation or fires, so the answer is (H).

5. **C** The question asks which scientists' theories are consistent with the results of the figure. The figure shows that exposure to forest fire smoke increases the percent of a hillside covered in scarlet larkspur blooms. Both Scientist 1 and Scientist 4 believe that the compounds in smoke released by forest fires increase the germination of scarlet larkspur seeds. The correct answer is (C).

6. **J** The question asks which scientist's theory is most consistent with the results of the study. Table 1 shows that the most scarlet larkspur blooms occurred on the hillsides with a recent forest fire and below average precipitation. This is consistent with Scientist 4's statement that *The greatest number of scarlet larkspur blooms will be found on hillsides that have experienced below average spring rainfall and a forest fire in the previous summer.* The correct answer is (J).

7. **B** The question asks for the question that CANNOT be directly answered by the results of the study shown in Table 1. Use POE. Table 1 shows that scarlet larkspur still bloomed even without the presence of a forest fire in the previous year, so (A) can be answered using Table 1; eliminate (A). The table shows that lower precipitation coincides with an increase in scarlet larkspur blooms, but it does not provide any information about the level of competition. Therefore, (B) cannot be directly answered by Table 1; keep (B). The hillsides with recent forest fires had more scarlet larkspur blooms, so eliminate (C). The hillsides with below average spring rainfall have more scarlet blooms, so eliminate (D). The correct answer is (B).

Passage II

1. **B** The question asks which pie chart is most consistent with Student 1's description of the distribution of nitrogen in a lake experiencing an HAB. Student 1 says that *A lake experiencing an HAB has approximately 90% of its nitrogen in useable form (70% from agricultural runoff and another 20% from microbial activity).* Eliminate (A) and (C) because they do not show 70% nitrogen from runoff. Eliminate (D) because it ignores the 10% of nitrogen that is trapped in the sediment in an unusable form. The correct answer is (B).

2. **H** The question asks which of the students, if either, states that decreasing oxygen levels leads to the release of nutrients from the sediment. Student 2 says that *When dissolved oxygen levels drop due to decreased water movement (such as during droughts or periods of decreased wind activity), a series of biochemical processes causes phosphorous to be released into the water.* Eliminate (F) and (G). While Student 1 does discuss decreasing dissolved oxygen levels, there is no mention of the release of nutrients from the sediment. Eliminate (J), and choose (H).

3. **A** The question asks which indicator species each student would expect to be more prevalent in a lake at the start of an HAB. Consider one student at a time and use POE. Student 1 says that HABs are started by excess nitrogen from runoff, and that the runoff initially increases dissolved oxygen levels. The dissolved oxygen levels do not begin to drop until after the algae bloom has killed aquatic plant life. Therefore, at the start of an HAB, the dissolved oxygen levels would be sufficient for *Ephemeroptera* to dominate. Eliminate (C) and (D). Student 2 says that HABs start after low dissolved oxygen levels trigger the release of phosphorous from the sediment. Therefore, Student 2 would expect the dissolved oxygen levels to be low prior to the start of the HAB, meaning that *Tubificidae* would flourish. Eliminate (B). The correct answer is (A).

4. **F** The question asks which student's theory is better supported by a study that showed that the majority of harmful algal blooms in a region occur annually in the beginning of summer and clear up by mid-fall without any intervention. Use POE. The study reveals that the HABs do not require intervention. Eliminate (G) and (J) because both say that HABs require human intervention. Student 2 states that *Without human intervention, an HAB is likely to spread until it consumes an entire lake.* This directly contradicts the idea that HABs clear up without intervention, so eliminate (H). The correct answer is (F).

5. **C**   The question asks which of the students, if either, would most likely believe that the dead zone created by an HAB could extend *below* the 50 m photic zone of a lake. Consider one student at a time and use POE. Student 1 says *Once the oxygen drops below a critical threshold, dead zones will sometimes form that extend from the surface to depths of almost 30 m.* The question states that the photic zone extends 50 m deep, so Student 1 does not think the dead zone will extend below the photic zone. Eliminate (B) and (D). Student 2 says that *HABs form on or near the surface, but they release toxic gases that kill so much aquatic life that dead zones can extend up to 90 m below the surface.* Therefore, Student 2 believes that the dead zone will extend below the 50 m deep photic zone. The correct answer is (C).

6. **J**   The question asks which of the students, if either, would likely agree that lake sediment contains phosphorous in a form that is readily available to aquatic life. Use POE. Student 1 states that *Heavy rains can lead to a significant increase in agricultural runoff, sending large amounts of nitrogen and phosphorous into a lake. In a healthy lake, the majority of both of these nutrients are trapped in an unusable form in the sediment.* Since Student 1 believes that phosphorous is in the sediment in an unusable form, eliminate (F) and (H). Student 2 says that *Nutrients such as nitrogen and phosphorous are concentrated in the sediment at the bottom of lakes.* Student 2's theory is that HABs are triggered when low dissolved oxygen levels trigger the release of these nutrients into the water. Therefore, it is reasonable to assume that under normal conditions they are not "readily available to aquatic life." Both students would agree with the third student's claim. The correct answer is (J).

7. **B**   The question asks for the limiting factor with regards to phytoplankton growth. A limiting factor is a naturally occurring element whose scarcity limits the growth of certain plants or animals in an ecosystem. Student 1 states *The growth of phytoplankton is curbed by the lack of available nitrogen.* This matches (B).

Passage III

1. **C**   The question asks which scientist believes that the availability of aquatic plants and algae will affect the color of the local flamingos. As the question asks about plantlife, look for references to diet. Both Scientist 1 and Scientist 2 state that *the diet and behavior of the flamingo has no effect on the development of pink coloring in its feathers.* Eliminate (A) and (B). Scientist 3 states *if the flamingo has a steady diet high in carotenoids, it will have dark pink coloring as an adult.* As the diet of the flamingo is mentioned as a factor in flamingo coloring, keep (C). Scientist 4 states that *all flamingos…eat the same diet, so neither genetics nor diet influence flamingo color.* Eliminate (D). The correct answer is (C).

2. **H**   The question asks which scientist's theory would be supported by the discovery that flamingos with darker pink coloring are more attractive to potential mates. Look for references to *mate* or *mating*. Scientist 3 never mentions mating, so this discovery cannot support Scientist 3's theory. Eliminate (F) and (G). Scientist 4 states that *flamingos that…have not yet found a mate engage in this behavior more frequently during mating season, causing their feathers to turn dark pink.* Eliminate (J), as it incorrectly identifies the color of the flamingos that are trying to attract a mate. The correct answer is (H).

3. **D** The question asks which answer choice is consistent with all of the scientists' theories. Look at the answer choices. The answers revolve around the question of which flamingos experience a change in feather color over time. The first sentence of each theory is *all flamingos are born with gray feathers that are retained for 2–3 years.* Each scientist then goes on to talk about why some flamingos later become light pink, while others become dark pink. All the scientists agree that flamingos start off gray and then become either light or dark pink. Eliminate (A), (B), and (C). The correct answer is (D).

4. **F** The question asks which scientists would agree that the conclusion of the mating season will cause a light pink flamingo to turn dark pink. Look for references to *mating season*. Only Scientist 4 mentions the *mating season.* Scientist 4 states that *once a dark pink flamingo has secured a mate or mating season ends, the flamingo will decrease the behavior and the feathers will return to a light pink color.* As this is the opposite of what the question states, eliminate (J). As Scientists 1–3 did not mention the mating season, eliminate (G) and (H). The correct answer is (F).

5. **B** The question asks which scientist's theory is best supported by the results of the study. In this study, 50 mated pairs of flamingos living under similar conditions produced 39 light pink offspring and 11 dark pink offspring. Look for information in each scientist's theory about the effect of genetics on feather coloring. Scientist 1 states that light pink flamingos only have the genotype *pp.* Two parents with only that genotype would have only light pink offspring. Eliminate (A). Scientist 2 states that light pink flamingos have genotypes of either *PP* or *Pp.* Two light pink *Pp* flamingos could produce both light pink and dark pink offspring. Keep (B). Scientist 3 says that feather color is determined by diet, so flamingos that *lived under the same conditions* should all be the same color. Eliminate (C). Scientist 4 believes dabbing behavior determines feather color, so all flamingos that *engaged in the same behaviors* should be the same color; eliminate (D). The correct answer is (B).

6. **H** The question asks what the Gene P genotype of one of the parents must be if a light pink and a dark pink flamingo mated and had both light pink and dark pink offspring. This question refers to Scientist 1, so look to find what the genotypes are for both dark pink and light pink. According to Scientist 1, light pink is *pp* and dark pink is either *PP* or *Pp.* Eliminate (F) and (G), as flamingos with those genotypes would be dark pink, not light pink. If the dark pink flamingo parent had the genotype *PP,* as in (J), all of the offspring would have the genotype *Pp* and dark pink coloring. Since some offspring have light coloring, eliminate (J). If a dark pink flamingo with *Pp,* as in (H), mated with a light pink flamingo with *pp* genotype, the offspring would be a mix of dark pink *Pp* and light pink *pp* flamingos. The correct answer is (H).

7. **B** The question asks which scientists would agree that flamingos given canthaxanthin could have either light pink or dark pink coloring. Look for references to *canthaxanthin*. Scientist 3 is the only scientist who mentions this. Scientist 3 states *if the flamingo has a steady diet high in carotenoids, it will have dark pink coloring as an adult* and then goes on to give *canthaxanthin* as an example of a carotenoid. Scientist 3 would not agree that a flamingo given canthaxanthin might have light coloring. Eliminate (C) and (D). The remaining 3 scientists do not believe that the amount of carotenoids a flamingo consumes affect flamingo color, so a flamingo given canthaxanthin could be either light pink or dark pink depending on their genes or mating status. The correct answer is (B).

Part III
Science Practice Tests

8   Science Practice Test 1
9   Science Practice Test 1: Answers and Explanations
10 Science Practice Test 2
11 Science Practice Test 2: Answers and Explanations
12 Science Practice Test 3
13 Science Practice Test 3: Answers and Explanations
14 Science Practice Test 4
15 Science Practice Test 4: Answers and Explanations

Chapter 8
Science Practice
Test 1

SCIENCE TEST

35 Minutes–40 Questions

Directions: There are six passages in this test. Each passage is followed by several questions. After reading a passage, choose the best answer to each question and fill in the corresponding oval on your answer document. You may refer to the passages as often as necessary.

You are NOT permitted to use a calculator on this test.

Passage I

As people age, they experience changes in their bone mineral density (the amount of bone mineral in bone tissue) and serum CTX levels (the amount of a particular marker for bone turnover in the blood). A study examined how treatment time for four different daily supplements affected the average bone mineral density and average serum CTX levels of patients. Table 1 shows how the average bone mineral density for patients treated with each supplement changed over time. Table 2 shows how the serum CTX levels of patients treated with each supplement changed over time. (Note: All of the patients were of the same gender and age at 0 months.)

	Table 1			
Brand of supplement	Average bone mineral density (in mg/cm³*) for patients treated with supplement daily for:			
	0 months	18 months	36 months	54 months
Bonegenic	130	120	117	116
Calcitrenix	128	125	121	118
Strength+	131	122	118	115
Vitagrow	127	123	116	113

*milligrams per cubic centimeter of bone

	Table 2			
Brand of supplement	Average serum CTX (in pg/mL*) for patients treated with supplement daily for:			
	0 months	18 months	36 months	54 months
Bonegenic	531	327	304	315
Calcitrenix	416	375	341	307
Strength+	507	389	363	371
Vitagrow	327	299	293	289

*picograms per milliliter of serum

1. Suppose that a doctor wants to prescribe the supplement that will help patients maintain as much of their initial bone density as possible when taken daily for 3 years. Based on Table 1, which of the 4 supplements tested would best meet the doctor's preferred specifications?

A. Bonegenic
B. Calcitrenix
C. Strength+
D. Vitagrow

2. According to Table 2, in the study, was the initial average serum CTX of patients given the Strength+ supplement equal to 510 pg/mL, greater than 510 pg/mL, or less than 510 pg/mL ?

F. Equal
G. Greater
H. Less
J. Cannot be determined from the given information

3. A scientist predicted that as the time of treatment with a supplement increased from 0 months through 54 months, the average serum CTX produced by patients would always decrease. According to Table 2, this prediction was consistent with the data for which of the 4 supplements?

A. Calcitrenix only
B. Calcitrenix and Vitagrow only
C. Strength+ and Vitagrow only
D. Bonegenic, Calcitrenix, Strength+, and Vitagrow

4. Based on Table 2, which of the following graphs best shows the average serum CTX for patients given the 4 supplements at a treatment time of 18 months?

F.

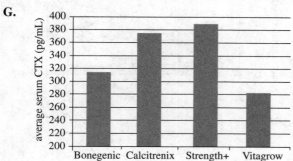

G.

H.

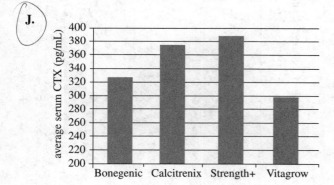

J.

5. Based on Table 1, patients of which of the 4 supplements showed the least change in average bone mineral density between 18 months and 36 months of treatment?

A. Bonegenic
B. Calcitrenix
C. Strength+
D. Vitagrow

6. Consider the statement "Among the 4 supplements tested, the supplement whose patients initially had the lowest average bone mineral density was also the supplement whose patients had the greatest average serum CTX at a treatment time of 54 months." Do the data in Tables 1 and 2 support this statement?

F. Yes; that supplement was Strength+.
G. Yes; that supplement was Vitagrow.
H. No; on average, Vitagrow patients initially had the lowest average bone mineral density, but Strength+ patients had the greatest average serum CTX at 54 months.
J. No; on average, Strength+ patients initially had the lowest average bone mineral density, but Vitagrow patients had the greatest average serum CTX at 54 months.

Passage II

Riverbed sediment deposition occurs when silt, sand, and gravel traveling in a river settle down and accumulate on the river bottom. Sediment accumulation patterns differ between *straight-channel rivers* and *meandering rivers* (see Figure 1).

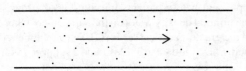

straight-channel river
(sediment accumulation is relatively
consistent along the riverbed)

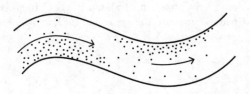

meandering river
(sediment accumulation is concentrated
more heavily along the inner curves)

Figure 1

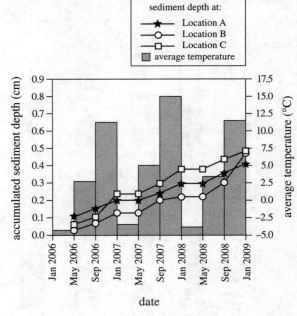

Figure 2

Researchers studied sediment accumulation in six locations along snowmelt-fed rivers: three locations were on a straight-channel river (Locations A–C) and three locations were on a meandering river (Locations D–F). The researchers measured the sediment depth along the center of the riverbed at each location every four months from January of 2006 to January of 2009 and used the values to calculate the accumulation of sediment throughout the study. Figures 2 and 3 show the results for Locations A–C and D–F, respectively. The average temperatures in the region over each 4-month interval are also shown in both figures.

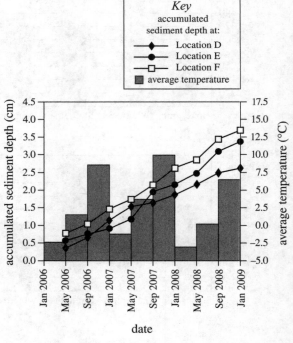

Figure 3

7. According to Figure 3, the increase in accumulated sediment depth at Location D was the least between which of the following months?

   A. September 2006 and January 2007
   B. May 2007 and September 2007
   C. September 2007 and January 2008
   D. January 2008 and May 2008

8. Which of the following best explains why researchers recorded temperature data along with accumulated sediment data?

   F. When temperatures are high, snowmelt may prevent any sediment from reaching the river.
   G. When temperatures are low, lack of snowmelt may limit the amount of sediment that flows into the river.
   H. When temperatures are high, snowmelt may limit the amount of sediment that flows into the river.
   J. When temperatures are low, lack of snowmelt may increase the amount of sediment that flows into the river.

9. According to Figure 3, which of the following graphs best shows the total accumulated sediment depth at Locations D–F by September 2007 ?

A.
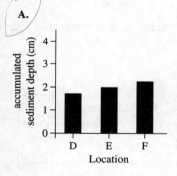

B.
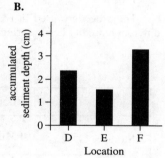

C.
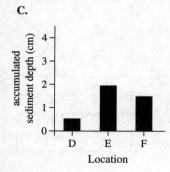

D.
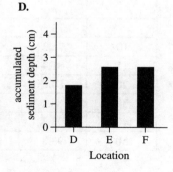

10. In Figure 2, consider the 4-month intervals during which there was no additional sediment accumulation at any of Locations A–C. The average temperature at each location during these time intervals was:

   F. less than –4°C.
   G. between –4°C and –2°C.
   H. between –2°C and 0°C.
   J. greater than 0°C.

11. Suppose the researchers had also measured, every four months, the accumulated sediment depth near the riverbank on the inner curve at Location E since January of 2006. Based on Figures 1 and 3, in September 2007, would they more likely have recorded an accumulated sediment depth of less than 2 cm or greater than 2 cm ?

   A. Less than 2 cm, because sediment concentrated more heavily along the center than on the inner curves.
   B. Less than 2 cm, because sediment concentrated more heavily along the inner curves than in the center.
   C. Greater than 2 cm, because sediment concentrated more heavily along the center than on the inner curves.
   D. Greater than 2 cm, because sediment concentrated more heavily along the inner curves than in the center.

12. According to Figures 2 and 3, over the study period, was the accumulated sediment depth in the straight-channel river greater than or less than the total sediment accumulation in the meandering river?

   F. Greater; sediment accumulated as much as 2.8 cm in the straight-channel river, whereas sediment accumulated as much as 0.3 cm in the meandering river.
   G. Greater; sediment accumulated as much as 3.7 cm in the straight-channel river, whereas sediment accumulated as much as 0.5 cm in the meandering river.
   H. Less; sediment accumulated as much as 0.5 cm in the straight-channel river, whereas sediment accumulated as much as 3.7 cm in the meandering river.
   J. Less; sediment accumulated as much as 0.3 cm in the straight-channel river, whereas sediment accumulated as much as 2.8 cm in the meandering river.

Passage III

Three experiments were performed to examine the flammability of acacia trees.

Experiment 1

Researchers collected 100 branches of similar shape and mass from 100 live acacia trees grown in a particular preserve. Each branch, with all of its attached foliage, was weighed and the *average sample initial mass* (SIM) was recorded. The branches were then placed in a storage room at a constant temperature and 25% humidity. After 5 days, 10 branches were removed from storage and placed in a glass burn chamber filled with dry air where they were ignited and allowed to burn for exactly 10 minutes. After burning, the remaining sample and all accumulated ash were removed and weighed. The *average sample final mass* (SFM) was calculated. This process was repeated 6 additional times at different storage intervals with 10 branches each time. The *percentage of mass burned* (PMB) for each group was calculated with the following equation:

$$PMB = \frac{SIM - SFM}{SIM} \times 100$$

The results for all groups are shown in Table 1.

Table 1	
Storage time (days)	PMB
5	64.3
10	68.5
15	71.2
20	73.1
30	75.6
40	76.4
50	78.9

Experiment 2

The procedure used in Experiment 1 was repeated except that the dry air in the burn chamber was compressed to three different pressures (see Table 2).

Table 2			
Storage time (days)	PMB at air pressure (in psi*) of:		
	20	40	80
5	67.6	68.2	72.1
10	70.3	71.4	75.9
15	72.8	74.5	78.2
20	75.7	76.7	80.3
30	77.2	79.6	83.5
40	79.5	81.8	84.7
50	82.9	84.4	89.6
*pounds of force per square inch of area			

Experiment 3

The procedure used in Experiment 1 was repeated at four different humidity levels during storage (see Table 3).

Table 3				
Storage time (days)	PMB at humidity (%) of:			
	10%	15%	20%	35%
5	73.3	70.5	66.2	61.7
10	76.2	73.6	70.5	63.4
15	81.4	77.1	72.3	66.6
20	84.6	79.2	75.8	68.5
30	88.1	82.4	77.7	69.9
40	93.3	86.7	80.4	71.1
50	95.8	90.3	82.2	73.9

13. Based on the results of Experiment 3, storing acacia branches at a constant temperature at what humidity and for what length of time resulted in the least amount of mass burned?

	humidity	storage time
A.	10%	5 days
B.	10%	20 days
C.	35%	5 days
D.	35%	20 days

14. If an air pressure of 60 psi had been tested in Experiment 2, the PMB at 20 days would most likely have been:

F. less than 76.7.
G. between 76.7 and 80.3.
H. between 80.3 and 83.5.
J. greater than 83.5.

15. Suppose the procedure of Experiment 1 is repeated at humidity of 30%. Based on the results of Experiments 1 and 3, a storage time of 10 days will most likely result in a PMB that is:

A. less than 63.4.
B. between 63.4 and 68.5.
C. between 68.5 and 70.5.
D. greater than 70.5.

16. Consider the branches in Experiment 1 that were stored for 30 days. If the accumulated ashes had *not* been collected from the burn chamber before the remaining sample was weighed, would their PMB more likely have been less than or greater than the PMB shown in Table 1 for a storage time of 30 days?

F. Less, because the SFM would have been less.
G. Less, because the SFM would have been greater.
H. Greater, because the SFM would have been less.
J. Greater, because the SFM would have been greater.

17. At the conclusion of Experiment 1, how many branches had *not* been burned in the burn chamber?

A. 20
B. 30
C. 50
D. 60

18. Examine the results of Experiments 1 and 2. Compared to the PMB of acacia burned in ordinary dry air, the PMB at any given storage time for acacia burned in compressed air was:

F. always greater.
G. always the same.
H. always less.
J. at times less and at times greater, depending on the air pressure.

19. Consider the SFM of any group of stored acacia branches in Experiment 1. Also consider the SIM of the group of acacia branches before storage. Was the SFM equal to, greater than, or less than the SIM ?

A. Equal
B. Greater
C. Less
D. Cannot be determined from the given information

Passage IV

Phenol red is a water-soluble dye that can be used to approximate the pH of an aqueous solution. A phenol red solution can be yellow, orange, or dark pink depending on the solution's pH. Table 1 shows the pH ranges that apply to each solution color in a phenol red solution.

Table 1	
Solution color	pH
yellow	< 6.6
orange	6.6 - 8.1
dark pink	> 8.1

Since an acid is produced when carbon dioxide dissolves in an aqueous solution, changes in the carbon dioxide concentration of a solution can be observed by monitoring pH changes. In an aquatic ecosystem, the concentration is affected by photosynthesis, which consumes carbon dioxide, and cellular respiration, which produces carbon dioxide. Photosynthesis and cellular respiration are demonstrated by equations 1 and 2, respectively.

1) carbon dioxide + water + sunlight → sugar + oxygen

2) sugar + oxygen → carbon dioxide + water + energy

A student conducted 3 experiments to determine the effect of the inclusion of aquatic plants and animals on the pH of aqueous solutions.

Experiment 1

The student prepared a solution of phenol red and water. The color of the solution was orange. The student added 20 mL of the phenol red solution to each of 2 glass vials. She also added a piece of *cabomba* (an aquatic plant) in both glass vials, capped the vials, and then incubated them at 20°C for 48 hr. During the 48 hr incubation, one of the vials was exposed to constant light while the other was kept in a dark room. After the incubation period, the color of the solution was noted (see Table 2).

Table 2			
Vial	Organism added	Exposed to light	Color after 48 hr
1	cabomba	yes	orange
2	cabomba	no	yellow

Experiment 2

The student repeated the same process from Experiment 1 except that a goldfish was placed in each vial instead of a piece of cabomba (see Table 3).

Table 3			
Vial	Organism added	Exposed to light	Color after 48 hr
3	goldfish	yes	yellow
4	goldfish	no	yellow

Experiment 3

The procedure for Experiment 1 was repeated except that the student used 4 vials, 2 of which contained both a piece of cabomba and a goldfish and 2 of which contained neither. Two of the vials were exposed to light and two were kept in the dark room (see Table 4).

Table 4				
Vial	Cabomba included	Goldfish included	Exposed to light	Color after 48 hr
5	yes	yes	yes	orange
6	yes	yes	no	yellow
7	no	no	yes	orange
8	no	no	no	orange

20. Suppose that the student wanted to conduct additional trials in Experiment 2 with a different type of animal species but did not have any remaining phenol red. Which of the following pieces of equipment could the student use to detect changes in the concentration of carbon dioxide in the solutions in the additional vials?

    F. Thermometer
    G. Digital scale
    H. pH sensor
    J. Light microscope

21. The pH of the solution in Vial 2 after the 48-hr incubation period was closest to which of the following values?

    A. 6.0
    B. 7.5
    C. 8.5
    D. 10.0

22. The experimental set-up for Experiment 2 differed from Experiment 1 in which of the following ways? In Experiment 2:

    F. each vial contained a primary producer, whereas in Experiment 1 each vial contained an omnivore.
    G. each vial contained an omnivore, whereas in Experiment 1 each vial contained a primary producer.
    H. both vials were exposed to light, whereas in Experiment 1 both vials were kept in a dark room.
    J. both vials were kept in a dark room, whereas in Experiment 1 both vials were exposed to light.

23. The student predicted that over the 48-hr incubation period, exposure to light in the absence of photosynthesis and cellular respiration would cause the phenol red to discolor and turn yellow. Are the results of Experiment 3 consistent with her prediction?

    A. No; after 48 hrs of incubation, the solution in Vial 6 was orange.
    B. No; after 48 hrs of incubation, the solution in Vial 7 was orange.
    C. Yes; after 48 hrs of incubation, the solution in Vial 6 was yellow.
    D. Yes; after 48 hrs of incubation, the solution in Vial 7 was yellow.

24. At the conclusion of the 48-hr incubation, why was the color of the phenol red solution in Vial 1 different from the color of the phenol red solution in Vial 2? The presence of light in Vial 1 was necessary for the cabomba to undergo:

    F. cellular respiration, which caused it to consume more carbon dioxide than the cabomba in Vial 2.
    G. cellular respiration, which caused it to consume less carbon dioxide than the cabomba in Vial 2.
    H. photosynthesis, which caused it to consume more carbon dioxide than the cabomba in Vial 2.
    J. photosynthesis, which caused it to consume less carbon dioxide than the cabomba in Vial 2.

25. After the 48-hr incubation period, another student removed the cabomba from Vial 1 and added 1 mL of an unknown solution. The student observed that the color of the phenol red solution changed to yellow. Is the unknown solution more likely acidic or basic?

    A. Basic, because the addition of the unknown solution led to an increase in the pH of the phenol red solution.
    B. Basic, because the addition of the unknown solution led to a decrease in the pH of the phenol red solution.
    C. Acidic, because the addition of the unknown solution led to an increase in the pH of the phenol red solution.
    D. Acidic, because the addition of the unknown solution led to a decrease in the pH of the phenol red solution.

26. Suppose that at the end of the incubation period in Experiment 3, the student added a tadpole to Vial 7. If Vial 7 had then been incubated for an additional 48 hrs with exposure to light, the color of the phenol red solution would most likely have been:

    F. yellow, because the tadpole would produce carbon dioxide while undergoing cellular respiration.
    G. yellow, because the tadpole would consume carbon dioxide while undergoing photosynthesis.
    H. dark pink, because the tadpole would produce carbon dioxide while undergoing cellular respiration.
    J. dark pink, because the tadpole would consume carbon dioxide while undergoing photosynthesis.

Passage V

An object at rest will stay at rest when the forces acting on it are balanced such that the *net force* is zero. In each trial of 2 experiments on forces, a helium balloon was at rest with balanced forces, as shown in Figure 1.

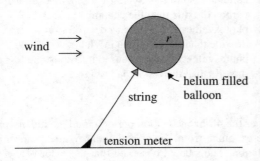

Figure 1

A spherical balloon with radius r is filled with helium and tied to a string tethered to the floor of a lab. A horizontal wind with constant speed V was generated. Once the string was stretched taut and returned to rest, a tension meter was used to measure the tension in the string. The *buoyant force* (upward force due to the low density of helium) was calculated. The forces acting on the balloon while it was at rest are shown in Figure 2.

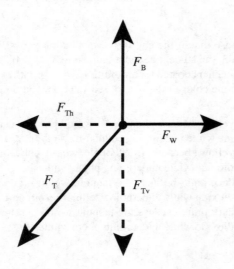

Figure 2

The buoyant force, F_B, was purely vertical, while the wind force, F_W, was purely horizontal. The tension force of the string, F_T, had both a horizontal component, F_{Th}, and a vertical component, F_{Tv}.

Experiment 1

In Trials 1–5, r was varied and V was 2.0 m/s. The values for r, in meters, for each trial are shown in Table 1 along with the values of F_B, F_W, F_{Th}, and F_{Tv}, in newtons (N).

Table 1					
Trial	r (m)	F_B (N)	F_W (N)	F_{Th} (N)	F_{Tv} (N)
1	0.3	1.22	0.28	−0.28	−1.22
2	0.4	2.89	0.49	−0.49	−2.89
3	0.5	5.64	0.77	−0.77	−5.64
4	0.6	9.75	1.11	−1.11	−9.75
5	0.7	15.48	1.51	−1.51	−15.48

Experiment 2

In Trials 6–10, r was 0.5 m and V was varied. The values for V, in meters per second, for each trial are shown in Table 2 along with the values of F_B, F_W, F_{Th}, and F_{Tv}, in newtons (N).

Table 2					
Trial	V (m/s)	F_B (N)	F_W (N)	F_{Th} (N)	F_{Tv} (N)
6	3.0	5.64	1.73	−1.73	−5.64
7	4.0	5.64	3.08	−3.08	−5.64
8	5.0	5.64	4.81	−4.81	−5.64
9	6.0	5.64	6.92	−6.92	−5.64
10	7.0	5.64	9.42	−9.42	−5.64

27. Based on the results of Experiment 2, as V increased, the wind force:

    A. increased only.
    B. decreased only.
    C. increased, then decreased.
    D. remained constant.

28. According to the results of Experiments 1 and 2, which of the following calculations would always result in zero?

    F. $F_B - F_{Tv}$
    G. $F_B - F_W$
    H. $F_B + F_{Tv}$
    J. $F_B + F_W$

29. Suppose that the method used to determine the wind force was only valid for wind forces greater than 0.4 N (meaning this method was unreliable to calculate forces less than 0.4 N). Based on the results of the experiments, was this method appropriate to use in all of these trials?

    A. No, because the value of F_W exceeded 0.4 N in all trials.
    B. No, because the value of F_W did not exceed 0.4 N in one of the trials.
    C. Yes, because the value of F_W exceeded 0.4 N in all trials.
    D. Yes, because the value of F_W did not exceed 0.4 in one of the trials.

30. According to the results of Experiment 2, approximately what speed should the horizontal wind be in order for the value of F_{Th} to be equal to F_{Tv}?

    F. 3.5 m/s
    G. 4.5 m/s
    H. 5.5 m/s
    J. 6.5 m/s

31. Suppose that in Experiment 1 a trial had been performed in which F_W was 1.65 N. The radius of the balloon in this trial would most likely have been:

    A. less than 0.6 m.
    B. between 0.6 m and 0.7 m.
    C. between 0.7 m and 0.8 m.
    D. greater than 0.8 m.

32. Which of the following statements about r or V indicates the main difference between the 2 experiments? In Experiment 1:

    F. r was held constant, while in Experiment 2, r was a dependent variable.
    G. r was held constant, while in Experiment 2, r was an independent variable.
    H. V was held constant, while in Experiment 2, V was a dependent variable.
    J. V was held constant, while in Experiment 2, V was an independent variable.

33. A vector quantity, such as force, can be expressed as $V = [V_x, V_y]$ where V_x is the horizontal component of the vector and V_y is the vertical component of the vector. For example, the force (in N) on the string in Trial 5 can be expressed as $V = [-1.51, -15.48]$. Which of the following gives the force (in N) of the *wind* during Trial 5 ?

    A. [1.51, 15.48]
    B. [1.51, 0.00]
    C. [-1.51, 15.48]
    D. [-1.51, 0.00]

Passage VI

In the year 79 BCE, Mt. Vesuvius erupted in a giant plume of ash. Records indicate that volcanic lightning was observed in the ash cloud following the eruption, with some branches of lightning extending up to 15 km above the volcanic vent. Two scientists debate whether *fractoemission* or *ice charging* generated the initial charges that lead to the lightning strikes during the Mt. Vesuvius eruption in 79 BCE.

Scientist 1

In the build-up to a volcanic eruption, as heated magma rises towards the vent on the surface, the decrease in pressure causes volatiles such as carbon dioxide and nitrogen in the magma to form bubbles. In silicate-rich magma, like that found at Mt. Vesuvius in 79 BCE, the bubbles expand faster than the magma can accommodate and the magma is forcibly fractured. When the magma is fractured, electrically charged ash particles are created in a process called fractoemission. Once the charged particles are expelled during the eruption, the positively charged particles travel faster and higher in the ash cloud than the negatively charged particles, causing a separation of charges. Within minutes, lightning bolts are generated to resolve the difference in charges. These lightning bolts always occur less than a kilometer downwind from the vent since they happen in the first few minutes after the eruption.

Volcanic lightning leads to the creation of Br radicals in the ash plume immediately surrounding the lightning strike. When the lightning is caused by fractoemission charging, evidence of locally high concentrations of these radicals can be found in the ash near the volcanic vent. The sediment found within a kilometer of Mt. Vesuvius contains evidence of high concentrations of Br radicals in the ash from 79 BCE.

Scientist 2

In violent volcanic eruptions, such as the Mt. Vesuvius eruption in 79 BCE, a large number of neutral ash particles are ejected in dense ash plumes at high speeds. These ash plumes have a high water vapor content, and even though the particles are ejected at temperatures of approximately 1,000°C, the water vapor eventually freezes once the particles rise above the freeze line (the altitude at which temperatures are low enough to freeze water droplets). The ice particles in the ash plume then collide with other ash particles and these collisions cause the particles to become charged in a process known as *ice charging*. As the charged particles move downwind, positively charged and negatively charged molecules travel at different speeds. Several minutes to hours after the initial eruption, the separation of charges eventually leads to lightning strikes slightly downwind from the vent and high in the ash plume.

When volcanic lightning occurs in the densely packed core of the ash cloud immediately following the eruption, as occurs with fractoemission charging, round crystals called lightning-induced volcanic spherules (LIVS) are produced. No spherules were found in the sediment from 79 BCE on Mt. Vesuvius, so the lightning observed must have been due to ice charging.

34. Both scientists discuss how the particles in the ash plume of the volcanic eruption initially gained a charge. The process described by each scientist is an example of:

F. combustion.
G. ionization.
H. weathering.
J. condensation.

35. A prominent researcher asserted that, on the day Mt. Vesuvius erupted in 79 BCE, based on the estimated temperature and wind patterns, the velocity of the ash particles would not have been sufficient enough for the ash plume to have crossed the freeze line prior to the observed volcanic lightning strikes. This information is *inconsistent* with the viewpoint(s) of which of the scientists, if either?

A. Neither scientist
B. Scientist 1 only
C. Scientist 2 only
D. Both Scientist 1 and Scientist 2

36. Consider Scientist 1's and Scientist 2's claims about the generation of the charges in the ash particles that led to the volcanic lightning seen in the Mt. Vesuvius eruption of 79 BCE. According to Scientist 1, were the charges generated prior to the eruption or after the eruption; and according to Scientist 2, were the charges generated prior to the eruption or after the eruption?

	Scientist 1	Scientist 2
F.	prior to the eruption	after the eruption
G.	prior to the eruption	prior to the eruption
H.	after the eruption	after the eruption
J.	after the eruption	prior to the eruption

37. Research has shown that particles charged through fractoemission will be discharged before they can reach an altitude of more than 10 km above a volcanic vent. Does this information support or weaken the viewpoint of Scientist 1 ?

A. It weakens Scientist 1's viewpoint because at least a couple of the lightning branches extended 15 km above the volcano vent.
B. It weakens Scientist 1's viewpoint because all of the lightning branches extended 15 km above the volcano vent.
C. It supports Scientist 1's viewpoint because some of the lightning branches extended more than 10 km above the volcano vent.
D. It supports Scientist 1's viewpoint because all of the lightning branches extended more than 10 km above the volcano vent.

38. The discovery of which of the following, if made today, would provide the most support for Scientist 1's viewpoint?

F. The formation of ice particles in the ash plume of a volcanic eruption
G. Lightning damage on trees 5 km downwind of Mt. Vesuvius
H. 2,100-year-old silicate-rich lava on Mt. Vesuvius
J. 2,100-year-old sediment with no LIVS on Mt. Vesuvius

39. Suppose that a volcanic lightning strike did occur in the densely packed core of the ash plume near the volcanic vent during the eruption of Mt. Vesuvius in 79 BCE. Would Scientist 1 agree that Br radicals might have been present in the Mt. Vesuvius ash in 79 BCE, and would Scientist 2 agree that LIVS might have been present in the Mt. Vesuvius ash in 79 BCE ?

	Scientist 1	Scientist 2
A.	no	no
B.	no	yes
C.	yes	no
D.	yes	yes

40. Based on Scientist 1's discussion, did the charging process that occurred during the fracture of magma have the effect of increasing the mass of the particles that became positively charged or decreasing the mass of the particles that became positively charged?

F. Increasing the mass, because the particles lost an electron.
G. Increasing the mass, because the particles gained a proton.
H. Decreasing the mass, because the particles lost an electron.
J. Decreasing the mass, because the particles gained a proton.

END OF TEST.
STOP! DO NOT TURN THE PAGE UNTIL TOLD TO DO SO.

Chapter 9
Science Practice
Test 1: Answers and
Explanations

SCIENCE PRACTICE TEST 1 ANSWER KEY

1. B	21. A
2. H	22. G
3. B	23. B
4. J	24. H
5. A	25. D
6. H	26. F
7. B	27. A
8. G	28. H
9. A	29. B
10. G	30. H
11. D	31. C
12. H	32. J
13. C	33. B
14. G	34. G
15. B	35. C
16. H	36. F
17. B	37. A
18. F	38. H
19. C	39. D
20. H	40. H

SCORE YOUR PRACTICE TEST

Step A
Count the number of correct answers: _____. This is your *raw score*.

Step B
Use the score conversion table below to look up your raw score. The number to the left is your *scale score:* _____.

Test 1 Scale Conversion Table

Scale Score	Raw Score	Scale Score	Raw Score	Scale Score	Raw Score
36	39–40	24	26–27	12	9
35	38	23	25	11	8
34	37	22	23–24	10	7
33	36	21	21–22	9	6
32	35	20	20	8	5
31	34	19	18–19	7	4
30	—	18	17	6	3
29	33	17	16	5	—
28	32	16	14–15	4	2
27	31	15	13	3	1
26	29–30	14	12	2	—
25	28	13	10–11	1	0

SCIENCE PRACTICE TEST 1 EXPLANATIONS

Passage I

1. **B** The question asks which supplement best meets the criteria that it will *maintain as much of (patients') initial bone density as possible* if it is taken for 3 years. Use Table 1 and compare the bone density between 0 months and 36 months for each supplement, as these are the *initial* value and the value at *3 years*. For Bonegenic, the bone density goes from 130 in month 0 to 117 in month 36 for a decrease in bone density of 13 mg/cm^3 over three years. For Calcitrenix, the value goes from 128 to 121 for a decrease of 7 mg/cm^3. For Strength+, the value goes from 131 to 118 for a decrease of 13 mg/cm^3. For Vitagrow, the values go from 127 to 116 for a decrease of 11 mg/cm^3. The smallest decrease occurred when patients took Calcitrenix. The correct answer is (B).

2. **H** The question asks for a comparison of the *initial average serum CTX of patients given the Strength+ supplement* in relation to *510 pg/mL*. Use Table 2 and look up the initial average serum CTX for Strength+ patients. At the *initial* time of 0 months, the average serum CTX is 507 pg/mL, which is less than 510 pg/mL. The correct answer is (H).

3. **B** The question asks which supplement(s) are consistent with the prediction given. The prediction is that as the time of treatment with a supplement increased, the average serum CTX would always decrease. Use Table 2 and check to see which supplements showed a decrease across time from 0 months to 54 months. For Bonegenic, the average serum CTX decreases each time from 0 months to 18 months to 36 months, but then it increases from 36 months to 54 months. Eliminate (D) because it includes Bonegenic. For Calcitrenix, the average serum CTX decreases at every time interval. Eliminate (C) because it does not include Calcitrenix. No remaining answers include Strength+, so check Vitagrow next to determine if (A) or (B) is the correct answer. For Vitagrow, the average serum CTX decreases at every time interval. Eliminate (A) because it does not include Vitagrow. The correct answer is (B).

4. **J** The question asks for the graph that best shows *the average serum CTX* across supplements at 18 months. Use Table 2 to find the values of average serum CTX for each supplement. At 18 months, Strength+ has the highest average serum CTX at 389 pg/mL. Eliminate (F) and (H) since these graphs do not show Strength+ as having the highest average serum. Compare the graphs for (G) and (J). The graphs show different values for Vitagrow. Check Table 2 for the average serum CTX at 18 months for Vitagrow; the average serum CTX is 299 pg/mL, which is shown on the graph for (J). The correct answer is (J).

5. **A** The question asks for the supplement that showed *the least change in average bone mineral density* from 18 months to 36 months of treatment. Use Table 1 to compare the values of bone mineral density between 18 months and 36 months for each supplement. For Bonegenic, the bone density goes from 120 in month 18 to 117 in month 36 for a difference of 3 mg/cm^3. For Calcitrenix, the bone density goes from 122 in month 18 to 121 in month 36 for a difference of 4 mg/cm^3. For Strength+, the bone

density goes from 122 in month 18 to 118 in month 36 for a difference of 4 mg/cm^3. For Vitagrow, the bone density goes from 123 in month 18 to 116 in month 36 for a difference of 7 mg/cm^3. Bonegenic has the least change in bone density. The correct answer is (A).

6. **H**   The question asks if the data in Tables 1 and 2 support the statement that patients with *the lowest average bone mineral density* initially took the same supplement as the patients who *had the greatest average serum CTX* at 54 months. Use Table 1 to find the supplement given to patients with the lowest average bone mineral density initially. At 0 months, patients given Vitagrow had the lowest average bone mineral density at 127 mg/cm^3. Next, use Table 2 to see if patients given Vitagrow had the greatest average serum CTX at 54 months. At 54 months, patients given Vitagrow had the lowest average serum, so the results do not support the statement. Eliminate (F) and (G) because they indicate that the statement is supported. Compare (H) and (J). Choice (J) incorrectly states that Strength+ patients initially had the lowest average bone mineral density. Eliminate (J). The correct answer is (H).

Passage II

7. **B**   The question asks for the range of months when the increase in accumulated sediment depth was the least at Location D. The accumulated sediment depth at Location D is shown in Figure 3. Look at Figure 3 and find the line showing the sediment depth for Location D. The smallest increase will be the line that is most horizontal. Out of the four answer choices, the line between May 2007 and September 2007 is the most horizontal. Eliminate (A), (C), and (D) since these time periods show a greater, rather than smaller, increase in accumulated sediment depth. The correct answer is (B).

8. **G**   The question asks why the researchers recorded average temperature. Read the answer choices for key terms and use POE. The answer choices all mention snowmelt. In the description of the study, it says the researchers studied *snowmelt-fed rivers*. Increased snowmelt would increase the sediment in the rivers, as sediment will be carried with the snowmelt into the river. Eliminate (F) and (H) because snowmelt would increase sediment rather than prevent or limit it. Eliminate (J) because lack of snowmelt would not increase sediment flow into rivers. The correct answer is (G).

9. **A**   The question asks for a graph that shows the accumulated sediment depth for Locations D–F in September 2007. The accumulated sediment depths for Locations D–F are shown in Figure 3. In September 2007, Location F had the highest accumulated sediment depth. Eliminate (C) because it shows Location E as having the highest accumulated sediment depth. Eliminate (D) because it shows Location E and Location F as having the same accumulated sediment depth. Based on Figure 3, Location D had the lowest accumulated sediment depth in September 2007. Eliminate (B) because it shows Location D as having a higher accumulated sediment depth than Location E. The correct answer is (A).

10. **G**   The questions asks for the temperature when there was no additional sediment accumulation at Locations A–C. The data for Locations A–C are shown in Figure 2. Use Figure 2 to find the times when the sediment accumulation did not increase, which will be the time periods when the line is horizontal. The sediment accumulation did not increase between January 2007 to May 2007 and between January 2008 to May 2008. In both of these time periods, the temperature, indicated by the bars, is less than –2.5°C. Eliminate (H) and (J). Both time periods are roughly halfway between –2.5°C and –5.0°C, which is greater than –4.0°C. The correct answer is (G).

11. **D**   The question asks whether the measured sediment at an inner curve of the river at Location E would be greater or less than 2 cm in September 2007. The data for Location E is shown in Figure 3. Based on Figure 3, the accumulated sediment depth at Location E in September 2007 was 2 cm. Based on Figure 1, for a meandering river such as Location E, the accumulation of sediment is greater along the inner curves of the river. Eliminate (A) and (B) because the accumulated sediment depth would be greater than 2 cm, not less. Eliminate (C) because it incorrectly states that the sediment concentration is greater in the center than along the inner curves. The correct answer is (D).

12. **H**   The question asks if the accumulated sediment depth in the straight-channel river was greater or less than the accumulated sediment depth in the meandering river. The passage states that Locations A–C *were on a straight-channel river* and Locations D–F *were on a meandering river*. Compare the accumulated sediment depth in Figure 2 (straight-channel river) to the accumulated sediment depth in Figure 3 (meandering river). In Figure 2, the accumulated sediment depth ranges from less than 0.1 cm to 0.5 cm. In Figure 3, the accumulated sediment depth ranges from less than 0.5 cm to about 3.5 cm. At each time interval, the accumulated sediment depth is less in the straight-channel river. Eliminate (F) and (G) because they incorrectly state that the sediment depth is greater in the straight-channel river. Eliminate (J) because it incorrectly states that the highest values for accumulated sediment depth for the straight-channel river is 0.3 cm and the meandering river is 2.8 cm. The correct answer is (H).

Passage III

13. **C**   The question asks for the humidity and storage time that resulted in the least amount of mass burned in Experiment 3. The results for Experiment 3 are shown in Table 3. The data shows PMB, which is described in the passage as *percentage of mass burned*. Look for the smallest PMB on Table 3. Note the trends. The PMB increases as the storage time increases, so 5 days will have a smaller PMB. Eliminate (B) and (D). PMB decreases as humidity increases, so 35% has a smaller PMB than 10% humidity. The correct answer is (C).

14. **G**   The question asks what the PMB would be for a storage time of 20 days and an air pressure of 60 psi in Experiment 2. Look for the data for the PMB at a storage time of 20 days in Table 2. The PMB is listed for air pressures of 20 psi, 40 psi, and 80 psi. The PMB values increase with higher air pressures. Thus, the PMB at an air pressure of 60 psi will fall between the values for 40 and 80 psi. At a storage time of 20 days, the PMB is 76.7% at 40 psi and 80.3% at 80 psi. The correct answer is (G).

15. **B** The question asks what the PMB would be with a storage time of 10 days and a humidity of 30% based on Experiments 1 and 3. Since humidity is not mentioned in Table 1, read the description of Experiment 1 to find the humidity percentage. The humidity for Experiment 1 was 25%. Based on Table 1, at 25% humidity and 10 days of storage time, the PMB was 68.5%. Based on Table 3, at 35% humidity and 10 days of storage time, the PMB was 63.4%. Therefore, the PMB at 30% humidity and 10 days of storage time would be between 63.4% and 68.5%. The correct answer is (B).

16. **H** The question asks how the PMB would have changed if the accumulated ashes had *not* been collected from the burn chamber before the remaining sample was weighed. Read the description of Experiment 1 to learn more about the accumulated ashes. The passage says that the *remaining sample and all accumulated ash were removed and weighed* to find the *average sample final mass* (SFM). If the accumulated ashes were not collected, the SFM would have been less. Eliminate (G) and (J) because they indicate the SFM would have been greater. Based on the equation $PMB = \dfrac{SIM - SFM}{SIM} \times 100$, a smaller SFM would result in a greater PMB. The correct answer is (H).

17. **B** The question asks how many branches were *not* burned at the conclusion of Experiment 1. Read the description of Experiment 1 to find out how many branches were burned. The passage says that *researchers collected 100 branches*. Later it states that *10 branches* were burned and that the *process was repeated 6 additional times*. Therefore, the total number of branches burned was 70. Since the researchers started with 100 branches, 30 branches were not burned. The correct answer is (B).

18. **F** The question asks how the PMB of acacia burned in ordinary dry air compared to the PMB of acacia burned in compressed air. These words do not appear in the tables, so skim the surrounding text to find the word *compressed*. This word appears in the description of Experiment 2, which was similar to Experiment 1 except that the *dry air…was compressed*. Compare the results of Table 1 to the results of Table 2 for each storage time. For the acacia stored in dry air for 5 days, the PMB is 64.3% and for the acacia stored in compressed air (20 psi) for 5 days, the PMB is 67.6%. The PMB in compressed air is greater. Eliminate (G) and (H) because these indicate that the PMB in compressed air is always the same as or always less than that of dry air. Compare the remaining data points in Table 1 to the data points with the same storage time for 20 psi in Table 2. For each storage time, the PMB in compressed air is greater. The correct answer is (F).

19. **C** The question asks how the SFM compared to the SIM in Experiment 1. Based on the description of Experiment 1, the average sample initial mass (SIM) and the average sample final mass (SFM) are used to calculate PMB using the equation $PMB = \dfrac{SIM - SFM}{SIM} \times 100$. Use POE to find the relationship. If the SFM and the SIM were equal, the equation would equal 0. Since none of the values on Table 1 are 0, the SFM and SIM were not equal; eliminate (A). If the SFM were greater than the SIM, the equation would result in a negative number. Since none of the values on Table 1 are negative, the SFM was not greater than the SIM; eliminate (B). If the SFM were less than the SIM, the equation would result in a positive number. Since all the values on Table 1 are positive, the SFM was always less than the SIM. The correct answer is (C).

Passage IV

20. **H** The question asks which of the devices listed could detect changes in the concentrations of carbon dioxide. Look for information about changes in carbon dioxide concentration. The passage says that *changes in the carbon dioxide concentration of a solution can be observed by monitoring pH changes*. A pH sensor would detect these changes whereas the other instruments listed would not. The correct answer is (H).

21. **A** The question asks for the approximate pH of the phenol red solution in Vial 2 after 48 hours. Table 2 shows that the color of the solution in Vial 2 after 48 hours is yellow. Refer to Table 1 for the relationship between solution color and pH. According to Table 1, a yellow solution has a pH of less than 6.6. Eliminate (B), (C), and (D) because all of these pH values are greater than 6.6. The correct answer is (A).

22. **G** The question asks how the set-up for Experiment 2 differed from the setup for Experiment 1. Look at Table 3 for the data for Experiment 2. According to Table 3, Vial 3 was exposed to light but Vial 4 was not. Eliminate (H) since it states that both vials in Experiment 2 were exposed to light, and eliminate (J) because it says that both of the vials were kept in the dark. The remaining answer choices use the term *primary producers*, which is an organism that produces sugars through photosynthesis. Eliminate (F) because the only organisms in Experiment 2 were goldfish, which are not primary producers. The correct answer is (G).

23. **B** The question asks whether Experiment 3 is consistent with the student's prediction that phenol red solution would turn yellow after 48 hours when exposed to light in the absence of cellular respiration and photosynthesis. Use POE. According to Table 4, after 48 hours, the solution in Vial 6 was yellow. Eliminate (A) since it states that the solution in Vial 6 was orange. The solution in Vial 7 was orange in Table 4. Eliminate (D). Table 4 also shows that Vial 7 was exposed to light, while Vial 6 was not. Since the question is about a solution that is exposed to light, eliminate (C). The correct answer is (B).

24. **H** The question asks why the color of the phenol red solution in Vial 1 differed from the color of the solution in Vial 2 after 48 hours. Refer to the passage and look for key terms in the answer choices. Equations 1 and 2 show the reactions of photosynthesis and cellular respiration, respectively. According to the equations, photosynthesis requires sunlight as a reactant, while cellular respiration does not, so eliminate (F) and (G) because they state that sunlight is necessary for cellular respiration. The passage states that photosynthesis consumes carbon dioxide. Eliminate (J), which states that photosynthesis would cause the cabomba in Vial 1 to consume less, rather than more, carbon dioxide than the cabomba in Vial 2. The correct answer is (H).

25. **D** The question asks whether an unknown solution that causes the phenol red solution in Vial 1 to turn yellow is likely to be acidic or basic. Table 2 shows that the solution in Vial 1 was orange after the 48-hour incubation period. Refer to Table 1 for the relationship between solution color and pH. According to Figure 1, orange solutions have a pH between 6.6 and 8.1 and yellow solutions have a pH below 6.6. This means that the pH of the solution decreased as it changed color from orange to

yellow. Eliminate (A) and (C), which state that the pH of the solution increased rather than decreased. To choose between the remaining choices, you need some outside knowledge. Acidic solutions have a pH less than 7.0, while basic solutions have a pH greater than 7.0. Eliminate (B) since addition of a basic solution would cause the pH to increase rather than decrease. The correct answer is (D).

26. **F**   The question asks for the color of the solution in Vial 7 after 48 hours with exposure to light if the vial had contained a tadpole. According to Table 4, Vial 7 contained neither a cabomba nor a goldfish, was not exposed to light, and remained orange after the 48-hour incubation period. A tadpole is an animal, so find the vial that was also exposed to light and contained an animal. Vial 3 was exposed to light and contained a goldfish. The solution in Vial 3 turned yellow after the 48-hour incubation period. Eliminate (H) and (J) since they both indicate that the solution would turn dark pink. Eliminate (G) since it incorrectly claims that the tadpole would undergo photosynthesis. The correct answer is (F).

Passage V

27. **A**   The question asks how the wind force varies as V is increased, based on the results of Experiment 2. The results of Experiment 2 are shown in Table 2. Use Table 2 and look for the relationship between the values of V and the wind force, F_w. For each trial in Table 2, the value for V increases, from 3.0 m/s in Trial 6 to 7.0 m/s in Trial 10. For F_w, the value is 1.73 N for Trial 6 and increases in every trial, ending with a maximum F_w of 9.42 N in Trial 10. The correct answer is (A).

28. **H**   The question asks which calculation would always result in zero, based on Experiments 1 and 2. The information for all variables in the answer choices is in Table 1, so choose any trial and plug in the values to calculate each answer. Start with (F). For (F), refer to Trial 1 in Table 1. When the value of −1.22 N for F_{Tv} is subtracted from the value of 1.22 N for F_B, the result is 1.22 − (−1.22), which does not equal zero. Eliminate (F). For (G), when the value of 0.28 N for F_w is subtracted from the value of 1.22 N for F_B, the result does not equal zero. Eliminate (G). For (H), when the value of −1.22 N for F_{Tv} is added to the value of 1.22 N for F_B, the result is 1.22 + (−1.22) which equals zero. Keep (H). For (J), when the value of −0.28 N for F_w is added to the value of 1.22 N for F_B, the result does not equal zero. Eliminate (J). The correct answer is (H).

29. **B**   The question asks whether a specific method of determining wind force would be an appropriate method to use in all the trials, given that the method *was only valid for wind forces greater than 0.4 N*. Begin by examining Table 1 and looking at the wind force F_w values for Trials 1 through 5. Trial 1 had a wind force value of 0.28 N, which is less than the 0.4 N stated in the question. Eliminate (A) and (C), which both state that *the value of F_w exceeded 0.4 N in all trials*. Since the method is unreliable to calculate forces less than 0.4 N, the method would be inappropriate for Trial 1. Eliminate (D) since it indicates that the method would be appropriate to use in Trials 1–10. The correct answer is (B).

30. **H**   The question asks at which horizontal wind speed the value of F_{Th} would be equal to F_{Tv} in Experiment 2. The results of Experiment 2 are shown in Table 2. Examine the columns for F_{Th} and F_{Tv} in Table 2. The value of F_{Tv} remains constant at −5.64 N. For the value of F_{Th} to equal the value of F_{Tv}, F_{Th} would also have to equal −5.64 N. The value −5.64 N is between −4.81 N in Trial 8 and −6.92 N in

Trial 9. The wind speed is likely between the values of the wind speed for these two trials. In Trial 8, $V = 5.0$ m/s, and in Trial 9, $V = 6.0$ m/s. The only value between 5.0 m/s and 6.0 m/s is 5.5 m/s in (H). The correct answer is (H).

31. **C** The question asks for the radius of the balloon in Experiment 1 corresponding to an experimental value, F_w, of 1.65 N. The results of Experiment 1 are shown in Table 1. Determine the relationship between the radius, r, and F_w. As seen in Table 1, as r increases, F_w also increases. The greatest value of F_w is 1.51 N, which is when $r = 0.7$ m. Since there is a direct relationship between r and F_w and 1.65 N is greater than 1.51 N, the radius will be larger than 0.7 m. Eliminate (A) and (B), which both indicate a radius less than 0.7 m. To choose between (C) and (D), look at the values of F_w to estimate the rate of increase. As seen in Table 1, the value of F_w increases by at least 0.2 N for every 0.1 m increase in the radius, r. Eliminate (D) since a radius greater than 0.8 meters would result in a value of F_w greater than 1.51 N + 0.2 N = 1.71 N. The correct answer is (C).

32. **J** The question asks for the statements about r or V that best indicates the main difference between the experiments. The first part of the answers refers to Experiment 1, so look at r and V in Experiment 1. In this experiment, the passage states that r was varied, and V was constant at 2.0 m/s. Eliminate (F) and (G), as they both incorrectly state that r was held constant rather than varied. Next examine Experiment 2. You need some outside knowledge here: an *independent variable* is also known as a manipulated variable because it is a variable whose value is manipulated by the experimenter. In Experiment 2, the value of V was manipulated by the scientists, so V is an independent variable. Eliminate (H). The correct answer is (J).

33. **B** The question asks for the vector notation of the force of the *wind*, in N, during Trial 5. The question states that the notation lists the horizontal component first followed by the vertical component. Since the question asks about wind force, look at F_w. The value for F_w = 1.51 N in Trial 5. The passage states that *the wind force, F_w, was purely horizontal*. This means that the value of the vertical component, V_y, must be zero. Eliminate (A) and (C) since they both have a non-zero vertical component (V_y). Eliminate (D), as it shows a negative V_x component of the vector. The correct answer is (B).

Passage VI

34. **G** The question asks which term accurately represents the process by which the charged particles were formed, according to both scientists. According to Scientist 1, *electrically charged ash particles are created in a process called fractoemission*, and according to Scientist 2, *collisions cause the particles to become charged in a process known as ice charging*. Eliminate (F) because neither explanation mentions combustion or burning. *Ionization* means the process of uncharged particles becoming charged, which is consistent with both explanations. There is no mention of weathering or condensation, so eliminate (H) and (J). The correct answer is (G).

35. **C**   The question asks which scientist's viewpoint, if either, is *inconsistent* with the assertion that the ash particles would not have crossed the freeze line before the lightning strikes. Scientist 2 states *the particles rise above the freeze line* prior to *lightning strikes slightly downwind from the vent and high in the ash plume*, which is inconsistent with the new information. Eliminate (A) and (B) because they do not include Scientist 2. Scientist 1 never mentions the freeze line. Eliminate (D). The correct answer is (C).

36. **F**   The question asks whether the charged particles were generated prior to or after the eruption, according to each scientist. Work one hypothesis at a time and use POE. According to Scientist 1, *when the magma is fractured, electrically charged ash particles are created*, then *charged particles are expelled during the eruption*. Therefore, Scientist 1 believes the particles are charged prior to the eruption. Eliminate (H) and (J). According to Scientist 2, *neutral ash particles are ejected in dense ash plumes at high speeds* and then after the plume has crossed the freeze line, *collisions cause the particles to become charged in a process known as ice charging*. Eliminate (G). The correct answer is (F).

37. **A**   The question asks whether Scientist 1's theory is strengthened or weakened by the new evidence that previously charged particles are discharged before they can reach an altitude of more than 10 km. Refer to the passage and look for data about altitude. According to the passage, *volcanic lightning was observed in the ash cloud following the eruption, with some branches of lightning extending up to 15 km above the volcanic vent*. There is no evidence that every one of the lightning branches was above a certain altitude. Eliminate (B) since it states that *all lightning* extended 15 km above the vent. Eliminate (D) since it states that *all* lightning extended *more than 10 km above* the vent. Scientist 1 claims that *lightning bolts are generated to resolve the difference in charges* of ash particles. However, if these particles are discharged before they reach 10 km, Scientist 1 would not expect the observed *lightning extending up to 15 km above the volcanic vent* during a volcanic eruption. Eliminate (C). The correct answer is (A).

38. **H**   The question asks which new evidence would most support Scientist 1's explanation. Refer to the passage and look for key terms in the answer choices. Choice (F) mentions the formation of ice particles. However, it is Scientist 2 who explains volcanic lighting as dependent on the formation of ice, while Scientist 1 never mentions ice particles. Eliminate (F) as it refers to the wrong hypothesis. Similarly, LIVS are only mentioned by Scientist 2, who states that the absence of LIVS means *the lightning observed must have been due to ice charging*. Eliminate (J) as it supports the wrong scientist's viewpoint. Scientist 1 claims that *lightning bolts always occur less than a kilometer downwind from the vent*. Eliminate (G) because evidence of lightning damage 5 km downwind of Mt. Vesuvius's vent would weaken Scientist 1's hypothesis. Choice (H) mentions *2,100-year-old silicate-rich lava on Mt. Vesuvius*. Scientist 1 states that fractures in *silicate-rich magma, like that found at Mt. Vesuvius in 79 BCE* caused the fractoemission charging. The correct answer is (H).

39. **D**   The question asks whether Scientist 1 would agree that Br radicals might have been present in the Mt. Vesuvius ash and whether Scientist 2 would agree that LIVS might have been present given the occurrence of lightning strikes in the core of the ash plume of Mt. Vesuvius in 79 BCE. Work one hypothesis at a time and use POE. According to the passage, Scientist 1 states that *volcanic lightning leads to the creation of Br radicals in the ash plume immediately surrounding the lightning strike,* and *sediment found within a kilometer of Mt. Vesuvius contains evidence of high concentrations of Br radicals in the ash from 79 BCE.* This supports the presence of Br radicals, so eliminate (A) and (B). Scientist 2 claims that *when volcanic lightning occurs in the densely packed core of the ash cloud immediately following the eruption, as occurs with fractoemission charging, round crystals called lightning-induced volcanic spherules (LIVS) are produced,* so eliminate (C), which says that Scientist 2 would not agree that LIVS might have been present in the ash when lightning did occur under these conditions. The correct answer is (D).

40. **H**   The question asks if the positively charged particles discussed by Scientist 1 would increase or decrease in mass as a result of becoming charged. A bit of outside knowledge could help, but is not really needed to answer the question. An atom, which is neutrally charged, becomes positively charged if it loses an electron. Without knowing that, use the information in the passages and POE. Scientist 1 says that *the positively charged particles travel faster and higher in the ash cloud,* indicating that they are lighter than the negatively charged particles. This implies that they have decreased in mass, so eliminate (F) and (G), which both indicate an increase in mass. According to (J), the particles gained a proton. But since protons have mass, this would involve an increase rather than a decrease in mass; eliminate (J). The correct answer is (H).

Chapter 10
Science Practice
Test 2

SCIENCE TEST

35 Minutes–40 Questions

Directions: There are six passages in this test. Each passage is followed by several questions. After reading a passage, choose the best answer to each question and fill in the corresponding oval on your answer document. You may refer to the passages as often as necessary.

You are NOT permitted to use a calculator on this test.

Passage I

Moth body coloration (see Figure 1) is a *hereditary* trait that can be passed from organisms to their offspring.

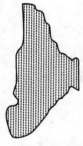 

white body coloration   black body coloration

Figure 1

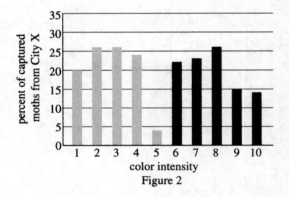

Figure 2

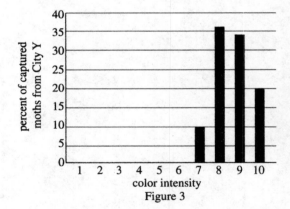

Figure 3

Scientists studied the body coloration of 2 subspecies of moths, *Biston betularia f. typica* and *Biston betularia f. carbonaria*. Both species live in City X. Only *B. betularia f. typica* lives in City Y, while only *B. betularia f. carbonaria* lives in City Z. Both subspecies live on trees found in temperate climates, such as birch. Moths with light body coloration are camouflaged from predators while living on light-colored trees but are not hidden in heavily polluted areas where the tree bark is darkened. Moths with dark body coloration are camouflaged from predators on trees that are darkened by pollution but not on light-colored trees.

Study 1

Scientists captured 100 *B. betularia f. typica* and 100 *B. betularia f. carbonaria* in City X. They labeled each one, recorded its color, and released it. Then they calculated the percent of moths having each of the body color intensities on a scale of 1 to 10, with 1 being completely white and 10 being completely black. The researchers followed the same methods with 100 *B. betularia f. typica* moths from City Y and 100 *B. betularia f. carbonaria* moths from City Z. The results of this study are shown in Figures 2–4.

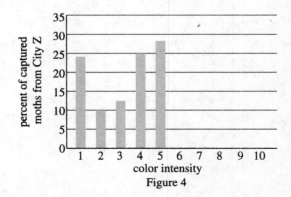

Figure 4

Study 2

After the end of Study 1, the scientists returned to City Y over the course of 10 years, from 1996–2005. During each visit, they captured at least 50 *B. betularia f. typica* moths and measured their body color intensities. They then calculated the average *B. betularia f. typica* body color intensity from the 1–10 scale for each of the 10 years. The scientists noted that during the 10-year period, 3 years were particularly wet, while 2 years were especially dry (see Figure 5). During wet years, pollutants tend to be washed from the surfaces of tree bark. During dry years, pollutants are more likely to concentrate on tree bark, and the tree bark itself tends to become thicker.

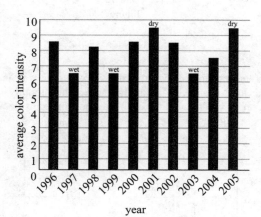

Figure 5

1. Based on the results from Study 1, the largest percentage of moths in City Y and City Z had a color intensity of:

	City Y	City Z
A.	8	1
B.	8	5
C.	9	4
D.	9	5

2. During which of the following years was birch bark most likely to be thickest in City Y ?

F. 2000
G. 2001
H. 2002
J. 2003

3. How was Study 1 different from Study 2 ?

A. *B. betularia f. carbonaria* moths were captured in Study 1 but not in Study 2.
B. *B. betularia f. typica* moths were captured in Study 1 but not in Study 2.
C. The moth body coloration was measured in Study 1 but not in Study 2.
D. The moth body coloration was measured in Study 2 but not in Study 1.

4. The scientists most likely labeled the moths in Study 1 to:

F. determine how body coloration was affected by pollution in City X.
G. determine the average wingspan of each population of moths.
H. make sure that the body coloration of each moth was measured only once.
J. make sure that the body coloration of each moth was measured multiple times.

5. Based on the results from Study 2, would a moth with a body color intensity measuring 6.5 or a moth with a body color intensity measuring 9.5 have had a greater chance of surviving in 2005 ?

A. A moth with a body color intensity of 6.5, because pollutants concentrate more on tree bark during dry years.
B. A moth with a body color intensity of 6.5, because pollutants are removed from tree bark during dry years.
C. A moth with a body color intensity of 9.5, because pollutants concentrate more on tree bark during dry years.
D. A moth with a body color intensity of 9.5, because pollutants are removed from tree bark during dry years.

6. A scientist hypothesized that there would be a greater range in body coloration in the *B. betularia f. typica* moths when they are forced to coexist with another subspecies of moths. Do the results from Study 1 support this hypothesis?

F. Yes; the range of body coloration for *B. betularia f. typica* moths was greater in City X than in City Y.
G. Yes; the range of body coloration for *B. betularia f. typica* moths was greater in City Y than in City X.
H. No; the range of body coloration for *B. betularia f. typica* moths was greater in City X than in City Y.
J. No; the range of body coloration for *B. betularia f. typica* moths was greater in City Y than in City X.

7. Based on the information in the passage, would the moth population in City Z have most likely been higher in wet years or dry years?

A. Wet, because the trees are darker and provide better camouflage.
B. Wet, because the trees are lighter and provide better camouflage.
C. Dry, because the trees are darker and provide better camouflage.
D. Dry, because the trees are lighter and provide better camouflage.

Passage II

Ions in seawater, such as Cl^-, SO_4^{2-}, Na^+, and Mg^{2+}, are carried down to the ocean floor through a process known as *marine deposition*. SO_4^{2-} and Mg^{2+} primarily come from the erosion of rocks, while Cl^- and Na^+ come from both mineral erosion and underwater volcanoes and hydrothermal vents.

Study 1

A fluid motion sensor was placed on a section of the seabed in the Atlantic Ocean, and data were collected over 12 months. At 6:00 A.M. every morning, the movement of water past the sensor was recorded, and a small amount of water was sequestered. Figure 1 shows the movement of water in millions of cubic meters (m^3) per second.

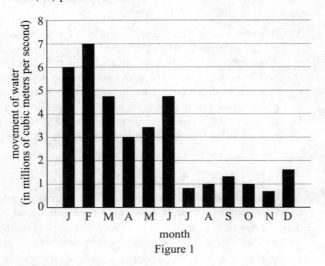

Figure 1

At the end of each month, the sequestered water was extracted by a scientific research crew, and a portion was analyzed for the concentrations of Cl^- and SO_4^{2-} ions. Using these data, the marine deposition was measured in kilograms (kg) per cubic meter (m^3) for each substance in each month (see Figure 2).

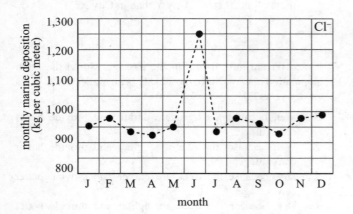

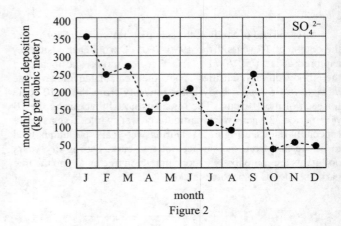

Figure 2

Study 2

Another portion of the monthly water sample was analyzed for concentrations of Na^+ and Mg^{2+} ions. The monthly marine deposition was calculated for each substance in equivalents (Eq) per m^3 (see Figure 3).

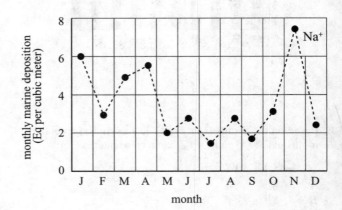

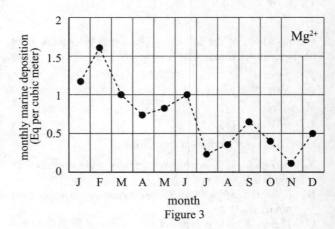

Figure 3

4 ○ ○ ○ ○ ○ ○ ○ ○ **4**

Study 3

The annual marine deposition of Cl^- and SO_4^{2-} ions over the 12-month period was calculated in kg/m^3 at the test site in the Atlantic Ocean, and also at two sites in the Arctic Ocean, located 2,000 and 4,000 kilometers due north, respectively (see Figure 4).

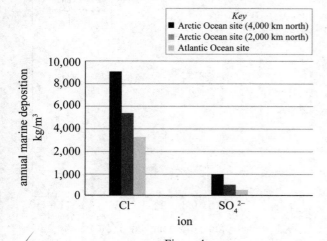

Figure 4

8. Based on the results from Study 1, the mean monthly marine deposition for Cl^- over the year of the study was:

   F. less than 900 kg/m^3.
   G. between 900 kg/m^3 and 1,100 kg/m^3.
   H. between 1,100 kg/m^3 and 1,200 kg/m^3.
   J. greater than 1,200 kg/m^3.

9. A student states, "The marine deposition of Na^+ is highest in the winter and lowest in the summer, since the winter features greater activity of volcanoes and hydrothermal vents." Is this statement supported by the results of Study 2 ?

   A. No, because marine deposition of Na^+ was, on average, greater between November and January than it was between June and August.
   B. No, because marine deposition of Na^+ was, on average, less between November and January than it was between June and August.
   C. Yes, because marine deposition of Na^+ was, on average, greater between November and January than it was between June and August.
   D. Yes, because marine deposition of Na^+ was, on average, less between November and January than it was between June and August.

10. Suppose that the study was repeated with the sensor placed in an underwater cave in the Atlantic Ocean where there is no movement of water. The information provided indicates that during this new study, the researchers would have measured:

   F. no marine deposition of any of the 4 substances.
   G. no marine deposition of Cl^- and SO_4^{2-}, but a high level of marine deposition of Na^+ and Mg^{2+}.
   H. high marine deposition of Cl^- and SO_4^{2-}, but no marine deposition of Na^+ and Mg^{2+}.
   J. high marine deposition of all 4 substances.

11. According to Study 3, as the distance from the fluid motion sensor in the Atlantic Ocean decreases, the annual marine deposition:

   A. decreases for both Cl^- and SO_4^{2-}.
   B. decreases for Cl^- but increases for SO_4^{2-}.
   C. increases for Cl^- but decreases for SO_4^{2-}.
   D. increases for both Cl^- and SO_4^{2-}.

12. Which of the following variables remained constant in Study 2 ?

   F. Marine deposition of SO_4^{2-}
   G. Marine deposition of Mg^{2+}
   H. Movement of water during the month
   J. Location of the study

13. According to Figure 1, during the year over which data were collected, the movement of water was greatest in February and least in November. According to Figures 2 and 3, the marine deposition of which ion was also greatest in February and least in November?

   A. Cl^-
   B. Mg^{2+}
   C. Na^+
   D. SO_4^{2-}

14. In Study 3, the marine deposition of Cl^- at a site 1,500 km due north of the Atlantic Ocean test site would most likely have been:

   F. less than 500 kg/m^3.
   G. between 500 and 1,000 kg/m^3.
   H. between 3,000 and 5,000 kg/m^3.
   J. greater than 5,000 kg/m^3.

Passage III

Oxidation-reduction titration is a method in which precise volumes of a *titrant* (an oxidizing or reducing agent) are added dropwise to a known volume of an *analyte* (a reducing or oxidizing agent, respectively, if the titrant is the oxidizing or reducing agent). This process can be monitored by adding a *redox indicator* (a substance that changes color over a certain range of electrode potentials) to the analyte or by measuring the sample's *voltage* using a potentiometer. Voltage (measured in kilovolts, kV) is a measure of the force of an electrical current that could be transmitted by the solution.

Two titration experiments were performed at 298 K using a 0.10 M iodine (I_2) solution and either a 0.0010 M sulfur dioxide (SO_2) solution or a 0.0010 M sodium thiosulfate solution (where M is the number of moles of oxidizing or reducing agent per liter of solution). All solutions were aqueous. A redox indicator solution of *starch* was also used. When iodine reacts with sulfur dioxide or sodium thiosulfate, the iodine is reduced to 2 iodide ions (I^-) and the sulfur dioxide or sodium thiosulfate is oxidized. Once the sulfur dioxide or sodium thiosulfate is fully oxidized, any additional iodine in the solution will bind with the starch and form a complex with a deep blue color.

Experiment 1

A drop of starch solution was added to an Erlenmeyer flask containing 100.0 mL of the sulfur dioxide solution. A potentiometer, which acts as a control input for electronic circuits, was placed in the solution. The iodine solution was incrementally added to the sulfur dioxide solution. After each addition, the sulfur dioxide solution was stirred and the solution's color and voltage were recorded (see Figure 1).

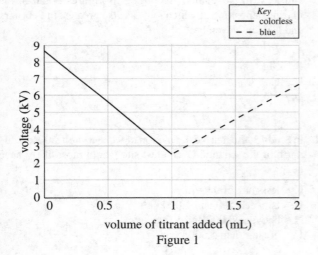

volume of titrant added (mL)
Figure 1

Experiment 2

Experiment 1 was repeated, except that the sodium thiosulfate solution was used instead of the sulfur dioxide solution (see Figure 2).

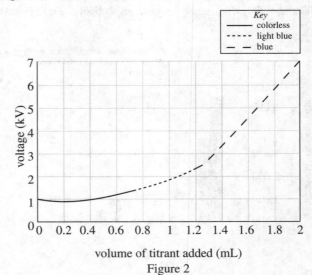

volume of titrant added (mL)
Figure 2

15. Suppose that in Experiment 1, the volume of sulfur dioxide solution used was 120.0 mL instead of 100.0 mL. Based on the information in the passage, how much titrant would need to be added before the solution turned blue?

   A. Less than 0.5 mL
   B. Between 0.5 mL and 1.0 mL
   C. Exactly 1.0 mL
   D. Between 1.0 mL and 1.5 mL

16. In Experiment 1, the analyte was blue at which of the following volumes of titrant added?

   F. 0.1 mL
   G. 0.5 mL
   H. 0.9 mL
   J. 1.5 mL

17. In Experiment 2, the analyte was in its fully oxidized form for which of the following volumes of titrant added?

    A. 0.3 mL
    B. 0.6 mL
    C. 0.9 mL
    D. 1.2 mL

18. In Experiment 1, if 2.5 mL of titrant was added to the analyte, the voltage would most likely have been:

    F. less than 1 kV.
    G. between 1 kV and 4 kV.
    H. between 4 kV and 7 kV.
    J. greater than 7 kV.

19. In Experiment 2, which solution was the titrant and which solution was the analyte?

titrant	analyte
A. sodium thiosulfate	iodine
B. sulfur dioxide	iodine
C. iodine	sodium thiosulfate
D. iodine	sulfur dioxide

20. In Experiments 1 and 2, the potentiometer that was placed in the analyte most likely did which of the following?

    F. Detected the concentration of starch in the solution
    G. Conducted an electric current initiated by ions in the solution
    H. Heated the solution to its boiling point
    J. Cooled the solution to its freezing point

21. A chemist states that in Experiment 2, the analyte was fully oxidized with 0.2 mL of titrant added, but not with 1.8 mL of titrant added. Do the results of Experiment 2 support this claim?

    A. Yes; at a value of 0.2 mL of titrant added, the analyte was blue, while at a value of 1.8 mL of titrant added, the analyte was colorless.
    B. Yes; at a value of 0.2 mL of titrant added, the analyte was colorless, while at a value of 1.8 mL of titrant added, the analyte was blue.
    C. No; at a value of 0.2 mL of titrant added, the analyte was blue, while at a value of 1.8 mL of titrant added, the analyte was colorless.
    D. No; at a value of 0.2 mL of titrant added, the analyte was colorless, while at a value of 1.8 mL of titrant added, the analyte was blue.

Passage IV

An astrophysics class is given the following facts about the burning out of stars.

1. The burning out of a star can be divided into 3 stages: *helium fusion*, *planetary nebula formation*, and *white dwarf development*.

2. Mid-sized stars fuse hydrogen nuclei (composed of protons) into helium nuclei at their centers, in a process known as helium fusion. These include yellow dwarves, like our Sun, and the slightly smaller orange dwarves. Helium fusion releases a significant amount of kinetic energy.

3. As kinetic energy continues to be released, a planetary nebula may form, in which colorful, ionized gas spreads out from the star's center.

4. The remaining material at the center of the planetary nebula condenses into a white dwarf, which is relatively cool and small in size.

5. Red dwarves are smaller stars that can also carry out helium fusion. These stars can develop into white dwarves sooner than yellow and orange dwarves, and they do not form planetary nebulas.

Two students discuss the eventual fate of three stars in the Alpha Centauri system: Alpha Centauri A, a 1.10-solar-mass yellow dwarf star, where one *solar mass* unit is equivalent to the mass of the Sun; Alpha Centauri B, a 0.91-solar-mass orange dwarf star; and Alpha Centauri C, a 0.12-solar-mass red dwarf star. Alpha Centauri A and B comprise a binary star system that revolves around a common center of mass, while Alpha Centauri C revolves around a nearby center of mass.

Student 1

The 3 stars of the Alpha Centauri system all formed at the same time from the same collection of matter. Alpha Centauri C was initially the most massive of the three stars, and Alpha Centauri A and Alpha Centauri B had the same size. The large Alpha Centauri C had more helium fusion than the other two stars, so it quickly became the smallest of the stars. More of its matter flowed to Alpha Centauri A than to Alpha Centauri B, making Alpha Centauri A slightly larger than Alpha Centauri B.

Student 2

Alpha Centauri A and Alpha Centauri B formed at a different time than Alpha Centauri C. Alpha Centauri A and Alpha Centauri B formed at the same time from a common collection of matter, and Alpha Centauri A was initially more massive than Alpha Centauri B. Alpha Centauri C formed later from a different, smaller collection of matter and never became bigger than a red dwarf. At some point, the small Alpha Centauri C was attracted to the other two stars, resulting in a triple star system.

22. Based on Student 2's discussion, Alpha Centauri C is part of the Alpha Centauri system because of which of the following forces exerted on Alpha Centauri C by the original binary star system?

F. Electromagnetism
G. Gravitation
H. Strong nuclear interaction
J. Weak nuclear interaction

23. Based on Student 1's discussion and Fact 2, while matter flowed between Alpha Centauri C and Alpha Centauri A, Alpha Centauri C released most of its energy by fusing:

A. helium nuclei into hydrogen nuclei at its core.
B. hydrogen nuclei into helium nuclei at its core.
C. helium nuclei into hydrogen nuclei at its periphery.
D. hydrogen nuclei into helium nuclei at its periphery.

24. Suppose that stars that form from the same collection of matter have similar chemical composition, but stars that form from different collections of matter have different chemical compositions. Student 2 would most likely agree with which of the following statements comparing chemical compositions of the stars in the current Alpha Centauri system at the time that they were formed?

F. Alpha Centauri A and Alpha Centauri B had the most similar compositions.
G. Alpha Centauri A and Alpha Centauri C had the most similar compositions.
H. Alpha Centauri B and Alpha Centauri C had the most similar compositions.
J. Alpha Centauri A, Alpha Centauri B, and Alpha Centauri C all had the same compositions.

25. If the mass of the Sun is 2.0×10^{30} g, what is the mass of Alpha Centauri A ?

A. 1.8×10^{30} g
B. 2.0×10^{30} g
C. 2.2×10^{30} g
D. 2.4×10^{32} g

26. Which of the following statements best explains why the process described in Fact 2 requires a high initial temperature and pressure?

F. All electrons are negatively charged, and like charges attract each other.
G. All electrons are negatively charged, and like charges repel each other.
H. All protons are positively charged, and like charges attract each other.
J. All protons are positively charged, and like charges repel each other.

27. Based on Fact 5, which of the three stars, if any, in the Alpha Centauri system would Student 1 expect to most likely develop into a white dwarf first?

A. Alpha Centauri A
B. Alpha Centauri B
C. Alpha Centauri C
D. The three stars will likely develop into white dwarves at the same time.

28. Based on Fact 5, would Student 2 agree that by the time Alpha Centauri B develops into a white dwarf, it will have spent as much time as a mid-sized star as Alpha Centauri A ?

F. Yes, because according to Student 2, Alpha Centauri A has always been less massive than Alpha Centauri B.
G. Yes, because according to Student 2, Alpha Centauri A has always been more massive than Alpha Centauri B.
H. No, because according to Student 2, Alpha Centauri A has always been less massive than Alpha Centauri B.
J. No, because according to Student 2, Alpha Centauri A has always been more massive than Alpha Centauri B.

Passage V

Three experiments were conducted using the gases nitrogen (N_2), nitrogen dioxide (NO_2), and xenon (Xe). For each gas:

1. A cap was placed on a 2 L metal chamber, containing sensors to measure temperature and pressure and a valve to allow gas to enter.

2. Air was pumped out of the chamber until the pressure inside was measured to be 0.00 mmHg.

3. The chamber was placed on an analytical balance, which was then reset to 0.00 g.

4. A specific mass of gas was added to the chamber.

5. When the gas in the vessel reached room temperature (298 K), the mass and pressure inside were recorded.

6. Steps 4 and 5 were repeated for different masses.

The experiments were repeated using a 4 L metal chamber (see Figures 1 and 2).

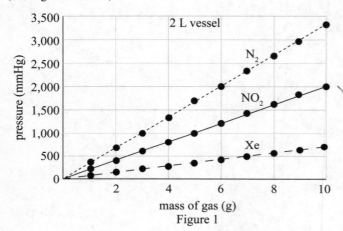
Figure 1

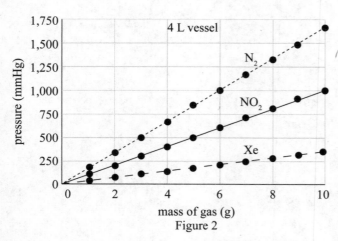
Figure 2

29. Based on Figure 2, if 12 g of Xe had been added to the 4 L vessel, the pressure would have been:

   A. less than 300 mmHg.
   B. between 300 and 600 mmHg.
   C. between 600 mmHg and 900 mmHg.
   D. greater than 1,200 mmHg.

30. Suppose the experiments had been repeated, except with a 3 L vessel. Based on Figures 1 and 2, the pressure exerted by 10 g of NO_2 would most likely have been:

   F. less than 1,000 mmHg.
   G. between 1,000 and 2,000 mmHg.
   H. between 2,000 and 2,500 mmHg.
   J. greater than 2,500 mmHg.

31. Based on Figures 1 and 2, for a given mass of N_2 at 298 K, how does the pressure exerted by the N_2 in a 4 L vessel compare to the pressure exerted by the N_2 in a 2 L vessel? In the 4 L vessel, the N_2 pressure will be:

   A. half as great as in the 2 L vessel.
   B. the same as in the 2 L vessel.
   C. twice as great as in the 2 L vessel.
   D. four times as great as in the 2 L vessel.

32. Which of the following best explains why equal masses of N_2 and NO_2 at the same temperature and in vessels of the same size had different pressures? The pressure exerted by the N_2 was:

   F. greater, because there were fewer N_2 molecules per gram than there were NO_2 molecules per gram.
   G. greater, because there were more N_2 molecules per gram than there were NO_2 molecules per gram.
   H. less, because there were fewer N_2 molecules per gram than there were NO_2 molecules per gram.
   J. less, because there were more N_2 molecules per gram than there were NO_2 molecules per gram.

33. Suppose the experiment involving N_2 and the 4 L vessel had been repeated, except at a temperature of 287 K. For a given mass of N_2, compared to the pressure measured in the original experiment, the pressure measured at 287 K would have been:

A. greater, because pressure is directly proportional to temperature.
B. greater, because pressure is inversely proportional to temperature.
C. less, because pressure is directly proportional to temperature.
D. less, because pressure is inversely proportional to temperature.

34. The table below shows the molar masses of N_2, NO_2, and Xe.

Gas	Molar mass (g/mol)
N_2	28.0
NO_2	46.0
Xe	131.3

The molar mass of O_2 is approximately 32 g/mol. Suppose that 6 grams of O_2 were placed into the 4 L chamber using the same procedure described in steps 1–6. Which of the following is most likely closest to the pressure of the O_2 at 298 K ?

F. 610 mmHg
G. 870 mmHg
H. 1,530 mmHg
J. 1,780 mmHg

Passage VI

The *absolute threshold pressure for hearing* is the minimum air pressure at each audio frequency that can produce a sound that is detectable by the human ear. The *pain threshold pressure for hearing* is the maximum air pressure at each audio frequency that the human ear can withstand without sensing pain.

Figure 1 below displays the absolute and pain threshold pressures for hearing in two media: air and water. The figure also shows P, the percentage increase in compression of the air or water with increasing sound pressure. Audio frequency is given in cycles per second (cyc/sec), and sound pressure level is given in decibels (db).

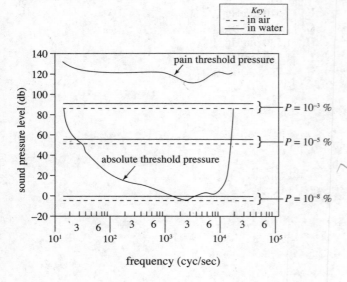

Figure 1

35. At which of the following frequencies can humans hear the widest range of sound pressure levels without pain?

A. 20 cyc/sec
B. 400 cyc/sec
C. 2,500 cyc/sec
D. 20,000 cyc/sec

36. According to Figure 1, which of the following is the closest to the highest frequency that can be heard by a human being?

F. 20 cyc/sec
G. 200 cyc/sec
H. 2,000 cyc/sec
J. 20,000 cyc/sec

37. Based on Figure 1, a sound of a given frequency will have the highest sound level pressure for which of the following sets of conditions?

	sound in	P
A.	air	$10^{-8}\%$
B.	air	$10^{-3}\%$
C.	water	$10^{-8}\%$
D.	water	$10^{-3}\%$

38. As humans grow older, there is often a loss in the ability to hear sounds at high frequencies. Which of the following figures best illustrates this?

F.

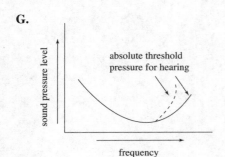

G.

H.

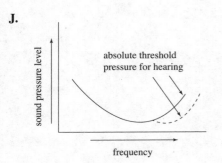

J.

39. A sound with a frequency of 3×10^3 cyc/sec causes pain at 115 db. Which of the following actions would eliminate the pain?

   I. Reducing the frequency to 10^3 cyc/sec

   II. Increasing the frequency to 10^4 cyc/sec

   III. Reducing the sound pressure level by 5 db

A. II only
B. I and III only
C. III only
D. I, II, and III

40. Based on Figure 1, does P depend on the frequency of sound at a given sound pressure level?

F. No, because as frequency increases, P increases.
G. No, because as frequency increases, P remains constant.
H. Yes, because as frequency increases, P increases.
J. Yes, because as frequency increases, P remains constant.

END OF TEST.
STOP! DO NOT TURN THE PAGE UNTIL TOLD TO DO SO.

Chapter 11
Science Practice
Test 2: Answers and
Explanations

SCIENCE PRACTICE TEST 2 ANSWER KEY

1. B		21. D	
2. G		22. G	
3. A		23. B	
4. H		24. F	
5. C		25. C	
6. F		26. J	
7. B		27. C	
8. G		28. J	
9. C		29. B	
10. F		30. G	
11. A		31. A	
12. J		32. G	
13. B		33. C	
14. H		34. G	
15. D		35. C	
16. J		36. J	
17. D		37. D	
18. J		38. G	
19. C		39. D	
20. G		40. G	

SCORE YOUR PRACTICE TEST

Step A
Count the number of correct answers: _____46_____. This is your *raw score*.

Step B
Use the score conversion table below to look up your raw score. The number to the left is your *scale score*: _____36_____.

Test 2 Scale Conversion Table

Scale Score	Raw Score	Scale Score	Raw Score	Scale Score	Raw Score
36	40	24	26–27	12	9
35	39	23	24–25	11	8
34	38	22	23	10	7
33	37	21	21–22	9	6
32	—	20	19–20	8	5
31	36	19	17–18	7	4
30	35	18	16	6	3
29	34	17	14–15	5	—
28	33	16	13	4	2
27	31–32	15	12	3	1
26	30	14	11	2	—
25	28–29	13	10	1	0

SCIENCE PRACTICE TEST 2 EXPLANATIONS

Passage I

1. **B** The question asks for the color intensity of the largest percentage of moths from City Y and City Z. The color intensity for the moths in City Y is shown in Figure 3, and the highest percentage of these moths had a color intensity of 8. Eliminate (C) and (D). The color intensity for the moths in City Z is shown in Figure 4, and the highest percentage of these moths had a color intensity of 5. Eliminate (A), and the only remaining answer is (B).

2. **G** The question asks in which year was birch bark likely to be the thickest in City Y. The blurb in Study 2 contains the following information: *During dry years, pollutants are more likely to concentrate on tree bark, and the tree bark itself tends to become thicker.* Therefore, bark is thickest during dry years, and of the years listed in the answer choices, only 2001 is identified on Figure 5 as a *dry* year, so (G) is the correct answer.

3. **A** The question asks how Study 1 differed from Study 2. Use POE. Moth color intensity is on the horizontal axis of Figures 2–4 from Study 1 and on the vertical axis of Figure 5 from Study 2. Eliminate (C) and (D) since moth color is measured in both studies. Now, read the text for reference to the type of moths used in each study. Study 2 contains the following information: *During each visit they captured at least 50* B. betularia f. typica *moths.* Eliminate (B). Only (A) remains.

4. **H** The question asks for the most likely reason that the scientists labeled the moths in Study 1. Use POE. Choice (F) is incorrect because pollution is discussed in the description of Study 2 not Study 1. Choice (G) is incorrect because wingspan is not measured in either study. You'll need to use a bit of science common sense here to choose between (H) and (J). In Study 1, the scientists are trying to count the number of moths in these various cities; therefore, in order to make this count accurate, they will need to make sure that each moth is counted only once. Eliminate (J). The correct answer is (H).

5. **C** The question asks if, according to Study 2, a moth with a body color intensity measuring 6.5 or a moth with a body color intensity measuring 9.5 would have a greater chance of surviving in 2005. Figure 5 shows that 2005 was a dry year, and the average color intensity was 9.5. Given that the average color intensity for both dry years shown in Figure 5 are higher than 9, it can be concluded that a moth with a color intensity of 9.5 is more likely to survive in a dry year. Eliminate (A) and (B). Then, notice that Study 2 contains the following information: *During dry years, pollutants are more likely to concentrate on tree bark.* The correct answer is (C).

6. **F** The question asks if the results of Study 1 would support the hypothesis that there would be a greater range in body coloration in the *B. betularia f. typica* moths when they are forced to coexist with another subspecies of moths. This question is difficult to answer *Yes* or *No* immediately, so work with the reasons given in each of the answer choices. In City X, the coloration of *B. betularia f. typica* ranges from 6 to 10. Note that in City Z, the *B. betularia f. carbonaria* species is found only at body

intensity colors from 1–5, so it is reasonable to assume that all of the body intensities of 6 and above in City X are of the *B. betularia f. typica* species. In City Y, the coloration of *B. betularia f. typica* ranges from only 7 to 10. Eliminate (G) and (J). The hypothesis that a greater range in body coloration is produced by a diversity in the subspecies is therefore supported by this information because City X contains two subspecies and City Y contains only one. The correct answer is (F).

7. **B**   The question asks if the moth population in City Z would most likely have been higher in wet years or dry years. Use POE on this question. Figure 4 shows that the moths in City Z are the lighter colored moths (*Betularia f. carbonaria*). Therefore, lighter trees would provide better camouflage. Eliminate (A) and (C). Study 2 states, *During wet years, pollutants tend to be washed from the surfaces of tree bark. During dry years, pollutants are more likely to concentrate on tree bark.* Since concentrated pollutants would darken the surface of a tree, the wet years will have lighter tree bark. The correct answer is (B).

Passage II

8. **G**   The question asks for the mean monthly marine deposition for Cl^- over the course of Study 1. Look carefully at Figure 2. The marine deposition of Cl^- is around 950 kg/m^3 except in June, at which point it is much higher. Because it has only this single outlier, you can reasonably expect that the *mean*, or *average*, monthly deposition will be only slightly higher than 950. The correct answer is (G).

9. **C**   The question asks if the statement *The marine deposition of Na^+ is highest in the winter and lowest in the summer, since the winter features greater activity of volcanoes and hydrothermal vents* is supported by the results of Study 2. Use POE with the reasons given in each of the answer choices. According to Figure 3, the monthly deposition of Na^+ is higher between November and January than it is between June and August. Eliminate (B) and (D). This information then *supports* the statement in the question that the *marine deposition of Na^+ is highest in the winter and lowest in the summer*, thus making (C) the correct answer.

10. **F**   The question asks what level of marine deposition the researchers would have measured if the study was repeated with the sensor placed in an underwater cave in the Atlantic Ocean where there is no movement of water. The introduction to the passage gives the following information: *Ions in seawater, such as Cl^-, SO_4^{2-}, Na^+, and Mg^{2+}, are carried down to the ocean floor through a process known as* marine deposition. Therefore, in order for there to be *marine deposition*, ions must be *carried down* somewhere. If the water does not move past the sensor, then no marine deposition will be measured at the sensor location. The correct answer is (F).

11. **A**   The question asks what happens to the annual marine deposition as the distance from the fluid motion sensor in the Atlantic Ocean decreases in Study 3. Make sure you pay careful attention to the key in Figure 4. According to Figure 4, the annual marine depositions of both ions were highest in the Arctic Ocean at the site farthest from the Atlantic Ocean. The annual marine depositions of both ions decrease as the sensor gets closer to the Atlantic Ocean site. The correct answer is (A).

12. **J**   The question asks which variable remained constant in Study 2. According to Figure 3, the marine deposition of SO_4^{2-} was not studied, eliminating (F). The marine deposition of Mg^{2+} changed during the study; eliminate (G). According to Figure 1, the movement of water during the month changed every month during the twelve-month period, eliminating (H). Only the location of the study, the Atlantic Ocean, was held constant. The location did not change until Study 3. The correct answer is (J).

13. **B**   The question asks which ion had the greatest marine deposition in February and least in November. Use POE. In Figures 2 and 3, only the marine deposition of Mg^{2+} is highest in February and lowest in November, making (B) the correct answer.

14. **H**   The question asks what the marine deposition of Cl^- at a site 1,500 km due north of the Atlantic Ocean test site in Study 3 would most likely have been. Refer to Figure 4. For Cl^-, marine deposition increases as the distance north of the Atlantic Ocean test site increases. At the Atlantic Ocean test site, the deposition is 3,000 kg/m^3, and at 2,000 km north of the Atlantic Ocean test site, the deposition is 5,000 kg/m^3. Therefore, the deposition at 1,500 km north would be between these two values. The correct answer is (H).

Passage III

15. **D**   The question asks how much titrant would need to be added to a sulfur dioxide solution of 120.0 mL before the solution turned blue. The passage states that *Once the sulfur dioxide or sodium thiosulfate is fully oxidized, any additional iodine in the solution will bind with the starch and form a complex with a deep blue color*. Therefore, the solution turns blue only after the iodine has reacted with all of the analyte. If the amount of sulfur dioxide were increased to 120.0 mL, the amount of titrant necessary to fully oxidize the sulfur dioxide would also increase. In Experiment 1, the solution currently turns blue at 1.0 mL of titrant, so it would require more than 1.0 mL if the sulfur dioxide volume were increased. The only possible answer is (D).

16. **J**   The question asks for a volume of titrant at which the analyte was blue in Experiment 1. Use Figure 1. The key in the corner of the graph says that anything graphed with a solid line is *colorless*, and anything graphed with a dotted line is *blue*. The curve shown in this graph changes from solid to dotted at 1 mL of titrant added, meaning that the solution at all values of titrant less than 1 mL will be colorless, and the solution at all values greater than 1 mL will be blue. Eliminate (F), (G), and (H) because they are not greater than 1 mL. The correct answer is (J).

17. **D**   The question asks for a volume of titrant in Experiment 2 at which the analyte was in its fully oxidized form. The passage states that *Once the sulfur dioxide or sodium thiosulfate is fully oxidized, any additional iodine in the solution will bind with the starch and form a complex with a deep blue color*. In other words, the analyte is not fully oxidized until the solution turns a deep blue color. According to Figure 2, the solution is blue (and therefore fully oxidized) above 1 mL of titrant added. The correct answer is (D).

18. **J**   The question asks what the voltage would most likely have been in Experiment 1 if 2.5 mL of titrant was added to the analyte. Figure 2 does not show the voltage at 2.5 mL of titrant added, but the curve follows a clear trend. As the volume of titrant added increases, the voltage increases as well. At 2 mL of titrant added, the voltage is equivalent to 7 kV. Therefore, at 2.5 mL of titrant added, the voltage will most likely be greater than 7 kV. The correct answer is (J).

19. **C**   The question asks which solution in Experiment 2 was the titrant and which solution was the analyte. Start by eliminating (B) and (D) because sulfur dioxide was not used in Experiment 2 at all. The passage describes oxidation-reduction titration as *a method in which precise volumes of a* titrant *(an oxidizing or reducing agent) are added dropwise to a known volume of an* analyte *(a reducing or oxidizing agent, respectively)*. In other words, one substance (the titrant) is added gradually to a certain amount of another substance (the analyte). Therefore, when Experiment 1 says that the iodine solution was incrementally added to the sulfur dioxide solution, it can be inferred that the iodine is the titrant, and the sulfur dioxide is the analyte. In Experiment 2, the sodium thiosulfate solution was used instead of the sulfur dioxide solution; therefore, in Experiment 2, the iodine is still the titrant, and the sodium thiosulfate solution is the analyte. The correct answer is (C).

20. **G**   The question asks what the potentiometer in Experiments 1 and 2 most likely did. Use POE. Experiment 1 contains the following information: *A potentiometer, which acts as a control input for electronic circuits, was placed in the solution*. The key phrase here is *electric circuits*. There's nothing to suggest that the potentiometer has anything to do with *concentration*, eliminating (F), or *freezing* or *boiling point*, eliminating (H) and (J). Only (G) contains any reference to *electric circuits*, so (G) is the correct answer.

21. **D**   The question asks if the results of Experiment 2 support the claim that in Experiment 2, *the analyte was fully oxidized with 0.2 mL of titrant added but not with 1.8 mL of titrant added*. Use POE. If you're not sure how to answer *Yes* or *No*, look at the reasons. At 0.2 mL of titrant added, the solution is colorless, and at 1.8 mL of titrant added, the solution is blue. Eliminate (A) and (C), which have answers that contradict this information. According to the introduction, a solution turns blue after it is fully oxidized, so the analyte was not yet oxidized at 0.2 mL; eliminate (B). The correct answer is (D).

Passage IV

22. **G**   The question asks, according to Student 2's discussion, which of the forces exerted on Alpha Centauri C by the original binary star system caused Alpha Centauri C to be part of the Alpha Centauri system. Student 2 concludes with the following sentence: *At some point, the small Alpha Centauri C was attracted to the other two stars, resulting in a triple star system*. Some outside knowledge is necessary here: gravity is the attraction between two objects with mass, so (G) is the correct answer.

23. **B**   The question asks, according to Student 1's discussion and Fact 2, while matter flowed between Alpha Centauri C and Alpha Centauri A, Alpha Centauri C released most of its energy by fusing which of the following? Student 1's hypothesis contains the following sentence: *The large Alpha Centauri C had more helium fusion than the other two stars, so it quickly became the smallest of the stars.* According to Fact 2, *Mid-sized stars fuse hydrogen nuclei (composed of protons) into helium nuclei at their centers, in a process known as helium fusion.* Only (B) matches the description of helium fusion in Fact 2, so (B) is the correct answer.

24. **F**   The question asks which statement Student 2 would most likely agree with. Student 2's hypothesis contains the following sentence: *Alpha Centauri A and Alpha Centauri B formed at the same time from a common collection of matter.* As the question suggests, stars that form from the same collection of matter have similar chemical compositions. Therefore, Student 2 would likely suggest that Alpha Centauri A and Alpha Centauri B have similar chemical compositions because they formed *from a common collection of matter.* Alpha Centauri C formed from a different collection of matter, eliminating (G), (H), and (J). The correct answer is (F).

25. **C**   The question asks what the mass of Alpha Centauri A is if the mass of the Sun is 2.0×10^{30} g. The introduction to this passage contains the following information: *Alpha Centauri A, a 1.10-solar-mass yellow dwarf star, where one* solar mass *unit is equivalent to the mass of the Sun.* The question states that the mass of the Sun is 2.0×10^{30} g. Therefore, the mass of Alpha Centauri A must be 1.10 times this value, given the definition of solar mass. Don't worry about calculating the exact value: you know that this value must be slightly greater than the mass of the Sun. Eliminate (A) and (B) because these are less than the mass of the Sun. Eliminate (D) because this is more than 100 times the mass of the Sun. The correct answer is (C).

26. **J**   The question asks which of the statements best explains why the process described in Fact 2 requires a high initial temperature and pressure. Use POE. This question involves a bit of outside knowledge, but it can be solved easily with a bit of common sense. First of all, Fact 2 states that the nuclei being fused are *composed of protons.* It is therefore not likely that the answer to this question will have anything to do with *electrons,* eliminating (F) and (G). *Helium fusion* describes the process by which these protons are *fused,* or put together. Think about it this way: if these protons are attracted to each other to begin with, do you think it would take a bunch of extra energy to put them together? Not likely! Eliminate (H). The correct answer is (J).

27. **C**   The question asks which of the three stars, if any, in the Alpha Centauri system Student 1 would expect to most likely develop into a white dwarf first based on Fact 5. Fact 5 contains the following information: *Red dwarves are smaller stars that can also carry out helium fusion. These stars can develop into white dwarves sooner than yellow and orange dwarves.* Student 1 states, *The large Alpha Centauri C had more helium fusion than the other two stars, so it quickly became the smallest of the stars.* Therefore, Student 1 would likely believe that the smallest star, Alpha Centauri C, would develop into a white dwarf first. The correct answer is (C).

28. **J**   The question asks if, according to Fact 5, Student 2 would agree that by the time Alpha Centauri B develops into a white dwarf it will have spent as much time as a mid-sized star as Alpha Centauri A. Use POE. If you're not sure how to answer *Yes* or *No*, look at the reasons. Student 2's hypothesis contains the following information: *Alpha Centauri A was initially more massive than Alpha Centauri B.* This eliminates (F) and (H) immediately. Fact 5 contains the following information: *Red dwarves are smaller stars that can also carry out helium fusion. These stars can develop into white dwarves sooner than yellow and orange dwarves.* Therefore, since the introduction indicates that currently Alpha Centauri B is smaller, it can develop into a white dwarf. Student 2 also states that *Alpha Centauri A and Alpha Centauri B formed at the same time.* Combine these facts together: if the stars formed at the same time and Alpha Centauri B will develop into a white dwarf sooner, then it will spend less time as a mid-size star. Eliminate (G). The correct answer is (J).

Passage V

29. **B**   The question asks what the pressure would have been in Figure 2 if 12 g of Xe had been added to the 4 L vessel. Figure 2 only gives the information up to 10 g of gas added, but fortunately, all these lines have a very consistent relationship: as the mass of gas goes up, the pressure goes up. In the 4 L vessel, when 10 g of Xe is added, the pressure is approximately 300 mmHg. At 12 g of Xe, the pressure should be slightly higher, somewhere around 450 mmHg. Only (B) gives a range that contains this value.

30. **G**   The question asks what the pressure exerted by 10 g of NO_2 would most likely have been, based on Figures 1 and 2, if the experiments had been repeated with a 3 L vessel. In the 2 L vessel in Figure 1, 10 g of NO_2 gives a pressure of approximately 2,000 mmHg. In the 4 L vessel in Figure 2, 10 g of NO_2 gives a pressure of approximately 1,000 mmHg. Therefore, in a 3 L vessel, 10 g of NO_2 should give a pressure between 1,000 and 2,000 mmHg. The correct answer is (G).

31. **A**   The question asks, according to Figures 1 and 2, how the pressure exerted by a given mass of N_2 at 298 K in a 4 L vessel compares to the pressure exerted by the N_2 in a 2 L vessel. Temperature is not mentioned in either figure, but the passage indicates that the experiments were conducted at 298 K, so use Figures 1 and 2. Since you need to compare the N_2 values from Figures 1 and 2, it's best to find values as exact as possible. Notice that at mass 6 g, the 2 L vessel has a pressure of 2,000 mmHg, and the 4 L vessel has a pressure of 1,000 mmHg. Therefore, the pressure in the 4 L vessel is *half as great as* the pressure in the 2 L vessel. The correct answer is (A).

32. **G**   The question asks which of the given statements best explains why equal masses of N_2 and NO_2 at the same temperature and in vessels of the same size had different pressures. Use POE. In Figures 1 and 2, the pressure when N_2 is used is consistently greater than the pressure when the NO_2 is used. Eliminate (H) and (J). Then you'll need some outside knowledge to complete the question. Simply stated, an N_2 molecule has fewer components than an NO_2 molecule, so it has a smaller mass. Therefore, in order to get the same mass of both molecules, you will need more N_2 molecules per gram, eliminating (F). The correct answer is (G).

33. **C**   The question asks what would happen to the pressure for a given mass of N_2 in a 4 L vessel if the experiment had been repeated at a temperature of 287 K. This question requires outside knowledge, but you can still eliminate some answers even without knowing the relationship between temperature and pressure. The question describes a scenario in which the temperature decreases, so there are only two possible answers: either the pressure increases because it's an inverse relationship, or the pressure decreases because it's a direct relationship. Eliminate (A) and (D). To choose between (B) and (C), you need to know the relationship between pressure and temperature: as pressure increases, so does temperature. This is a *direct* relationship; eliminate (B). As the temperature decreases from 298 K to 287 K, the pressure will decrease also. The correct answer is (C).

34. **G**   The question asks what the pressure would most likely be if 6 grams of O_2 at 298 K were placed into the 4 L chamber using the same procedure described in Steps 1–6 given that the molar mass of O_2 is approximately 32 g/mol. First, compare the given table with Figure 2 to find the link between molar mass and pressure. Notice that N_2 has the lowest molar mass, but the highest pressure at every mass. Xe has the highest molar mass and the lowest pressure at every mass. Therefore, molar mass is inversely related to pressure. The molar mass of O_2 is between those of N_2 and NO_2, so the pressure will be between those of N_2 and NO_2 at 6 grams, which are approximately 1,000 mmHg and approximately 625 mmHg, respectively. Only (G) falls within this range. The correct answer is (G).

Passage VI

35. **C**   The question asks at which frequency humans can hear the widest range of sound pressure levels without pain. Use POE. The difference between the pain threshold pressure and the absolute threshold pressure represents the full range of sound pressure levels that a human can hear at a given frequency. Notice that the numbers on the x-axis are a logarithmic scale instead of a linear scale. For each order of magnitude, the hashmarks indicate 1×10^n, 2×10^n, 3×10^n, etc. So 20 cyc/sec is the hashmark following the one for 1×10^1. At this point, the pain threshold pressure is approximately 130 db and the absolute threshold pressure is approximately 80 db. This leads to a range of 50 db that humans can hear without pain. Once you understand the concept of this question, you can ballpark this visually without calculating every amount. Of the four choices given, the two lines are furthest apart at 2,500 cyc/sec (just before the "3" hashmark at the 10^3 order of magnitude). The correct answer is (C).

36. **J**   The question asks which of the following frequencies is the closest to the highest frequency that can be heard by a human being, according to Figure 1. The first line of the passage states the following: *The* absolute threshold pressure for hearing *is the minimum air pressure at each audio frequency that can produce a sound that is detectable by the human ear.* In other words, humans cannot hear any sounds below the absolute threshold pressure for hearing at any given frequency. In order to answer this question, you will need to use Figure 1 and the curve labeled *absolute pressure threshold,* and you will need to find its maximum frequency, listed on the x-axis. Notice that the numbers on the x-axis are a logarithmic scale instead of a linear scale. For each order of magnitude (10^n), the hashmarks indicate 1×10^n, 2×10^n, 3×10^n, etc. According to Figure 1, this curve becomes vertical right around 2×10^4 cyc/sec, or 20,000 cyc/sec, indicating that humans cannot hear any frequencies beyond this point. The correct answer is (J).

37. **D** The question asks with which of the sets of conditions will a sound of a given frequency have the highest sound level pressure. Use POE. Note the key at the top of Figure 1. According to this key, *in water* is shown on the graph with a solid line, and *in air* is shown on the graph with a dotted line. The solid line is consistently higher than the dotted, suggesting that *water* has a higher sound level pressure at each value of *P*, eliminating (A) and (B). Then note the *P*-values on the right side of the graph. The *P*-value closest to the top of the graph, where sound pressure levels are higher, is 10^{-3} %. The correct answer is (D).

38. **G** The question asks which of the figures best illustrates the information that as humans grow older, there is often a loss in the ability to hear sounds at high frequencies. Use POE. The graph will need to show a change at high frequency, rather than low frequency. Based on this information alone, you can eliminate (F) and (H). The dotted curve (*after hearing loss*) should indicate some kind of hearing loss at high frequencies, so it should show a curve that does not quite reach the highest frequencies. Eliminate (J). The correct answer is (G).

39. **D** The question asks which of the actions listed would eliminate the pain caused by a sound with a frequency of 3×10^3 cyc/sec at 115 db. Note the exponential scale on the *x*-axis of Figure 1. The hashmark labeled *3* between 10^3 and 10^4 represents 3×10^3 cyc/sec. At this point, the pain threshold pressure is 111 db, which means that anything over 111 db will cause pain. Use POE. If the frequency was reduced to 10^3, the pain threshold would increase to 119 db, and a sound at 115 db would no longer be painful. Eliminate (A) and (C) because you know that (I) works. Now check (II). If the frequency was increased to 10^4, the pain threshold pressure increases to approximately 121 db. This means that (II) would eliminate the pain as well. Eliminate (B). The correct answer is (D).

40. **G** The question asks if, based on Figure 1, *P* depends on the frequency of sound at a given sound pressure level. Use POE. If you're unsure whether to answer *Yes* or *No*, check the reasons. Use Figure 1. Frequency appears on the *x*-axis, and sound pressure level appears on the *y*-axis. According to the lines showing the pressure *in air* and *in water*, the increasing frequency has no effect on *P*. Eliminate (F) and (H). *P* does *not* depend on the frequency, making (G) the correct answer.

Chapter 12
Science Practice
Test 3

SCIENCE TEST

35 Minutes–40 Questions

Directions: There are six passages in this test. Each passage is followed by several questions. After reading a passage, choose the best answer to each question and fill in the corresponding oval on your answer document. You may refer to the passages as often as necessary.

You are NOT permitted to use a calculator on this test.

Passage I

The apoptotic index (AI) for a group of dividing cells is calculated as shown below:

$$AI = \frac{\text{number of cells undergoing } apoptosis \text{ (cell death)}}{\text{total number of cells}}$$

Figure 1 shows the *AI* for a culture of fibroblast cells as a function of the surrounding concentration, in parts per million (ppm), of a cell toxin.

One thousand actively dividing fibroblast cells in culture were studied. Figure 2 shows the distribution of the cells in each of the stages of the dividing cell cycle.

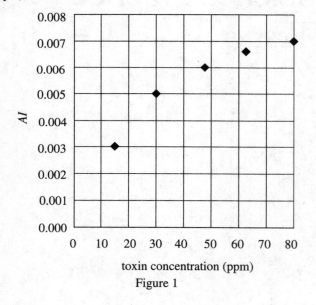

Figure 1

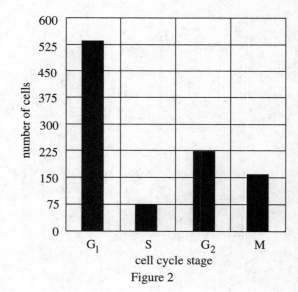

Figure 2

Electron micrographs were taken of the fibroblasts in culture. Figure 3 shows an example of cells in each of the 4 stages of the dividing cell cycle. Although the cells are *not* arranged in the sequence of the cell cycle, each stage is shown only once.

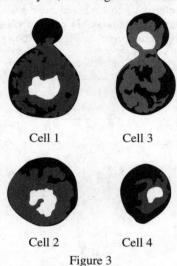

Cell 1   Cell 3

Cell 2   Cell 4

Figure 3

1. Which cell in Figure 3 is most likely in the stage of the cell cycle during which cytokinesis is occurring as mitosis nears completion?

A.   Cell 1
B.   Cell 2
C.   Cell 3
D.   Cell 4

2. Based on Figure 1, if a culture of fibroblast cells was surrounded by a toxin concentration of 90 ppm, the percent of those cells that would undergo apoptosis is most likely:

F.   less than 0.5%.
G.   between 0.5% and 0.6%.
H.   between 0.6% and 0.7%.
J.   greater than 0.7%.

3. Which of the following cells in Figure 3 is most likely in the first stage of the actively dividing cell cycle?

A.   Cell 1
B.   Cell 2
C.   Cell 3
D.   Cell 4

4. According to Figure 2, how did the number of fibroblast cells in stage G_2 compare with the number of cells in stage S? The number in G_2 was approximately:

F. $\frac{1}{4}$ as great as the number in S.

G. $\frac{1}{3}$ as great as the number in S.

H.   3 times as great as the number in S.

J.   4 times as great as the number in S.

5. Based on Figure 2, of the fibroblast cells that were in the actively dividing cell cycle, the proportion that were in G_1 is closest to which of the following?

A. $\frac{540}{1000}$

B. $\frac{300}{540}$

C. $\frac{1000}{540}$

D. $\frac{540}{300}$

6. Suppose that 3,000 cells are cultured in a surrounding toxin concentration of 30 ppm. Based on Figure 1, the number of these cells undergoing apoptosis is most likely closest to:

F.   1.5.
G.   15.
H.   150.
J.   1,500.

Passage II

A *polymorphism* is the persistent occurrence of different appearances for a particular trait in a species. All humans have slight differences in their *genotypes* (genetic code) that result in different *phenotypes* (observable characteristics). Genetic polymorphisms are persistent variations in gene sequences at a particular location in chromosomes, such as those accounting for different blood types. Variations that cannot be observed with the naked eye require techniques such as *capillary electrophoresis* (the separation of genetic or protein material based on charge characteristics using an electric field).

The label on a vial of blood from a hospital patient was lost. The sample just tested positive for a disease of the blood protein hemoglobin that is very common in the hospital population. The sample was traced to a room with 4 patients who were subsequently tested to determine the source of the initial vial.

Tests and Results

Smears of the blood from the unidentified patient (P) and from the 4 newly tested patients (1–4) were observed under the microscope for the presence of any cells with an abnormal appearance (target or sickle cells). Results are shown in Table 1.

Table 1	
Patient	Blood smear findings
P	Sickle cells
1	Target cells
2	Sickle cells
3	No abnormal cells
4	Sickle cells

Serum was isolated from the blood of Patient P and from Patients 1–4 and placed in separate tubes. A buffer was added to each vial to establish a pH of 8.6. One at a time, samples from each tube were injected into the capillary electrophoresis device set at 7.5 kilovolts (kV) to separate the types of hemoglobin present into peaks. The hemoglobin proteins composing a peak had similar charge characteristics. Figure 1 shows the peaks that resulted from all 5 samples.

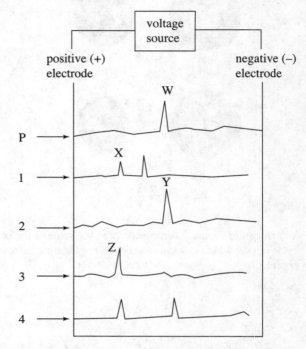

Note: Each peak is made up of hemoglobin proteins. W, X, Y, and Z are 4 specific peaks.

Figure 1

7. What is the most likely reason that the serum samples were treated with a buffer to bring pH to 8.6 ?

   A. Hemoglobin protein breaks down at that pH.
   B. All bacteria and viruses are destroyed at that pH.
   C. Capillary electrophoresis separation of hemoglobin functions best at that pH.
   D. Capillary electrophoresis separation of hemoglobin does not function at that pH.

8. Are the data in Table 1 consistent with the hypothesis that Patient 4 and Patient P are the same person?

   F. Yes; Patient 4 has the same blood cell appearance as Patient P.
   G. Yes; Patient 4 has different blood cell appearance as Patient P.
   H. No; Patient 4 has the same blood cell appearance as Patient P.
   J. No; Patient 4 has different blood cell appearance as Patient P.

9. Based on the information in the introduction and test results, do Patients 2 and 4 likely have the same genotype?

   A. Yes, because the blood smear findings of Patients 2 and 4 are the same.
   B. Yes, because Patients 2 and 4 have the same protein peak patterns.
   C. No, because the blood smear findings of Patients 2 and 4 are different.
   D. No, because Patients 2 and 4 have different protein peak patterns.

10. Sickle cells are caused by certain hemoglobin genotype combinations of 3 different alleles. The Hb^A allele is responsible for normal hemoglobin, the Hb^S allele is responsible for one variant that results in sickle cells, and the Hb^C allele is responsible for a different variant also resulting in sickle cells. Based on Table 1, the genotype of Patient 4 could be which of the following?

     I. $Hb^A \, Hb^A$
     II. $Hb^A \, Hb^S$
     III. $Hb^A \, Hb^C$

   F. II only
   G. I or III only
   H. II or III only
   J. I, II, or III

11. According to Figure 1, the pattern of protein peaks produced by serum from Patient P most closely resembles the pattern produced by the serum sample from:

   A. Patient 1.
   B. Patient 2.
   C. Patient 3.
   D. Patient 4.

12. Based on Figure 1, the hemoglobin proteins in which of the following two peaks were most likely closest in charge characteristics?

   F. W and X
   G. W and Z
   H. X and Y
   J. X and Z

13. During the capillary electrophoresis, all the hemoglobin proteins started with some quantity of charge before migrating from left to right in Figure 1. Therefore, the proteins resulting in peaks furthest to the left must have been the most:

   A. negative, as opposite charges attract each other.
   B. negative, as opposite charges repel each other.
   C. positive, as opposite charges attract each other.
   D. positive, as opposite charges repel each other.

Passage III

Carboxylic acids are organic compounds containing a *carboxyl* (–COOH) group. These molecules are acidic since they are able to donate protons in solution. The acidity and other physical properties of carboxylic acids are affected by the composition of the atoms bound to the carboxyl group. Table 1 lists the freezing points and boiling points for several carboxylic acids.

Table 1			
Formula	Name	Freezing point (°C)	Boiling point (°C)
CHOOH	Formic acid	8.4	101
CH₃COOH	Acetic acid	16.6	118
CH₃CH₂COOH	Propionic acid	–20.8	141
CH₃(CH₂)₂COOH	Butyric acid	–5.5	164
CH₃(CH₂)₃COOH	Valeric acid	–34.5	186

Figure 1 shows how the vapor pressure (in mm Hg) of 3 carboxylic acids changes as a function of temperature.

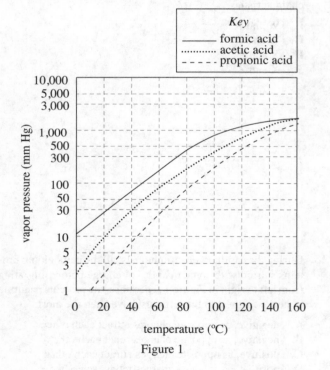

Figure 1

Figure 2 shows how the vapor pressure of the same 3 carboxylic acids changes as a function of concentration when mixed with water at 20°C.

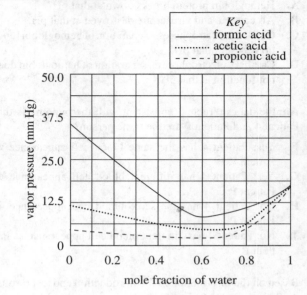

Figure 2

14. Which of the carboxylic acids listed in Table 1 has the *highest* melting point?

   F. Propionic acid
   G. Valeric acid
   H. Acetic acid
   J. Formic acid

15. A carboxylic acid not listed in Table 1, pyruvic acid, has a boiling point of 165°C. Based on Table 1 and Figure 1, the vapor pressure of pyruvic acid at 40°C is most likely:

   A. less than 10 mm Hg.
   B. between 10 and 100 mm Hg.
   C. between 100 and 500 mm Hg.
   D. greater than 500 mm Hg.

16. According to Figure 2, the vapor pressure of a 0.5 mole fraction solution of water in formic acid is closest to the vapor pressure of which of the following water in formic acid solutions?

    F. 0.4 mole fraction
    G. 0.6 mole fraction
    H. 0.8 mole fraction
    J. 0.9 mole fraction

17. According to Figure 2, as the mole fraction of water in an acetic acid and water solution increases from 0 to 1, the vapor pressure:

    A. decreases, then increases.
    B. increases, then decreases.
    C. decreases only.
    D. increases only.

18. $CH_3(CH_2)_4COOH$ is the chemical formula for the carboxylic acid named hexanoic acid. Based on Table 1, this compound most likely boils at a temperature:

    F. lower than 180°C.
    G. between 180°C and 215°C.
    H. between 215°C and 250°C.
    J. higher than 250°C.

19. According to Figure 1, does acetic acid or formic acid resist vaporization more at 60°C ?

    A. Formic acid, because formic acid has the lower vapor pressure.
    B. Formic acid, because formic acid has the higher vapor pressure.
    C. Acetic acid, because acetic acid has the lower vapor pressure.
    D. Acetic acid, because acetic acid has the higher vapor pressure.

Passage IV

A solenoid is a device that creates a magnetic field from electric current and can be used to exert a force on a nearby bar magnet to activate a mechanical device.

Scientists performed experiments on the solenoid apparatus shown in Figure 1.

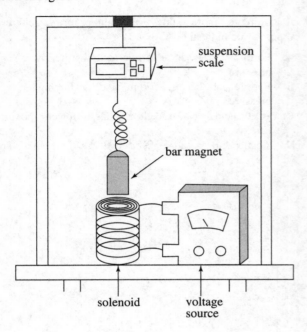

Figure 1

A wire carrying current from a voltage source was coiled into a hollow cylinder to form a solenoid with a length of XY. A solid cylinder bar magnet was suspended near the top of the solenoid as shown in Figure 2.

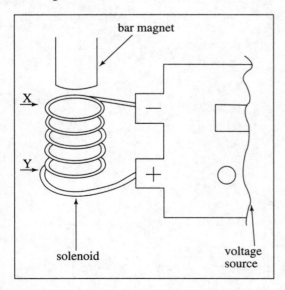

Figure 2

When the voltage source was turned on, the solenoid exerted a measurable force on the suspended bar magnet.

The bar magnet was attached to a digital suspension scale that measured weight in newtons (N). With the voltage source off, the scale read 4.7000 N. Prior to the start of each experimental trial, the scale was adjusted to read 5.0000 N.

Experiment 1

The scientists applied various levels of voltage in volts (V) to the circuit and recorded the weight indicated by the suspension scale for each trial. Results were recorded in Table 1.

Table 1	
Voltage (V)	Weight (N)
7.25	5.0078
8.00	5.0095
8.75	5.0113

Experiment 2

The scientists removed the bar magnet, inverted it, and reattached it to the suspension scale so that the opposite end was now facing the solenoid. The procedures of Experiment 1 were repeated and results were recorded in Table 2.

Table 2	
Voltage (V)	Weight (N)
7.25	4.9922
8.00	4.9905
8.75	4.9887

Experiment 3

The bar magnet was returned to the original alignment it was in during Experiment 1. The length XY of the solenoid coil was varied while a voltage of 8.00 V was applied to the circuit. Weights were recorded in Table 3.

Table 3	
Solenoid length XY (cm)	Weight (N)
7.50	5.0169
8.50	5.0131
9.50	5.0105

20. Based on the results of Experiments 1 and 3, the length XY of the solenoid coil in Experiment 1 was most likely:

    F. shorter than 7.50 cm.
    G. between 7.50 cm and 8.50 cm.
    H. between 8.50 cm and 9.50 cm.
    J. longer than 9.50 cm.

21. In Experiments 1 and 2, the orientation of the bar magnet relative to the solenoid opening determined which of the following?

    A. Solenoid length XY
    B. Direction of the force exerted by the solenoid on the bar magnet
    C. Density of the bar magnet
    D. Magnetic field strength of the solenoid

22. Which of the following provides the best explanation for the results of Experiment 3 ? The force exerted on the bar magnet by the solenoid magnetic field:

    F. increased as the voltage applied to the circuit increased.
    G. decreased as the voltage applied to the circuit increased.
    H. increased as the length XY of the solenoid increased.
    J. decreased as the length XY of the solenoid increased.

23. Suppose the scientists maintained the same bar magnet orientation in Experiment 3 as in Experiment 2. Based on the results of Experiments 1 and 2, with the solenoid length XY equal to 9.50 cm, the weight on the scale would most likely have been:

    A. 4.9831 N.
    B. 4.9895 N.
    C. 5.0105 N.
    D. 5.0169 N.

24. Prior to all experiments, the suspension scale was calibrated to read exactly 0 N when nothing was attached. Once the bar magnet was attached, the scientists made which of the following adjustments to the scale reading for each of the experimental trials?

    F. The displayed weight was adjusted downward by approximately 1.3 N.
    G. The displayed weight was adjusted upward by approximately 1.3 N.
    H. The displayed weight was adjusted downward by approximately 0.3 N.
    J. The displayed weight was adjusted upward by approximately 0.3 N.

25. Which of the following graphs best depicts the results of Experiment 3 ?

    A.
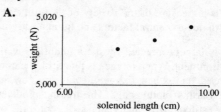

    B.
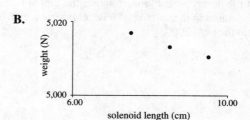

    C.
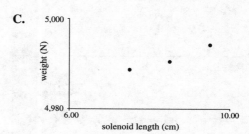

    D.
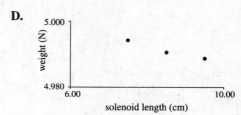

26. Suppose another trial had been conducted in Experiment 2 in which the voltage was 6.50 V. The weight measured on the scale would most likely have been closest to which of the following?

    F. 4.9908 N
    G. 4.9918 N
    H. 4.9928 N
    J. 4.9938 N

Passage V

Biodiversity is a measure of the variety of life in the world, and it can vary both due to natural factors and human activities.

Biodiversity is largely affected by the amount of available oxygen in the environment. When oxygen is plentiful, the number of species increases, but when oxygen levels are low, mass extinctions lower Earth's biodiversity. The marine biodiversity over time can be estimated by analyzing sediment and fossils found beneath the ocean floor. Figure 1 shows the global marine biodiversity, measured in the number of invertebrate genera, from the year 1500 to the year 2000.

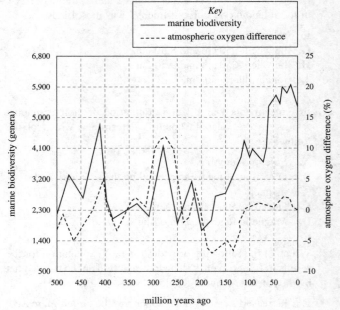

Figure 2

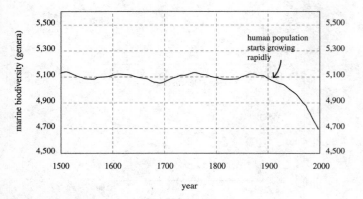

Figure 1

Figure 2 shows the global marine biodiversity and the atmospheric oxygen difference over the past 500 million years. The atmospheric oxygen difference is equal to:

(atmospheric oxygen concentration at a specific time) − (current atmospheric oxygen concentration)

Two ecology students describe their theories on the loss of marine biodiversity since 1900.

Student 1

The rapid loss in marine biodiversity since 1900 is caused by human activities. Figure 1 shows that the marine biodiversity was stable for centuries until the human population surged upward, quadrupling between 1900 and present day. The deforestation and large-scale industry necessary to support the large population has led to a decrease of 0.50% in the atmospheric oxygen concentration since 1900. As a result, marine biodiversity has decreased at a rate faster than any other time in the past 500 million years. Since 2000, marine biodiversity has fallen by approximately 2% per decade.

Student 2

The loss in marine biodiversity is part of a natural cycle of growth and loss that has occurred many times over the past 500 million years. As natural processes such as volcanic eruptions, asteroid impacts, and weathering cause decreases and increases in the atmospheric oxygen levels, marine biodiversity follows the same trend (see Figure 2). Human activities have very little effect on the atmospheric oxygen concentration, so the human impact on marine biodiversity is negligible.

27. Given Figure 1, Student 1 would most likely claim that from the year 1500 to the year 1900, the atmospheric oxygen concentration:

A. increased by more than 1.0%.
B. decreased by more than 1.0%.
C. changed by 1.0%.
D. changed by less than 1.0%, remaining relatively constant.

28. According to Figure 2, over which of the following time intervals did the atmospheric oxygen concentration decrease more than 10 times as much as Student 1 claims it has decreased since 1900?

F. 440 to 420 million years ago
G. 330 to 310 million years ago
H. 260 to 240 million years ago
J. 30 to 10 million years ago

29. Student 1 claims that current marine biodiversity is falling at a faster rate than it did at any time in the past 500 million years. Does Figure 1 give sufficient basis for that claim?

A. No; Figure 1 shows the marine biodiversity level for the past few centuries only.
B. No; Figure 1 shows the marine biodiversity for the past 500 million years.
C. Yes; Figure 1 shows the marine biodiversity level for the past few centuries only.
D. Yes; Figure 1 shows the marine biodiversity for the past 500 million years.

30. According to Student 1, marine biodiversity has been decreasing at a constant rate since 2000. Given the marine biodiversity level in the year 2000 in Figure 1, Student 1 would most likely conclude that the marine biodiversity in the year 2020 was closest to which of the following?

F. 4,500 genera
G. 4,600 genera
H. 4,800 genera
J. 4,900 genera

31. Suppose Student 2 stated that there have been times over the past 500 million years at which the atmospheric oxygen concentration has been lower than it is today. To support this statement, Student 2 would most likely cite oxygen data in Figure 2 for which of the following times?

A. 405 million years ago
B. 330 million years ago
C. 180 million years ago
D. 70 million years ago

32. Assume that the current atmospheric oxygen concentration is 21%. Given Figure 2, the two students would most likely claim that the atmospheric oxygen concentration 300 million years ago was closest to which of the following?

F. 15%
G. 19%
H. 24%
J. 27%

33. Which of the following statements about marine biodiversity would Student 2 most likely agree with?

A. Marine biodiversity generally increases as the oxygen concentration decreases.
B. Marine biodiversity generally decreases as the oxygen concentration decreases.
C. Marine biodiversity is affected only by human activities.
D. Marine biodiversity has remained constant for the past 500 million years.

Passage VI

The force per unit area resulting from the separation of solutions of different concentrations by a selectively permeable membrane is called *osmotic pressure*. Molecules, including water, have a tendency to move from regions of high concentration to regions of low concentration. Selectively permeable membranes act as filters, only allowing molecules below a certain threshold size to pass through. Osmotic pressure is the pressure required to stop water from moving across such a membrane from a region of high to low water concentration.

Cupric ions (Cu_2+) and glucose were dissolved separately in equal volumes of water to make two solutions. The glucose solution was more dilute, meaning that it had a higher percentage of water molecules than the cupric ion solution. Of the three molecules used for the solutions, water is the smallest and glucose is the largest. Water and glucose solutions are colorless while cupric ion solutions are blue. However, mixing glucose and cupric ions results in a red solution.

Experiment 1

A U-shaped tube contains a selectively permeable membrane, dividing it into equal halves. Glucose solution is poured in the left and an equal volume of cupric ion solution is poured in the right. Over 2 hours, the water level fell on the left and rose on the right. At this time, the left-sided solution was red and the right-sided was blue.

Experiment 2

Cupric ion solution is poured in the left side of the U-shaped tube and an equal volume of pure water is poured in the right. Over 2 hours, the water level fell on the right and rose on the left. At this time, both sides of the tube contained blue-colored solutions.

Experiment 3

Glucose solution is poured in the left side of the U-shaped tube and an equal volume of pure water is poured in the right. Over 2 hours, the water level fell on the right and rose on the left. At this time, both sides of the tube contained colorless solutions.

34. Which of the following diagrams could represent the results of Experiment 1 after the two hours had passed?

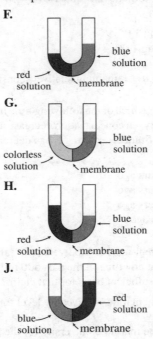

F. blue solution / red solution / membrane

G. colorless solution / blue solution / membrane

H. red solution / blue solution / membrane

J. blue solution / red solution / membrane

35. Albumin molecules do not pass through the selectively permeable membrane used in Experiments 1–3 and form clear solutions in water. If Experiment 2 were repeated, but the left side was filled with an albumin solution, the solution levels would:

A. fall on the left and rise on the right, resulting in a left-sided red solution and right-sided clear solution.
B. rise on the left and fall on the right, resulting in red solutions on both sides.
C. fall on the left and rise on the right, resulting in red solutions on both sides.
D. rise on the left and fall on the right, resulting in clear solutions on both sides.

36. In Experiments 1 and 2, cupric ion particles were able to move:

F. through the membrane into both the glucose solution and pure water.
G. through neither membrane into neither the glucose solution nor the pure water.
H. only through the membrane separating it from the glucose solution.
J. only through the membrane separating it from pure water.

37. In Experiments 2 and 3, what did the left side of the U-tube contain at the start of the experiment?

Experiment 2	Experiment 3
A. cupric ion solution	pure water
B. glucose solution	pure water
C. cupric ion solution	glucose solution
D. glucose solution	cupric ion solution

38. In Experiment 1, if a selectively permeable membrane that cupric ions, glucose, and water molecules could all pass through had been used, how, if at all, would the results have differed?

F. The water level would have fallen on the right and risen on the left.

G. A red color would have appeared on both sides of the U-tube.

H. A blue color would have appeared on both sides of the U-tube.

J. The same results would have been observed.

39. After watching Experiment 1 only, an observer asserted that since the left-sided solution ended up red, cupric ions must be bigger than water molecules. Is this a valid assertion?

A. No; the results show only that cupric ions and water molecules are smaller than glucose molecules.

B. No; the results show only that cupric ions and water molecules are larger than glucose molecules.

C. Yes; the results show that water molecules but not cupric ions can pass through the selectively permeable membrane.

D. Yes; the results show that both water molecules and cupric ions can pass through the selectively permeable membrane.

40. In Experiment 1, before the molecules began to move through the semi-permeable membrane, the appearance of the right-sided solution in the U-tube was:

F. clear.

G. blue.

H. red.

J. purple.

END OF TEST.
STOP! DO NOT TURN THE PAGE UNTIL TOLD TO DO SO.

Chapter 13
Science Practice
Test 3: Answers and
Explanations

SCIENCE PRACTICE TEST 3 ANSWER KEY

1.	C	21.	B
2.	J	22.	J
3.	D	23.	A
4.	H	24.	J
5.	A	25.	B
6.	G	26.	J
7.	C	27.	D
8.	F	28.	H
9.	D	29.	A
10.	H	30.	F
11.	B	31.	C
12.	J	32.	J
13.	A	33.	B
14.	H	34.	F
15.	A	35.	D
16.	H	36.	F
17.	A	37.	C
18.	G	38.	G
19.	C	39.	A
20.	J	40.	G

SCORE YOUR PRACTICE TEST

Step A

Count the number of correct answers: _____. This is your *raw score*.

Step B

Use the score conversion table below to look up your raw score. The number to the left is your *scale score*: _____.

Test 3 Scale Conversion Table

Scale Score	Raw Score	Scale Score	Raw Score	Scale Score	Raw Score
36	39–40	24	26	12	9
35	38	23	24–25	11	8
34	37	22	22–23	10	7
33	—	21	20–21	9	5–6
32	36	20	18–19	8	4
31	35	19	17	7	—
30	34	18	15–16	6	3
29	33	17	14	5	2
28	32	16	13	4	—
27	31	15	12	3	1
26	29–30	14	11	2	—
25	27–28	13	10	1	0

SCIENCE PRACTICE TEST 3 EXPLANATIONS

Passage I

1. **C**   The question asks for the cell in Figure 3 that is most likely in the stage of the cell cycle in which mitosis is nearing completion. Read the description of Figure 3 to learn more about the images. The passage says the four images represent *cells in each of the 4 stages of the dividing cell cycle*. Since the question asks for a cell near the end of mitosis, look for the cell that has almost finished dividing into two cells. Cell 3 shows the clearest division into two cells. The correct answer is (C).

2. **J**   The question asks for an *AI* value for fibroblast cells in a toxin concentration of 90 ppm based on Figure 1. Look at the horizontal axis that shows toxin concentration in Figure 1. A concentration of 90 ppm is beyond the range of the graph, so extrapolate the pattern. At a toxin concentration of 80 ppm, the *AI* is approximately 0.007. The *AI* increases as toxin concentration increases, so the *AI* for 90 ppm would be a little higher than 0.007. The answer choices are all percentages, and the *AI* is a proportion, so it needs to be converted into a percentage. To convert *AI* to a percentage, multiply the *AI* by 100%, or 0.007(100%) = 0.7%, so the percentage for 90 ppm would be a little higher than 0.7%. Eliminate (F), (G), and (H) as these are not higher than 0.7%. The correct answer is (J).

3. **D**   The question asks for the cell that is in the first stage based on Figure 3. Read the description of Figure 3 to learn more about the images. The passage states that the four images represent *cells in each of the 4 stages of the dividing cell cycle*. Since the question asks for a cell in the *first stage* of the cycle, use POE to determine the correct cell. Cells 1 and 3 show visible signs of division, so they represent stages near the end of the cell cycle. Eliminate (A) and (C). Compare the remaining answer choices. Cells 2 and 3 are similar in appearance, but Cell 2 is larger. Cell 2 is also very similar in appearance to Cell 1, which is beginning to divide. Therefore, it is logical that Cell 2 is closer in the cycle to the division stage than Cell 1. Therefore, Cell 1 must be closer to the beginning of the cycle. The correct answer is (D).

4. **H**   The question asks how the number of fibroblast cells in stage G_2 compares to the number of cells in stage S based on Figure 2. Look for the data for the number of cells in each cell cycle stage in Figure 2. Approximately 75 cells are in stage S, and approximately 225 cells are in stage G_2. There are more cells in stage G_2, so eliminate (F) and (G). Try (H): 75 times 3 is 225. The correct answer is (H).

5. **A**   The question asks for the proportion of cells in the cell cycle that were in stage G_1 based on Figure 2. Look for the data for the number of cells in the G_1 stage in Figure 2. Approximately 540 cells are in stage G_1. Use POE. The proportion must have the number of cells in stage G_1 in the numerator, so eliminate (B) and (C). The proportion must have the total number of cells in the denominator, which must be greater than the number of cells in stage G_1, so eliminate (D). The correct answer is (A).

6. **G**   The question asks for the number of cells out of a sample of 3,000 cells that are undergoing apoptosis in a toxin concentration of 30 ppm. Look for 30 ppm along the horizontal axis in Figure 1. At 30 ppm, the *AI* is 0.005. The passage says the *AI* is calculated using the formula

$AI = \dfrac{number\ of\ cells\ undergoing\ apoptosis}{total\ number\ of\ cells}$, so this is a proportion. Start with POE. Eliminate (J) because 1,500 cells would be half of the cells, which is 0.5 instead of 0.005. Eliminate (H), as this is 1/10 of (J), which would mean a proportion of 0.05 instead of 0.005. In (G), this is 1/100 of (J), which is 0.005. The correct answer is (G).

Passage II

7. **C** The question asks for the rationale behind treating samples with a buffer to reach a pH of 8.6. Since pH is not mentioned in either figure, look for where pH is mentioned in the passage. In the 4th paragraph, the passage states that *a buffer was added to each vial to establish a pH of 8.6*. Immediately after adding the buffer, the passage says *samples from each tube were injected into the capillary electrophoresis device.* Since the buffer is added right before the samples are run through the capillary electrophoresis device, the buffer must have something to do with this process. Eliminate (A) and (B) since they don't mention capillary electrophoresis. If a pH of 8.6 did not allow the electrophoresis separation to occur, there would be no purpose for the scientists to add the buffer. Eliminate (D). If electrophoresis occurs best at a pH of 8.6, this explains why the buffer would have been added. The correct answer is (C).

8. **F** The question asks if the information in Table 1 is consistent with the hypothesis that Patient 4 and Patient P are the same person. Refer to Table 1 and use POE. Since Patient P's blood smear and Patient 4's blood smear both contain sickle cells, they have the same blood cell appearance. Eliminate (G) and (J). Since the blood cell appearance is the same, they could be the same person. Eliminate (H). The correct answer is (F).

9. **D** The question asks whether the information and data in the passage indicate that Patient 2 and Patient 4 likely have the same genotype. Look for information about genotypes in the passage. The first paragraph states that *all humans have slight differences in their genotypes (genetic code) that result in different phenotypes (observable characteristics).* Since genotypes *cannot be observed with the naked eye*, scientists must rely on *capillary electrophoresis* to analyze the genetic code of different patients. Therefore, the data that will support or contradict a claim on genotypes must be in Figure 1, since that is the data from the capillary electrophoresis process. Eliminate (A) and (C) since they use data from Table 1 instead of Figure 1. Patient 2 has one large peak labeled Y, and Patient 4 has two smaller peaks in different locations. Eliminate (B) because the patients do not have protein peaks in the same locations. The correct answer is (D).

10. **H** The question asks for possible genotypes of Patient 4. Look for information about genotypes in the passage. The first paragraph says *all humans have slight differences in their genotypes (genetic code) that result in different phenotypes (observable characteristics).* Table 1 says Patient 4 has sickle cells in his or her blood smear. Therefore, Patient 4 must have a genotype that results in sickle cells. The question says that the Hb^A allele results in normal cells, and both the Hb^S and Hb^C alleles result in sickle cells.

Genotype I has two copies of the normal Hb^A allele, so this genotype cannot result in sickle cells. Eliminate (G) and (J). Both alleles Hb^S and Hb^C cause sickle cells, so Patient 4 could have either genotype II or genotype III. Therefore, the correct answer is (H).

11. **B** The question asks for a comparison between two samples represented in Figure 1. Patient P has one large peak labeled *W*. The only other sample with a single peak in a similar location is Patient 2. The correct answer is (B).

12. **J** The question asks which protein peaks are *closest in charge characteristics* based on Figure 1. Look for the term *charge characteristics* in the description of Figure 1. The passage says *the hemoglobin proteins composing a peak had similar charge characteristics*, so the proteins with similar charge characteristics should be located in a similar location on the figure. Peaks X and Z are in similar locations, and peaks W and Y are in similar locations. Out of these two pairs, only X and Z are linked in an answer choice. The correct answer is (J).

13. **A** The question asks for the charge of the proteins that resulted in peaks furthest to the left in Figure 1. Refer to Figure 1. The electrode on the left of the diagram is labeled *positive*, and the electrode on the right of the figure is labeled *negative*. Use POE to eliminate the illogical answers. Since the electrode on the left is positive, the proteins nearest to that electrode would be negative only if opposite charges attract. If opposite charges repel, the proteins would be positive. Eliminate (B) and (D) because they reverse this logic. To choose between the remaining answers, you need some outside knowledge. Opposite charges attract each other, so the proteins located nearest to the positive electrode would be negatively charged. Eliminate (C) since it says the proteins on the left are positive. The correct answer is (A).

Passage III

14. **H** The question asks for the acid with the highest melting point based on data in Table 1. Look at the variables in Table 1. Melting point is not listed, but freezing point is. Melting and freezing occur at the same temperature since both processes transition between liquids and solids at this temperature. Therefore, the acid with the highest freezing point also has the highest melting point. The highest freezing point listed on Table 1 is for acetic acid at 16.6°C. The correct answer is (H).

15. **A** The question asks for the value of the vapor pressure of an additional acid at 40°C based on its boiling point and the data in Table 1 and Figure 1. Look for the trends for boiling point and vapor pressure in Table 1 and Figure 1. In Table 1, formic acid has the lowest boiling point and propionic acid has the highest boiling point. In Figure 1, formic acid has the highest vapor pressure and propionic acid has the lowest vapor pressure. Therefore, boiling point and vapor pressure exhibit an inverse relationship: as one variable increases, the other variable decreases. The 165°C boiling point of pyruvic acid is greater than the boiling point of any of the three acids in Table 1 and Figure 1. Since vapor pressure decreases as boiling point increases, pyruvic acid should have a lower vapor pressure than any of the three acids. Find 40°C on the horizontal axis of the graph, and trace up to the dashed line for propionic acid. Read across to the vertical axis and note that propionic acid has a vapor pressure between 9 and 10 mm Hg. Pyruvic acid must have an even lower vapor pressure. The correct answer is (A).

16. **H** The question asks, based on Figure 2, for the concentration of the formic acid solution that has the vapor pressure closest to that of a 0.5 mole fraction formic acid solution. Look for the vapor pressure of a 0.5 mole fraction of water formic acid solution in Figure 2. A 0.5 mole fraction of water formic acid solution, represented by the solid line, has a vapor pressure of approximately 10 mm Hg. Draw a horizontal line at this vapor pressure to see where else the formic acid solution has this value. The formic acid solution line intersects the 10 mm Hg vapor pressure line again at a mole fraction of 0.8. The correct answer is (H).

17. **A** The question asks how the vapor pressure changes as the mole fraction of water increases from 0 to 1 in an acetic acid solution, based on Figure 2. Look for the trend between vapor pressure and mole fraction of water in Figure 2, making sure to use the dotted line for acetic acid. As the concentration increases from a mole fraction of 0 to 0.6, the vapor pressure decreases, and then from a mole fraction of 0.6 to 1, the vapor pressure increases. The correct answer is (A).

18. **G** The question asks for the boiling point of an additional acid based on its chemical formula and the data in Table 1. Look for the trend between chemical formula and boiling point in Table 1. As the number of CH_2 groups increases, the boiling point increases. In Table 1, valeric acid has the highest boiling point of 186°C and the greatest number of CH_2 groups. The chemical formula of hexanoic acid has one more CH_2 group than valeric acid, so hexanoic acid has a higher boiling point than valeric acid. Eliminate (F). For each additional CH_2 group added to the chemical formula, the boiling point increases by just over 20°C. Hexanoic acid has one more CH_2 group than valeric acid, so the boiling point of hexanoic acid should be approximately 23°C more than the boiling point of valeric acid, or 186°C + 23°C = 209°C. This boiling point falls within the range of 180°C and 215°C. The correct answer is (G).

19. **C** The question asks whether acetic acid or formic acid resists vaporization more at 60°C, based on Figure 1. Look for the data for vapor pressure in Figure 1, making sure to use the appropriate lines for each acid based on the key. At 60°C, the solid line for formic acid shows a vapor pressure of approximately 200 mm Hg, and the dotted line for acetic acid shows a vapor pressure of approximately 80 mm Hg. Eliminate (A) and (D) since both indicate that formic acid has a lower vapor pressure than acetic acid. Compare the remaining answer choices. For an acid to *resist* vaporization more, it must have the lower vapor pressure. Since acetic acid has the lower vapor pressure, the correct answer is (C).

Passage IV

20. **J** The question asks for the length of the solenoid coil in Experiment 1 based on the results of Experiments 1 and 3. Table 1 shows the results of Experiment 1, and Table 3 shows the results of Experiment 3. Since the question asks to synthesize information from two tables, look for the link between the data. Table 3 shows the weights for various solenoid lengths, while Table 1 shows the weights at various voltages. Read the description of Table 3 to find the voltage used in Experiment 3. The passage says *a voltage of 8.00 V was applied to the circuit.* Look for the weight for a voltage of 8.00 V

in Table 1. At this voltage, the weight exerted on the suspension scale is 5.0095 N. Now, look at Table 3 to determine how solenoid length affects weight. As the solenoid length increases, the weight decreases. A weight of 5.0095 N is lower than any weight listed on Table 3, so the solenoid length must be longer than any length listed on Table 3. Since the maximum solenoid length listed is 9.50 cm, the solenoid length used in Experiment 1 must be longer than 9.50 cm. The correct answer is (J).

21. **B**   The question asks which variable was determined by the orientation of the bar magnet in Experiments 1 and 2. Look for where bar magnet orientation is mentioned in the passage. In the description for Experiment 2, the passage says *the scientists removed the bar magnet, inverted it, and reattached it*, but everything else stayed the same as Experiment 1. Compare the data from Experiment 2 to Experiment 1 to see how the change in bar magnet orientation affected the data. In Experiment 1, as the voltage increases, the weight increases. In Experiment 2, as the voltage increases, the weight decreases. Use POE. Choice (A) mentions *solenoid length*. Since the procedures are kept the same except for changing the orientation of the bar magnet, solenoid length is not affected. Eliminate (A). Choice (B) mentions *direction of the force exerted by the solenoid on the bar magnet*. Since Experiment 1 shows an increasing force, and Experiment 2 shows a decreasing force, this is consistent. Keep (B), but check the other answers just in case. Choice (C) mentions the *density of the bar magnet* which is calculated by dividing mass by volume. Reorienting the bar magnet will not change its mass or volume, so eliminate (C). Choice (D) mentions the *magnetic field strength of the solenoid*. Since only the direction of the magnet changed, the magnetic field strength would not change. Eliminate (D). The correct answer is (B).

22. **J**   The question asks how the force exerted on the magnet by the solenoid electric field is changed as another variable is changed in Experiment 3. The results of Experiment 3 are shown in Table 3. The description of Table 3 states that *a voltage of 8.00 V was applied to the circuit*. Since the voltage is constant, eliminate (F) and (G). Since weight is a measure of force, look for the data in Table 3 to determine how solenoid length affects weight. As the solenoid length increases, the weight decreases. A lower weight indicates a lower force pulling the magnet downward. Therefore, the force decreased as the solenoid length increased. The correct answer is (J).

23. **A**   The question asks what the weight on the scale for a solenoid length of 9.50 cm would have been if Experiment 3 used the same bar magnet orientation as Experiment 2. In the description for Experiment 2, the passage says *the scientists removed the bar magnet, inverted it, and reattached it*, but everything else stayed the same as Experiment 1. Compare the data from Experiment 2, found in Table 2, to the data from Experiment 1, found in Table 1, to see how the change in bar magnet orientation affected the data. In Experiment 1 the weight increases from the 5.000 N as voltage increases, while in Experiment 2 it decreases from 5.000 N as voltage increases. Therefore, the bar magnet orientation in Experiment 2 causes weight to decrease instead of increase. In the description for Experiment 3, the passage says *the bar magnet was returned to the original alignment it was in during Experiment 1*. If instead Experiment 3 had used the bar magnet orientation from Experiment 2, Experiment 3 would have exhibited the same pattern of decreasing weight instead of increasing weight. Eliminate (C) and (D) because they are greater than 5.000 N. At a solenoid length of 9.50 cm, the weight recorded in Experiment 3 was 5.0105 N, which is an increase 0.0105 N from 5.000 N. The new orientation should cause a decrease of 0.0105 N instead: 5.0000 N − 0.0105 N = 4.9895 N. The correct answer is (A).

24. **J**   The question asks how scientists performed a calibration on the suspension scale. Look for where adjustment of the suspension scale is mentioned in the passage. In the fifth paragraph, the passage says *with the voltage source off, the scale read 4.7000 N.* The passage then states that *prior to the start of each experimental trial, the scale was adjusted to read 5.0000 N.* Eliminate (F) and (H) because they mention a downward adjustment, and the value of the scale reading increases. Find the difference between the two weights to determine the adjustment, or 5.0000 N – 4.7000 N = 0.3 N. The procedure would require an adjustment upward of approximately 0.3 N. The correct answer is (J).

25. **B**   The question asks for a graph that best conveys the results of data from Experiment 3. The results for Experiment 3 are in Table 3. In Table 3, as the solenoid length increases, the weight decreases. Eliminate (A) and (C), since these graphs show weight increasing as solenoid length increases. Compare the remaining answer choices. Choice (D) shows all of the weights below 5.000 N, but Table 3 shows all of the weights above 5.000 N. Eliminate (D). The correct answer is (B).

26. **J**   The question asks for the likely weight if an additional trial had been performed in Experiment 2 with a voltage of 6.50 V. Experiment 2 is represented by Table 2. As the voltage increases in Table 2, the weight decreases. An additional trial at 6.50 V is lower than any voltages listed in the table, so the additional trial should have a higher weight than the highest weight in the table, which is 4.9922 N. Eliminate (F) and (G). Compare the values in Table 2 to determine how much higher the weight should be. A voltage of 6.50 V is 0.75 V below the first voltage listed on Table 2. To find the corresponding weight increase, determine the pattern of weight differences between voltages that are 0.75 V apart. As the voltage decreases from 8.75 V to 8.00 V, the weight increases from 4.9887 to 4.9905, which is an increase of 0.0018 N. As the voltage decreases from 8.00 V to 7.25 V, the weight increases from 4.9905 to 4.9922, which is an increase of 0.0017 N. Therefore, the approximate increase in weight from 7.50 V to 6.75 V should be 0.0016 N. Add this value to the weight at 7.25 V: 4.9922 + 0.0016 = 4.9938 N. The correct answer is (J).

Passage V

27. **D**   The question asks what Student 1 would most likely claim about the atmospheric oxygen concentration from 1500 to 1900 based on Figure 1. Figure 1 shows the biodiversity over time. Based on Figure 1, marine biodiversity was relatively stable between 1500 and 1900. Look at Student 1's theory. Student 1 states that *the marine biodiversity was stable for centuries until the human population surged upward, quadrupling between 1900 and present day.* Student 1 goes on to say that this population surge caused *a decrease of 0.50% in the atmospheric oxygen concentration since 1900*, which resulted in a decrease in biodiversity. If the change in oxygen concentration caused the change in marine biodiversity, then when the marine biodiversity is stable, the oxygen concentration should also be stable. Therefore, the student believes atmosphere oxygen concentrations were relatively stable prior to the population surge after the year 1900. The correct answer is (D).

28. **H**   The question asks for an interval on Figure 2 that shows an oxygen concentration decrease that is *more than 10 times* the amount mentioned by Student 1. Look for information about oxygen concentration decreases in Student 1's theory. Student 1 says human actions have led to *a decrease of 0.50% in the atmospheric oxygen concentration since 1900*. The question asks for a time interval that shows an *atmospheric oxygen concentration decrease more than 10 times* this, so multiply 0.50% by 10 to get a 5% decrease. Look at Figure 2. Atmospheric oxygen difference, which is the difference between atmospheric oxygen concentration at a given time and current atmospheric oxygen concentration, corresponds to the *y*-axis on the right side of the graph and the dotted line. Use POE. Choice (F) refers to the period from 440 to 420 million years ago. At that time, atmospheric oxygen concentration was increasing, not decreasing. Eliminate (F). Choice (G) refers to the period from 330 to 310 million years ago. During that time, atmospheric oxygen decreased from 2.5% more than present day to approximately 1% more than present day. This is only a 1.5% difference, so eliminate (G). Choice (H) refers to the period from 260 to 240 million years ago. During that time, atmospheric oxygen concentration ranged from about 11% more than present day to about 1% less than present day for a decrease of about 12%. Keep (H), but check (J) just in case. Choice (J) refers to the period from 30 to 10 million years ago. During that time, atmospheric oxygen concentration ranged from about 2.5% to about 1%. Eliminate (J). The correct answer is (H).

29. **A**   The question asks if Figure 1 supports a student's claim that marine biodiversity is falling at a rate faster than it has at any point over the last 500 million years. Look for the data for marine biodiversity in Figure 1. The *x*-axis ranges from the years 1500 to 2000, which is only a period of 500 years. Eliminate (B) and (D) since both say the figure describes the last 500 *million* years. Compare the remaining answer choices. Since Figure 1 only covers approximately 500 years, it can't be used to provide evidence for the last 500 million years. Eliminate (C). The correct answer is (A).

30. **F**   The question asks what Student 1 would conclude about marine biodiversity in 2020 based on Figure 1. Look at the marine biodiversity values in Figure 1. Trace up from the year 2000 to determine the biodiversity in 2000: just under 4,700 genera. Student 1 states that *since 2000, marine biodiversity has fallen by approximately 2% per decade*. Eliminate (H) and (J) since both show an increase in the number of genera. Since 1% of 4,700 is 47, then 2% of 4,700 is 47 × 2 = 94. Therefore, the number of genera will drop almost 100 between 2000 and 2010 to approximately 4,600. The question asks about 2020 not 2010, so eliminate (G). The number of genera would fall by a little less than 100 again between 2010 and 2020. The correct answer is (F).

31. **C**   The question asks for the time period in Figure 2 that Student 2 would most likely cite the oxygen data for in order to support the claim that there have been times over the past 500 million years in which oxygen concentration was lower than it is today. Look for the data for atmospheric oxygen difference in Figure 2. Atmospheric oxygen difference corresponds to the *y*-axis on the right side of the graph and the dotted line. Atmospheric oxygen difference is calculated by subtracting the current atmospheric oxygen concentration from the atmospheric oxygen concentration at a specific time. For the atmospheric oxygen concentration to be *lower than it is today*, the difference must be negative. Look for where the dotted line dips below 0%, which is between 200 and 120 million years ago. Eliminate (A), (B), and (D) because they do not fall in this range. The correct answer is (C).

32. **J**   The question asks for the value of atmospheric oxygen concentration 300 million years ago based on Figure 2, given that the current atmospheric oxygen concentration is 21%. Figure 2 graphs *atmospheric oxygen difference*. The equation in the introduction defines atmospheric oxygen difference as (atmospheric oxygen concentration at a specific time) − (current atmospheric oxygen concentration). Look at Figure 2 to find 300 million years ago along the *x* -axis. Draw a vertical line upward until you reach the dotted line, which represents oxygen level. Now draw a line to the right until you reach the vertical axis. The atmospheric oxygen difference at 300 million years ago is approximately 6%. Plug this value and the 21% present day value into the atmospheric oxygen difference equation to solve for the atmospheric oxygen concentration: 6% = (atmospheric oxygen concentration 300 million years ago) −21%. The atmospheric oxygen concentration 300 million years ago is equal to 27%. The correct answer is (J).

33. **B**   The question asks which statement about marine biodiversity Student 2 would most likely agree with. Use POE. Student 2 believes that *the loss in marine biodiversity is part of a natural cycle of growth and loss* and *the human impact on marine biodiversity is negligible*. Eliminate (D) because a cycle of growth and loss means the biodiversity is not constant. Eliminate (C) as Student 2 believes it is natural rather than caused by humans. Compare the remaining answer choices. The only difference between (A) and (B) is how marine biodiversity changes as oxygen concentration decreases. Student 2 states that *as natural processes such as volcanic eruptions, asteroid impacts, and weathering cause decreases and increases in the atmospheric oxygen levels, marine biodiversity follows the same trend*, which means that marine biodiversity and oxygen concentration exhibit a direct relationship: as one increases, so does the other. Eliminate (A). The correct answer is (B).

Passage VI

34. **F**   The question asks for a diagram that represents the results of Experiment 1 after two hours. Read the description for Experiment 1 to determine the results. The passage states that *the water level fell on the left and rose on the right*. Eliminate (G) and (H) because they do not show a higher water level on the right. The passage also states that *the left-side solution was red and the right-sided was blue*. Eliminate (J) because it has the colors reversed. The correct answer is (F).

35. **D**   The question asks how repeating Experiment 2 with an albumin solution on the left would affect the results. Use POE. According to the description of Experiment 2, Experiment 2 uses cupric ion on the left side and water on the right side. If the cupric ion solution on the left was replaced with an albumin solution, then only albumin and water would be in the tube. The question states that albumin molecules form clear solutions in water, so both sides would have to be clear. Eliminate (B) and (C). In the first paragraph, the passage says *molecules, including water, have a tendency to move from regions of high concentration to regions of low concentration*. The albumin particles cannot pass through the membrane, but the water molecules on the right side of the tube will move to the lower concentration on the left side, so the water level will rise on the left. Eliminate (A). The correct answer is (D).

36. **F**   The question asks how cupric ion particles move in Experiments 1 and 2. In Experiment 1, *glucose solution is poured in the left and an equal volume of cupric ion solution is poured in the right.* At the end of the experiment, *the left-sided solution was red and the right-sided was blue.* The introduction states that *mixing glucose and cupric ions results in a red solution.* Therefore, the only way the left solution would end up red is if cupric ion particles passed through the selectively permeable membrane into the glucose solution. Eliminate (G) and (J) since both contradict this idea. Compare the remaining two answer choices. The only difference is whether the cupric particles were also able to move into pure water. Read the description for Experiment 2. In Experiment 2, *cupric ion solution is poured on the left and an equal volume of pure water is poured in the right.* At the end of the experiment, *both sides of the tube contained blue-colored solution.* The introduction states that *cupric ion solutions are blue,* so the only way both solutions would be blue is if cupric ion particles passed through the selectively permeable membrane into the pure water. Eliminate (H). The correct answer is (F).

37. **C**   The question asks for the substance in the left half of the U-tube at the start of Experiments 2 and 3. Read the description for Experiment 2 to determine the substance. In Experiment 2, *cupric ion solution is poured in the left side.* Eliminate (B) and (D) since they say the substance on the left was glucose. Next, check the description for Experiment 3. In Experiment 3, *glucose solution is poured in the left,* so eliminate (A). The correct answer is (C).

38. **G**   The question asks how the results of Experiment 1 would have been different if a selectively permeable membrane that allows cupric ions, water, and glucose to pass had been used. Read the description for Experiment 1 to determine the solutions used for the experiment. In Experiment 1, *glucose solution is poured in the left and an equal volume of cupric ion solution is poured in the right.* In the original experiment, *the left-side solution was red and the right-sided was blue* after two hours. According to the introduction, *mixing glucose and cupric ions results in a red solution.* The only way the solution on the left would end up red is if cupric ion particles passed through the selectively permeable membrane into the glucose solution. The glucose particles must not have passed from the left to the right side though. In the new experiment, glucose can also pass through the selectively permeable membrane, resulting in a mixture of cupric and glucose ions on both sides of the membrane. This would cause red solutions to occur on both sides. The correct answer is (G).

39. **A**   The question asks if the assertion that cupric ions are bigger than water molecules is valid based on Experiment 1. In Experiment 1, *glucose solution is poured in the left and an equal volume of cupric ion solution is poured in the right.* At the end of the experiment, *the left-side solution was red and the right-sided was blue* after two hours. According to the introduction, *mixing glucose and cupric ions results in a red solution.* The only way the left solution would end up red is if cupric ion particles passed through the selectively permeable membrane into the glucose solution. Eliminate (C) because it says cupric ion particles can't pass through the membrane. Look through the introduction for a reference to the size of molecules. The introduction states that *selectively permeable membranes act as filters allowing only particles below a certain threshold size to pass through* and *of the three molecules used for the solutions, water is the smallest and glucose is the largest.* Eliminate (B), as it says water molecules and cupric ions are larger than glucose molecules. Consider the reasons for the remaining choices. Choice (D) says

that both water and cupric ions can pass through the selectively permeable membrane. If both can pass through the membrane, then that would not provide any evidence about whether cupric ions were larger than water molecules. Eliminate (D). Experiment 1 only shows that both cupric ions and water are small enough to pass through the membrane, but that glucose is too large to pass through the membrane. The correct answer is (A).

40. **G**   The question asks for the color of the substance in the right side of the tube at the beginning of Experiment 1. Read the description for Experiment 1 to determine the substance. In Experiment 1, *cupric ion solution is poured in the right*. Read the introduction to determine the color of cupric ion solution. The passage says *cupric ion solutions are blue*. The correct answer is (G).

Chapter 14
Science Practice
Test 4

SCIENCE TEST

35 Minutes–40 Questions

Directions: There are six passages in this test. Each passage is followed by several questions. After reading a passage, choose the best answer to each question and fill in the corresponding oval on your answer document. You may refer to the passages as often as necessary.

You are NOT permitted to use a calculator on this test.

Passage I

Two ways to measure the quality of soil are *bulk density* and the *soil organic matter test*, SOM (a measure of the active organic content). High quality soil provides structure to plants and moves water and nutrients, so plants grow in larger quantities, leading to higher crop yields at harvest.

Bulk density is measured as the dry weight of a sample of soil divided by the volume of the sample. A bulk density measure above 1.33 g/cm³ can negatively affect soil quality. Figure 1 shows the bulk density levels for 5 different years at Fields A and B.

Table 1 shows how soil quality varies with SOM. Table 2 shows the average SOM of each field for each of the 5 years.

Table 1	
SOM	Soil quality rating
<0.25	poor
0.25 to 0.50	fair
0.51 to 0.75	good
>0.75	excellent

Table 2	
Field	Average SOM
A	0.89
B	0.28

Figure 2 shows the total crop yield at each field at the end of the 5 years.

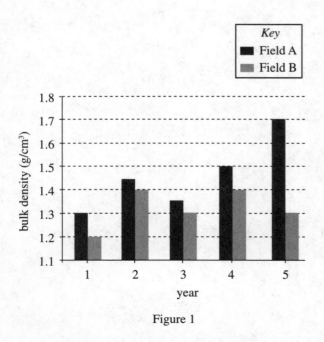

Figure 1

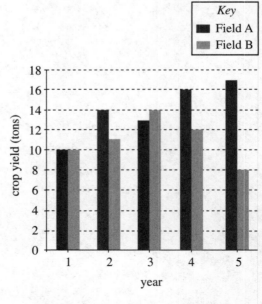

Figure 2

1. Which set of data best supports the claim that Field A has *lower* soil quality than Field B ?

   A. Figure 1
   B. Figure 2
   C. Table 1
   D. Table 2

2. If 8 tons or fewer in crop yields were considered a failed harvest, in which year and in which field would there have been a failed harvest?

   Z. Field A in Year 1
   G. Field A in Year 3
   H. Field B in Year 4
   J. Field B in Year 5

3. Suppose a new crop rotation for Field B included legumes and other deep-rooted and high-residue crops. The SOM of this field will most likely change in which of the following ways? The SOM will:

   A. decrease, because soil quality is likely to increase.
   B. decrease, because soil quality is likely to decrease.
   C. increase, because soil quality is likely to increase.
   D. increase, because soil quality is likely to decrease.

4. Based on Figures 1 and 2, consider the average bulk density and the average crop yields for Fields A and B over the study period. Which site had the lower average crop yield, and which site had the lower average bulk density?

	lower crop yield	lower bulk density
F.	Field A	Field A
G.	Field B	Field B
H.	Field A	Field B
J.	Field B	Field A

5. As soil quality improves, the number of earthworms increases. Students hypothesized that more earthworms would be found in Field B than in Field A. Are the data presented in Table 2 consistent with this hypothesis?

   A. Yes; based on SOM, Field B had a soil quality rating of excellent and Field A had a soil quality rating of fair.
   B. Yes; based on SOM, Field B had a soil quality rating of fair and Field A had a soil quality rating of poor.
   C. No; based on SOM, Field B had a soil quality rating of fair and Field A had a soil quality rating of excellent.
   D. No; based on SOM, Field B had a soil quality rating of poor and Field A had a soil quality rating of fair.

6. The restrictive bulk-density threshold of a soil is the maximum bulk density under which plants roots can still grow effectively. The restrictive bulk-density threshold for two types of soil is shown below.

Soil type	Restrictive threshold (g/cm^3)
Sand	1.80
Clay	1.55

   Based on the table above and the information in the Figures 1 and 2, is the soil in Field A more likely primarily sand or clay?

   F. Sand, because in Year 3 the bulk density of Field A was less than 1.55 and the crop yield was high.
   G. Sand, because in Year 5 the bulk density of Field A was greater than 1.55 and the crop yield was high.
   H. Clay, because in Year 3 the bulk density of Field A was less than 1.55 and the crop yield was high.
   J. Clay, because in Year 5 the bulk density of Field A was greater than 1.55 and the crop yield was high.

Passage II

Ferric oxide (Fe_2O_3) is more commonly known as rust. This is produced in a reaction between iron, a common metal, and water, H_2O.

$$2Fe + 3\,H_2O \longrightarrow Fe_2O_3 + 3H_2$$

Table 1 shows the amount of Fe_2O_3, in grams, produced over time in various salt solutions at 20°C. In 3 separate trials, 15 grams of Fe were added to 100 mL of a salt solution. Solutions A–C were identical except for the difference in salt concentration, which was measured in mass percent.

		Mass of Fe_2O_3 (g) produced by:			
Solution	Salt concentration	Day 1	Day 2	Day 3	Day 4
A	0.5%	0.11	0.23	0.51	0.73
B	1.5%	0.46	0.81	1.21	1.74
C	4.5%	0.76	2.03	2.65	3.21

Table 1

The Solution C trial was repeated 4 times, but in each trial, an equal amount of 1 of 4 rust inhibitors was added to the solution (see Figure 1).

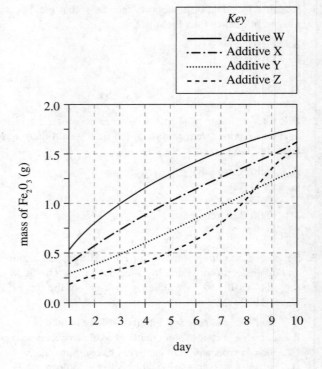

Key
— Additive W
—·—·— Additive X
·········· Additive Y
- - - - Additive Z

Figure 1

7. Which of the following rust inhibitors was *most* effective at inhibiting rust over the first 5 days?

A. Additive W
B. Additive X
C. Additive Y
D. Additive Z

8. Based on Table 1, if the amount of Fe_2O_3 produced by Day 5 had been measured for Solution B, it would most likely have been:

F. less than 1.21 g.
G. between 1.21 g and 1.74 g.
H. between 1.74 g and 2.65 g.
J. greater than 2.65 g.

9. In the experiments shown in Table 1 and Figure 1, by measuring the amount of Fe_2O_3, the experimenters could also determine the rate at which:

A. H_2 was converted into H_2O.
B. H_2O was converted into H_2.
C. Fe was converted into H_2O.
D. H_2O was converted into Fe.

10. Consider the amount of Fe_2O_3 produced by Solution C without any added inhibitors on Day 1. Based on Table 1 and Figure 1, the Solution C sample with Additive X produced approximately the same amount of Fe_2O_3 by which of the following days?

F. Day 1
G. Day 3
H. Day 6
J. Day 10

11. According to Table 1, what was the amount of Fe_2O_3 produced by Solution A from the time the amount was measured on Day 2 until the time the amount was measured on Day 3 ?

A. 0.23 g
B. 0.28 g
C. 0.51 g
D. 0.74 g

12. Based on Table 1, which graph best shows how the amount of Fe_2O_3 produced by Solution C without any additives changed over time?

F.

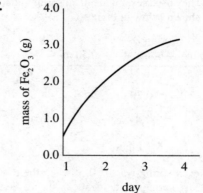

G.

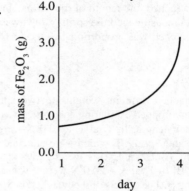

H.

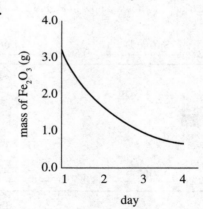

J.

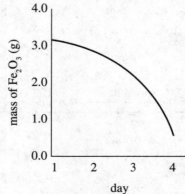

Passage III

Some physics students conducted experiments to study forces and springs. They used several identical springs attached to a horizontal board, shown below in Figure 1.

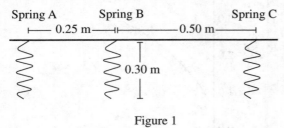

Figure 1

The length of each spring was 0.30 m when there were no weights attached. The springs had identical spring constants. When weights were attached, the length of the springs increased as the force of the weights stretched the springs downwards. The length the springs stretched was proportional to the force of the weight.

Experiment 1

The students attached different weights to two springs at once. When the springs stopped oscillating and came to a rest, the students measured their length. In Trial 1, a 10.0 N weight was attached to Spring A and Spring B, which were attached 0.25 m apart on the board. In Trial 2, a 15.0 N weight was attached to Spring A and Spring B. In Trial 3, a 20.0 N weight was attached to Spring A and Spring B. The effects of the weights on Springs A and B for the three trials are shown below in Figure 2.

Trial 1:

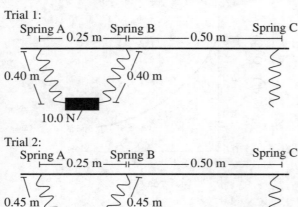

Trial 2:

Trial 3:

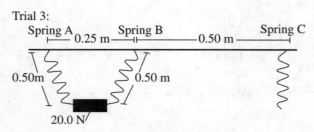

Figure 2

Experiment 2

The students attached a 0.25 m board with a high friction surface to Spring B and Spring C (see Figure 3). The students then placed a 5.0 N weight at different locations along the board. Because of the high friction surface, the weights stayed in place when the board was at an angle.

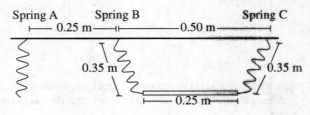

Figure 3

In each of these 3 trials, a 5.0 N weight was placed at various distances along the board from the attachment with Spring B (see Figure 4). In Trial 4, the weight was placed so its center was 0.075 m along the board from the attachment with Spring B. In Trial 5, the weight was placed so its center was 0.125 m along the board from the attachment with Spring B. In Trial 6, the weight was placed so its center was 0.200 m along the board from the attachment with Spring B. The effects of the weight position on the lengths of Springs B and C for the 3 trials are also shown in Figure 4.

Trial 4:

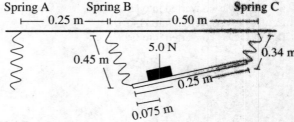

Trial 5:

Trial 6:

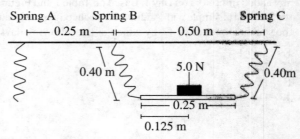

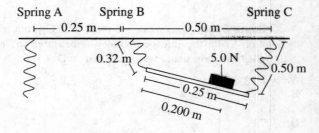

Figure 4

13. In a new study, suppose the students had placed a 10.0 N weight on Spring A only. Which of the following drawings most likely represents the results of this experiment?

A.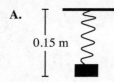
0.15 m

B.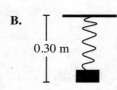
0.30 m

C.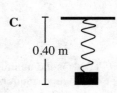
0.40 m

D.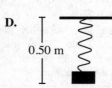
0.50 m

14. In Experiment 2, as the distance between the 5.0 N weight and the attachment of the board to Spring B increased, the force exerted on Spring B:

   F. increased only.
   G. decreased only.
   H. increased, then decreased.
   J. decreased, then increased.

15. Which of the following statements best describes the most likely reason that the students used identical springs in Trials 1–3 ?

   A. To ensure that the springs stretched similarly when a weight was attached
   B. To ensure that the springs did not share the weight evenly
   C. To compensate for the effects of oscillation on the results of the experiment
   D. To compensate for the weight of the board exerted on each of the springs

16. Based on the results of Trials 1 and 5, the weight of the board used in Experiment 2 was:

   F. 0 N.
   G. 2.5 N.
   H. 5.0 N.
   J. 10.0 N.

17. In which of the following trials in Experiment 2, if any, was the force exerted by the weight and the board equally distributed between Springs B and C ?

   A. Trial 4
   B. Trial 5
   C. Trial 6
   D. None of the trials

18. The elastic potential energy of a spring is determined by both the spring constant and the amount of deformation the spring is experiencing. Assume that the spring constant is the same in all of the trials in Experiment 2. Was the elastic potential energy of Spring C higher in Trial 5 or Trial 6 ?

   F. In Trial 5, because the force of the weight on Spring C was greater in Trial 5.
   G. In Trial 5, because the force of the weight on Spring C was less in Trial 5.
   H. In Trial 6, because the force of the weight on Spring C was greater in Trial 6.
   J. In Trial 6, because the force of the weight on Spring C was less in Trial 6.

19. Suppose another trial had been conducted in Experiment 2 in which the same weight had been placed 0.150 m from the attachment of the board to Spring B. Spring B would most likely have extended:

   A. less than 0.32 m.
   B. between 0.32 m and 0.40 m.
   C. between 0.40 and 0.45 m.
   D. more than 0.45 m.

Passage IV

Sodium chloride, or salt, is used to de-ice roads and sidewalks during the winter because it lowers the freezing point of water. Water with sodium chloride freezes at a lower temperature than water alone, so putting sodium chloride on icy sidewalks and roads can cause the ice to melt. Sodium chloride is highly effective as a de-icer and is given a *de-icer proficiency rating* of 100. Distilled water is ineffective as a de-icer and is given a de-icer proficiency rating of 0.

Different proportions of sodium chloride and distilled water were combined to create mixtures with de-icer proficiency ratings between 0 and 100.

Table 1		
De-icer proficiency rating	Volume of distilled water	Volume of sodium chloride
100	0 ml	50 ml
80	10 ml	40 ml
60	20 ml	30 ml
40	30 ml	20 ml
20	40 ml	10 ml
0	50 ml	0 ml

Experiment 1

A 5 g cube of ice, frozen from distilled water, was submerged in 50 mL of each de-icing mixture listed in Table 1. After 300 seconds, the portion of the cube that had not been melted was removed and weighed. The de-icing rate was calculated by determining the weight of ice melted per second. By doing this, it was possible to determine the de-icer proficiency rating for a solution based on the rate at which ice was melted.

Experiment 2

The addition of magnesium chloride to a de-icer changes its de-icer proficiency rating. Different amounts of magnesium chloride were added to 50 mL samples of sodium chloride. Each de-icing mixture was tested under the same conditions as Experiment 1, and the measured de-icing rate was used to calculate the de-icer proficiency rating. The results are shown in Figure 1.

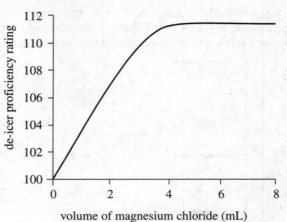

Figure 1

Experiment 3

The *temperature de-icing minimum* (TDM) is the minimum de-icer proficiency rating necessary for a de-icing solution to have any effect on ice at a given temperature. Four 50 mL samples were prepared of each De-icers A and B and a 5 g of cube of ice was placed into each sample. The samples were then placed in freezers at four different temperatures. Table 2 shows the de-icer proficiency rating determined for each de-icer at each freezer temperature and the known TDM for that temperature.

Table 2			
Freezer temperature	TDM	Proficiency rating of:	
		De-icer A	De-icer B
−10 C	24.1	90.3	70.1
−25 C	36.9	78.9	64.9
−50 C	49.7	68.8	59.7
−75 C	52.3	56.6	51.7

20. Suppose a mechanic wants to produce a sodium chloride and magnesium chloride de-icing solution with a proficiency rating of 106. If the mechanic includes 5 *liters* of sodium chloride in the solution, based on Figure 1 and the information in the passage, how many *milliliters* of magnesium chloride should be included?

F.　　0.20
G.　　200
H.　2,000
J.　20,000

21. Suppose a trial had been performed in Experiment 3 with a freezer temperature of –30 C. At this temperature, which of the following sets of proficiency ratings would most likely have been determined for De-icer A and De-icer B ?

	De-icer A	De-icer B
A.	68.8	59.7
B.	70.1	70.5
C.	75.5	61.8
D.	78.9	64.9

22. Based on Table 1, if 3 mL distilled water were added to 7 mL sodium chloride, the proficiency rating of this mixture would be:

F. 3.
G. 7.
H. 30.
J. 70.

23. Based on Experiment 3, as temperature decreases, the minimum proficiency rating for a de-icer to be effective:

A. increases only.
B. decreases only.
C. increases, then decreases.
D. decreases, then increases.

24. Which of the following expressions is equal to the proficiency rating for each de-icer mixture listed in Table 1 ?

F. $\dfrac{\text{volume of sodium chloride}}{\text{volume of water}} \times 100$

G. $\dfrac{\text{volume of water}}{\text{volume of sodium chloride}} \times 100$

H. $\dfrac{\text{volume of sodium chloride}}{(\text{volume of water} + \text{volume of sodium chloride})} \times 100$

J. $\dfrac{\text{volume of water}}{(\text{volume of water} + \text{volume of sodium chloride})} \times 100$

25. Based on Table 1 and Experiment 2, if 6 mL magnesium chloride were added to a mixture of 10 mL distilled water and 40 mL sodium chloride, the proficiency rating of the resulting de-icer would most likely be:

A. less than 60.
B. between 60 and 80.
C. between 80 and 112.
D. greater than 112.

26. Which of the 2 de-icers from Experiment 3 would be better to use to melt ice if the temperature were between –10 C and –75 C ?

F. De-icer A, because its proficiency rating was lower than the TDM at each temperature tested.
G. De-icer A, because its proficiency rating was higher than the TDM at each temperature tested.
H. De-icer B, because its proficiency rating was lower than the TDM at each temperature tested.
J. De-icer B, because its proficiency rating was higher than the TDM at each temperature tested.

Passage V

Comets originate from regions of our solar system that are very far from the Sun. The comets are formed from debris thrown from objects in the solar system: they have a nucleus of ice surrounded by dust and frozen gases. When comets are pulled into the Earth's atmosphere by gravitational forces and become visible, they are called *meteors*. Meteors become visible about 50 to 85 km above the surface of Earth as air friction causes them to glow. Most meteors vaporize completely before they come within 50 km of the surface of Earth.

Recently, images taken by two instruments, UVA and VIS, revealed dark spots and streaks in the Earth's atmosphere. The significance of these dark spots and streaks is not fully understood. The Small Comet Theory asserts that these spots and streaks are due to a constant rain of small ice comets, but some scientists argue that the spots are just random technological noise.

UVA and VIS technologies provide images of energy that cannot be seen by the human eye. Both instruments take images in the magnetosphere, in which they orbit. The layers of Earth's atmosphere are shown in Figure 1.

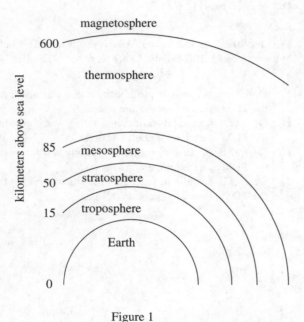

Figure 1

Two scientists debate whether there is a constant rain of comets burning up in Earth's magnetosphere.

Scientist 1

Small comets are pulled into Earth's atmosphere by gravitational effects and burn up in the magnetosphere. Small comets are about 20 to 30 feet in diameter and burn up in the magnetosphere because they are much smaller than the comets that become meteors. Comets with larger diameters will burn up in portions of the atmosphere much closer to Earth. About 30,000 small comets enter the Earth's magnetosphere every day. The dark spots and streaks on UVA and VIS images occur when the small comets begin to boil in the magnetosphere, releasing krypton and argon and creating gaseous H_2O, which interacts with hydroxyl, OH^-, radicals. Images taken by these instruments at different points in time show the same frequency of dark spots and streaks and give conclusive evidence in favor of the Small Comet Theory. If the spots and streaks were due to random technological noise, then the frequency of their appearance would fluctuate.

Scientist 2

The dark spots and streaks in the UVA and VIS images are due to technological noise, not small comets. If the Small Comet Theory were true, and 20 small comets bombarded Earth's atmosphere per minute, there would be a visible bright object at least twice every five minutes. This is because, as objects enter the Earth's mesosphere, they burn up, creating large clouds of ice particles. As the ice particles vaporize, they become approximately as bright in the sky as Venus. Because comets rarely enter Earth's atmosphere, such bright flashes are rare, occurring far less than two times every five minutes. Therefore, the Small Comet Theory cannot be correct. Further, since comets originate from regions of space beyond the orbit of the farthest planet, they contain argon and krypton. If the Small Comet Theory were true and Earth were bombarded by 30,000 comets per day, there would be 500 times as much krypton in the atmosphere as there actually is.

27. According to Scientist 2, which of the following planets in our solar system is most likely the closest to the region of space where comets originate?

    A. Jupiter
    B. Neptune
    C. Saturn
    D. Venus

28. Based on Scientist 1's viewpoint, a comet that burns up in the thermosphere would have a diameter of:

   F. 5–10 ft.
   G. 10–20 ft.
   H. 20–30 ft.
   J. greater than 30 ft.

29. Which of the following generalizations about small comets is most consistent with Scientist 1's viewpoint?

   A. No small comet ever becomes a meteor.
   B. Some small comets become meteors.
   C. Small comets become meteors twice every five minutes.
   D. All small comets become meteors.

30. During the *Perseids*, an annual meteor shower, more than 1 object visibly burns up in the atmosphere per minute. According to the information provided, Scientist 2 would classify the Perseids as:

   F. typical comet frequency in the magnetosphere.
   G. unusual comet frequency in the magnetosphere.
   H. typical meteor frequency in the mesosphere.
   J. unusual meteor frequency in the mesosphere.

31. Given the information about meteors in the introduction, at which of the following altitudes above the sea level on Earth would a meteor NOT be visibly glowing?

   A. 55 km
   B. 70 km
   C. 85 km
   D. 100 km

32. Suppose that a study of meteors of various sizes revealed that a large meteor observed during the study period was visible in the stratosphere before it vaporized completely. How would the findings of this study most likely affect the scientists' viewpoints, if at all?

   F. It would not affect either scientist's viewpoint.
   G. It would strengthen Scientist 1's viewpoint only.
   H. It would strengthen Scientist 2's viewpoint only.
   J. It would weaken both scientists' viewpoints.

33. Scientist 1 would most likely suggest that astronomers attempting to take pictures of small comets in the atmosphere should use enhanced imaging technology to look in which region?

   A. The region between 15 km above sea level and 50 km above sea level
   B. The region between 50 km above sea level and 85 km above sea level
   C. The region between 85 km above sea level and 600 km above sea level
   D. The region above 600 km above sea level

Passage VI

A cotton fiber is composed of one very long cell with two cell walls. During a one-to three-week period of cell life called elongation, cotton fibers grow 3 to 6 cm. The level of hydrogen peroxide in cotton fiber cells during elongation is very high. Scientists wanted to study whether the level of hydrogen peroxide affected the length of the cotton fiber.

The amount of hydrogen peroxide is controlled by an enzyme called *superoxide dismutase* (SOD). This enzyme turns superoxide into hydrogen peroxide. Four identical strains of cotton fiber plants were created. Three of the strains were then manipulated such that each was able to express only one of three types of superoxide dismutase. The gene for SOD1 was active in S1, the gene for SOD2 was active in S2, and the gene for SOD3 was active in S3.

Experiment

Five cotton plants of each strain were grown in a nutrient solution until cotton fibers completed the elongation period. The average length of cotton fibers and the average concentration of hydrogen peroxide were determined on each day. Table 1 shows the data gathered on the first day.

Table 1			
	On the first day of elongation period:		
Strain	Day of elongation period	Average amount of hydrogen peroxide (μmol/mg)	Average cotton fiber length (cm)
S1	1	1.2	0.2
S2	1	6.0	0.5
S3	1	5.7	0.1
S4	1	1.9	0.2

Next, the scientists used the average elongation period length to determine the midpoint of elongation for each strain. Table 2 shows the average amount of hydrogen peroxide and average cotton fiber length for each strain at the midpoint of its elongation period.

Table 2			
	At the midpoint of elongation period:		
Strain	Day of elongation period	Average amount of hydrogen peroxide (μmol/mg)	Average cotton fiber length (cm)
S1	4	4.1	2.7
S2	2	5.3	1.0
S3	10	12.4	2.0
S4	6	8.7	3.2

Finally, Table 3 shows the average elongation period, the average amount of hydrogen peroxide, and the average cotton fiber length for all four strains at the end of the elongation period.

Table 3			
	At the end of elongation period:		
Strain	Average elongation period length (days)	Average amount of hydrogen peroxide (μmol/mg)	Average cotton fiber length (cm)
S1	8	2.1	3.6
S2	4	0.2	1.4
S3	20	5.6	5.9
S4	12	2.3	4.5

34. For S2, as the elongation period moved from the first day to the end, the amount of hydrogen peroxide:

F. increased only.
G. decreased only.
H. increased, then decreased.
J. decreased, then increased.

35. Which of the following is a dependent variable in the experiment?

    A. The length of the cotton fiber
    B. The type of superoxide dismutase the plant could express
    C. The point in time during the elongation period
    D. The type of cotton plant

36. A cotton fiber contains both a primary and a secondary cell wall. Which one of the following cell types does NOT have a cell wall?

    F. Animal
    G. Fungal
    H. Bacterial
    J. Algal

37. One plant had an average cotton fiber length of 0.6 cm, and the average amount of hydrogen peroxide in its fibers was 5.9 μmol/mg. Which of the following most likely describes this plant?

    A. It was from S1 and at the midpoint of its elongation period.
    B. It was from S1 and at the end of its elongation period.
    C. It was from S2 and at the beginning of its elongation period.
    D. It was from S2 and at the end of its elongation period.

38. The scientists used one of the four strains of cotton plants as a control. Which strain was most likely the control?

    F. S1
    G. S2
    H. S3
    J. S4

39. Suppose the data for all the plants were plotted on a graph with the time of the elongation period on the x-axis and the average length of the cotton fiber on the y-axis. Suppose also that the best-fit line for these data was determined. Which of the following would most likely characterize the slope of this line?

    A. The slope would be positive.
    B. The slope would be negative.
    C. The slope would be zero.
    D. The slope would be undefined because the line would be vertical.

40. Consider the average cotton fiber length and the average amount of hydrogen peroxide 4 days into the elongation period for S1 and S2 shown in Tables 1 and 2. After 4 days, which strain had more hydrogen peroxide and which strain had a longer average cotton fiber length?

	more hydrogen peroxide	longer fiber length
F.	S1	S1
G.	S1	S2
H.	S2	S1
J.	S2	S2

END OF TEST.
STOP! DO NOT TURN THE PAGE UNTIL TOLD TO DO SO.

Chapter 15
Science Practice
Test 4: Answers and
Explanations

SCIENCE PRACTICE TEST 4 ANSWER KEY

1. A
2. J
3. C
4. G
5. C
6. G
7. D
8. H
9. B
10. G
11. B
12. F
13. D
14. G
15. A
16. H
17. B
18. H
19. B
20. G

21. C
22. J
23. A
24. H
25. C
26. G
27. B
28. J
29. A
30. J
31. D
32. F
33. D
34. G
35. A
36. F
37. C
38. J
39. A
40. F

SCORE YOUR PRACTICE TEST

Step A
Count the number of correct answers: _____. This is your *raw score*.

Step B
Use the score conversion table below to look up your raw score. The number to the left is your *scale score:* _____.

Test 4 Scale Conversion Table

Scale Score	Raw Score	Scale Score	Raw Score	Scale Score	Raw Score
36	39–40	24	26	12	9
35	37–38	23	24–25	11	8
34	36	22	23	10	7
33	—	21	21–22	9	6
32	35	20	19–20	8	5
31	34	19	17–18	7	4
30	33	18	15–16	6	3
29	32	17	14	5	—
28	31	16	13	4	2
27	30	15	12	3	1
26	29	14	11	2	—
25	27–28	13	10	1	0

SCIENCE PRACTICE TEST 4 EXPLANATIONS

Passage I

1. **A**   The question asks which data set shows Field A as having *lower* soil quality than Field B. Use POE and check each set of data. Figure 1 shows the bulk density of the two fields. The passage states that *a bulk density measure above 1.33 g/cm³ can negatively affect soil quality*. Figure 1 shows Field A as having a higher bulk density than Field B each year, with most years measuring above 1.33 g/cm³. Therefore, Figure 1 shows Field A as having lower soil quality than Field B. Keep (A). Figure 2 shows the crop yield for the two fields. For most years, Field A has a higher crop yield than Field B, which doesn't indicate a lower soil quality. Eliminate (B). Table 1 does not include any data regarding Field A or Field B, so eliminate (C). Table 2 shows Field A as having a higher SOM than Field B. Based on Table 1, a higher SOM indicates a higher rather than lower soil quality, so eliminate (D). The correct answer is (A).

2. **J**   The question asks which field in which year had a failed harvest. Based on the information given in the question, a failed harvest is a harvest of *8 tons or fewer in crop yields*. Figure 2 shows the crop yields for each field. Look at each year to find when there was a harvest of 8 tons or fewer. In Year 5, Field B had a crop yield of 8 tons, thus making it a failed harvest. Eliminate (F), (G), and (H), as those years and fields all show a crop yield of greater than 8 tons. The correct answer is (J).

3. **C**   The question asks how a new crop rotation in Field B would affect the SOM. Use POE and check each answer choice. Based on Table 1, a higher SOM indicates higher soil quality. Eliminate (A) and (D) because they indicate the opposite relationship. A crop rotation of *legumes and other deep-rooted and high-residue crops* would likely increase the organic content of the soil, thus increasing the SOM and soil quality. Eliminate (B) because it states that the SOM will decrease. The correct answer is (C).

4. **G**   The question asks which site had the lower average crop yield and the lower average bulk density. The first part of the answers refers to Figure 2, so refer to Figure 2 to find the site that had the lower average crop yield. For most of the years, Field B had a lower crop yield than Field A; therefore, Field B had a lower average crop yield. Eliminate (F) and (H) because they incorrectly state that Field A had a lower average crop yield. Next, use Figure 1 to find the site that had the lower average bulk density. For each year, Field B had a lower bulk density than Field A; therefore, Field B had a lower average bulk density. Eliminate (J) because it incorrectly states that Field A had a lower average bulk density. The correct answer is (G).

5. **C**   The question asks if Table 2 supports the hypothesis that Field B has more earthworms, given that as the number of earthworms increases, the soil quality also increases. Compare the SOM values of Fields A and B in Table 2 to the ranges of soil quality in Table 1 to determine the soil quality of Fields A and B. Field A has a SOM of 0.89, which is a soil quality rating of excellent according to Table 1. Field B has a SOM of 0.28, which is a soil quality rating of fair. Since Field B has a lower soil quality

than Field A, Field B would have fewer earthworms, and the hypothesis is not supported. Eliminate (A) and (B) because they incorrectly state that the hypothesis is supported. Eliminate (D) because it incorrectly states the soil quality ratings for Fields A and B. The correct answer is (C).

6. **G** The question asks whether the soil in Field A is more likely primarily sand or clay. Use POE and check each answer choice. The answer choices focus on the bulk density and crop yield of Field A in Years 3 and 5. Start with the easiest piece of information, which is the crop yield. Crop yield is shown in Figure 2. The crop yield of Field A in Year 5 was the second lowest crop yield for Field A in those five years, while the crop yield of Field A in Year 5 was the highest. Eliminate (F) and (H) because they both incorrectly state that the crop yield in Year 3 was high. Both of the remaining answers reference Year 5, so look at Figure 1 to find the bulk density of Field A in Year 5. Figure 1 shows the bulk density of Field A in Year 5 was 1.70 g/cm³. Based on the table given in the question, the *restrictive bulk density threshold*, which is the *maximum bulk density under which plants roots can still grow effectively*, is 1.80 g/cm³ for sand and 1.55 g/cm³ for clay. The high crop yield in Field A in Year 5 indicates that the plant roots were still able to grow effectively at a bulk density above 1.55 g/cm³. Therefore, the soil in Field A is likely not primarily clay. Eliminate (J). The correct answer is (G).

Passage II

7. **D** The question asks for the most effective rust inhibitor over the first five days. Figure 1 shows the amount of rust, Fe_2O_3, produced in the presence of each of the rust inhibitors. Look for the rust inhibitor that had the lowest mass of Fe_2O_3 over the first five days. The dashed line representing Additive Z had the lowest amount of rust over the first five days. The correct answer is (D).

8. **H** The question asks for the mass of Fe_2O_3 in Solution B if it had been measured on Day 5. The mass of Fe_2O_3 in the solutions is shown in Table 1. Look in the second row for the relationship between the mass of Fe_2O_3 in Solution B and time from Day 1 to Day 4. The mass of Fe_2O_3 in Solution B increases from 0.46 g to 1.74 g over the first 4 days. The mass of Fe_2O_3 in Solution B will likely continue to increase after Day 4, so the amount of Fe_2O_3 in Solution B on Day 5 would most likely be greater than 1.74 g. Eliminate (F) and (G), as these have values less than 1.74 g. To choose between the remaining answers, look at the mass of Fe_2O_3 each day to estimate the rate of increase. The daily increases in mass were 0.35, 0.40, and 0.53. In order to reach above 2.65 g by Day 5, as in (J), the increase from Day 4 to Day 5 would have to be over 0.90. This is too big of an increase given the trend from the first four days, so eliminate (J). The correct answer is (H).

9. **B** The question asks what else the experimenters could determine based on the amount of Fe_2O_3 measured. The answer choices contain parts of the reaction equation, so look at the equation, and use POE. Based on the equation Fe and H_2O are converted into Fe_2O_3 and H_2. So, when Fe_2O_3 is produced, H_2 is also produced. Eliminate (A) because it reverses the conversion of H_2O and H_2. Keep (B) because it correctly shows the conversion of H_2O into H_2. Eliminate (C) because Fe converts into Fe_2O_3, not H_2O. Eliminate (D) because H_2O converts into H_2. The correct answer is (B).

10. **G** The question asks on which day Solution C with Additive X produced the same amount of Fe_2O_3 as on Day 1 without an additive. The mass of Fe_2O_3 in each solution without additives is shown in Table 1. Use Table 1 to find the amount of Fe_2O_3 produced by Solution C on Day 1 without any additives. On Day 1, Solution C produced 0.76 g of Fe_2O_3. In Figure 1, Fe_2O_3 is on the y-axis. Find the value 0.76 g on the y-axis and draw a horizontal line to the curve for Solution C with Additive X, which is the line with dots and dashes. Draw a vertical line down to the x-axis to determine that the mass of Fe_2O_3 is approximately 0.76 on Day 3. The correct answer is (G).

11. **B** The question asks how much Fe_2O_3 Solution A produced between Day 2 and Day 3. The mass of Fe_2O_3 in each solution is shown in Table 1. According to Table 1, by Day 2, Solution A had produced 0.23 g and by Day 3, Solution A had produced 0.51 g. To find the amount of Fe_2O_3 produced between Day 2 and Day 3, subtract 0.23 g from 0.51 g to get 0.28 g. The correct answer is (B).

12. **F** The question asks for a graph showing the relationship between time and the mass of Fe_2O_3 produced by Solution C without any additives. The mass of Fe_2O_3 in the solutions without additives is shown in Table 1. Look at Table 1 to find the trend between time and amount of Fe_2O_3. For all solutions, the amount of Fe_2O_3 and time have a direct relationship; as one increases, so does the other. Eliminate (H) and (J) because these show an inverse relationship. Both (F) and (G) show a direct relationship and start at the same value, but they have different values for Days 2 and 3. Look back at Table 1 to find that the amount of Fe_2O_3 produced by Solution C on Day 2 is 2.03 g. Eliminate (G) because it incorrectly shows the amount of Fe_2O_3 as less than 1 g on Day 2. The correct answer is (F).

Passage III

13. **D** The question asks for a drawing that represents a 10.0 N weight on Spring A only. Based on Figure 1, the length of Spring A with no weight is 0.30 m. Eliminate (A) and (B) because the length of the spring will be greater than 0.30 m with the weight attached. Based on Trial 1 in Experiment 1, the length of Spring A is 0.40 m when a 10.0 N weight is shared with Spring B. If Spring A only has the 10.0 N weight, the spring length will be longer than 0.40 m; eliminate (C). The correct answer is (D).

14. **G** The question asks how the force exerted on Spring B changes as the distance between the weight and the attachment to Spring B increases, according to Experiment 2. Trials 4, 5, and 6 show the results of Experiment 2. Use these trials in Experiment 2 to determine the relationship between the force exerted in Spring B and the distance between the weight and the attachment to Spring B. The distance between the weight and the attachment to Spring B increases from Trial 4 to Trial 6. The length of Spring B decreases in each trial from Trial 4 to Trial 6. Additionally, the passage states that *the length of the springs increased as the force of the weights stretched the springs downwards.* Therefore, as distance between the weight and the attachment increased, the length of Spring B decreased, because the force exerted on Spring B decreased. The correct answer is (G).

15. **A** The question asks for the most likely reason the students used identical springs in Trials 1–3. Use POE and eliminate answers that don't make sense. Keep (A) because the passage states that *the springs had identical spring constants*. Eliminate (B) because the passage states that the students used *identical springs;* it wouldn't make sense that identical springs would not share the weight evenly. Eliminate (C) because the passage states that the students measured the length *when the springs stopped oscillating,* so the students didn't need to compensate for oscillation. Eliminate (D) because the board was used in Trials 4–6, not Trials 1–3. The correct answer is (A).

16. **H** The question asks for the weight of the board used in Experiment 2. Experiment 1 varies the weight of the masses attached to the spring, whereas Experiment 2 varies the position of the board and mass. Find the trial in Experiment 1 that is most similar to a trial in Experiment 2. Use Trial 5 for Experiment 2 since the weight is attached in the middle of the board, just as in Experiment 1. In Trial 5, Spring A and Spring B both have a length of 0.40 m. Find the Trial in Experiment 1 where Spring A and Spring B also both have a length of 0.40 m. In Trial 1, Spring A and Spring B both have a length of 0.40 m for a 10.0 N weight. Therefore, the combined weight of the board and the 5.0 N weight should be 10.0 N in Trial 5. Since the weight weighs 5.0 N, the board weighs the remaining 5.0 N. The correct answer is (H).

17. **B** The question asks if the weight was distributed evenly between Spring B and Spring C in any of the trials in Experiment 2. Look at Trials 4–6 to find the different weight distributions between Springs B and C. For the weight distribution to be even, the springs need to be the same length. In Trial 5, the lengths of Springs B and C are both 0.40 m; therefore, the weight is distributed evenly. The correct answer is (B).

18. **H** The question asks whether the elastic potential energy of Spring C was higher in Trial 5 or Trial 6. The question states that the elastic potential energy is determined by the spring constant and the amount of deformation of the spring. Since the spring constant is constant in all trials, the only remaining factor to affect the elastic potential energy of Spring C is the deformation of the spring. Figure 1 shows the length of the spring *when there were no weights attached.* Without a weight, the length of Spring C is 0.30 m. Spring C stretched beyond 0.30 m will show spring deformation. In Trial 5, Spring C is 0.40 m, and in Trial 6, Spring C is 0.50 m. Since Spring C is more stretched in Trial 6, Spring C has more spring deformation and thus a higher elastic potential energy in Trial 6 than in Trial 5. Eliminate (F) and (G). The passage states that *the length of the springs increased as the force of the weights stretched the springs downwards.* Since Spring C is longer in Trial 6, it has a greater force exerted on it. Eliminate (J) because it incorrectly states that Spring C has less force exerted on it. The correct answer is (H).

19. **B** The question asks what the stretched length of Spring B would be if the weight was placed 0.150 m away from Spring B's attachment in Experiment 2. Use Trials 4–6 in Experiment 2 to find the relationship between stretched length and weight placement. In Trial 4, the distance is 0.075 m and Spring B is stretched to 0.45 m. In Trial 5, the distance is 0.125 m and Spring B is stretched to 0.40 m. As the distance increases, Spring B is stretched less. Since a distance of 0.150 m is between the distances in Trials 5 and 6, Spring B will be stretched between 0.32 m and 0.40 m. The correct answer is (B).

Passage IV

20. **G**   The question asks how many *milliliters* of magnesium chloride is needed for a solution with a 106 proficiency rating. Figure 1 shows how the addition of magnesium chloride changes the proficiency rating of a solution. At a proficiency rating of 106, 2 mL of magnesium chloride was added. Read the description of Experiment 2 to find the amount of sodium chloride used. In Experiment 2, the amount of sodium chloride is 50 mL. In the question, the mechanic has 5 L of sodium chloride. Since 1 L = 1,000 mL, 5 L is 5,000 mL. To find the correct amount of magnesium chloride, divide 5,000 mL by 50 mL to find that the volume of the mechanic's solution is 100 times greater than the volume used in Experiment 2. Multiply 2 mL of magnesium chloride by 100 to get 200 mL of magnesium chloride. The correct answer is (G).

21. **C**   The question asks what the proficiency ratings of De-icers A and B are at −30°C. Table 2 shows the proficiency ratings at different temperatures. De-icer A has a proficiency rating of 78.9 at −25°C and 68.8 at −50°C, so the proficiency rating at −30°C will be between 78.9 and 68.8. Eliminate (A) and (D) because those are the proficiency ratings for De-icer A at −50°C and −25°C. De-icer B has a proficiency rating of 64.9 at −25°C and 59.7 at −50°C, so the proficiency rating at −30°C will be between 64.9 and 59.7. Eliminate (B). The correct answer is (C).

22. **J**   The question asks for the proficiency rating of a mixture of 3 mL distilled water and 7 mL sodium chloride. Table 1 shows the proficiency ratings for different mixtures of distilled water and sodium chloride. Since there is more sodium chloride than water, look for the proficiency ratings for mixtures with more sodium chloride. The proficiency ratings of 0, 20, and 40 are all for mixtures that have more water than sodium chloride. Therefore, the proficiency rating of a mixture with more sodium chloride than water will be above 40. Eliminate (F), (G), and (H) because they are all below 40. The correct answer is (J).

23. **A**   The question asks how the minimum proficiency rating for a de-icer to be effective changes as temperature decreases. Table 2 shows temperature, TDM, and the proficiency ratings for two de-icers. The description of Experiment 3 says that TDM, or the temperature de-icing minimum, is the *minimum de-icer proficiency rating necessary for a de-icing solution to have any effect on ice*. As the temperature decreases (becomes more negative), the TDM always increases. The correct answer is (A).

24. **H**   The question asks which expression is equal to the proficiency rating for each de-icer mixture in Table 1. To find the correct expression, plug in numbers from Table 1. A proficiency rating of 100 has 0 mL of distilled water and 50 mL of sodium chloride. Start with (F). Plugging in the values makes the expression 50/0 × 100. Dividing by 0 is not possible, so eliminate (F). For (G), 0/50 × 100 equals 0, rather than the actual proficiency rating of 100. Eliminate (G). For (H), 50/(0 + 50) × 100 equals 100. Keep (H). For (J), 0/(0 + 50) × 100 equals 0. Eliminate (J). The correct answer is (H).

25. **C**   The question asks how adding 6 mL of magnesium chloride would change the proficiency rating of a mixture of 10 mL water and 40 mL sodium chloride. Figure 1 shows how magnesium chloride changes the proficiency rating of a mixture of 50 mL sodium chloride and 0 mL water. Each of the

mixtures in Figure 1 has a proficiency rating above 100. Based on Table 1, 50 mL of sodium chloride has a proficiency rating of 100, so adding magnesium chloride must increase the proficiency rating. Based on Table 1, a mixture 10 mL water and 40 mL sodium chloride has a proficiency rating of 80. Adding magnesium chloride will increase the rating above 80. Eliminate (A) and (B). According to Figure 1, adding 6 mL of magnesium chloride to a pure sodium chloride solution with a proficiency rating of 100 results in a proficiency rating below 112. Since a 40 mL sodium chloride and 10 mL water mixture has a lower proficiency than pure sodium chloride, it would also have a proficiency below 112 after the addition of 6 mL of magnesium chloride. Eliminate (D). The correct answer is (C).

26. **G**   The question asks which de-icer would be better to use to melt ice between –10°C and –75°C. Use POE by checking each answer choice against Table 2. De-icer A has a higher proficiency rating than the TDM at each temperature. Eliminate (F) as it contradicts this. De-icer B has a higher proficiency rating than the TDM at most temperatures except at –75°C, when De-icer B's proficiency rating is lower than the TDM. Eliminate (H) and (J), as De-icer B's proficiency rating is higher than the TDM at some temperatures, but lower than the TDM at one temperature. The correct answer is (G).

Passage V

27. **B**   The question asks which planet is closest to the region of space where comets originate according to Scientist 2. Look for the phrase *region of space* in Scientist 2's paragraph. Scientist 2 says, *comets originate from regions of space beyond the orbit of the farthest planet*. Outside knowledge is needed to know that the farthest planet in the solar system is Neptune. The correct answer is (B).

28. **J**   The question asks for the diameter of a comet that burns up in the thermosphere according to Scientist 1. Look for mentions of the size of comets in Scientist 1's explanation. According to Scientist 1, *small comets are about 20 to 30 feet in diameter and burn up in the magnetosphere*, and *comets with larger diameters will burn up in portions of the atmosphere much closer to Earth*. Figure 1 shows the portions of the atmosphere. Based on Figure 1, the thermosphere is closer to Earth than the magnetosphere, so a comet that burns up in the thermosphere will have a diameter bigger than 30 feet. Eliminate (F), (G), and (H). The correct answer is (J).

29. **A**   The question asks which statement about small comets is most consistent with Scientist 1's viewpoint. Every answer choice mentions *meteor* so look for *meteor* in Scientist 1's paragraph. Scientist 1 says, *small comets are about 20 to 30 feet in diameter and burn up in the magnetosphere because they are much smaller than the comets that become meteors*. This is consistent with the claim that no small comets become meteors, which matches (A). Eliminate (B), (C), and (D), which all mention small comets becoming meteors. The correct answer is (A).

30. **J**   The question asks how Scientist 2 would classify the *Perseids* meteor shower. According to the information provided in the question, during the *Perseids* meteor shower, *more than 1 object visibly burns up in the atmosphere per minute*. Scientist 2 says that the bright flashes of meteors burning up

in the atmosphere occur *far less than two times every five minutes*, so more than 1 object per minute during the *Perseids* is an unusual frequency. Eliminate (F) and (H) because the frequency is not typical. According to Scientist 2, *as objects enter the Earth's mesosphere, they burn up*. Eliminate (F), which claims that the meteor activity would occur in the magnetosphere and uses the incorrect term *comet*. The correct answer is (J).

31. **D**   The question asks at what altitude a meteor would NOT be visibly glowing. The first paragraph of the passage states that m*eteors become visible about 50 to 85 km above the surface of Earth as air friction causes them to glow*. Therefore, a meteor would not be visibly glowing above 85 km. Eliminate (A), (B), and (C) because those numbers are all at or below 85 km and thus in the range where meteors are visibly glowing. The correct answer is (D).

32. **F**   The question asks how a large meteor visible in the stratosphere would affect the scientists' viewpoints, if at all. The discussion of when meteors are visible is in the introduction, which says, *Meteors become visible about 50 to 85 km above the surface of Earth as air friction causes them to glow. Most meteors vaporize completely before they come within 50 km of the surface of Earth*. The use of the term *most* means that a few do not. Therefore, the observation of a large meteor that does not burn up before the stratosphere does not contradict any information in the introduction. Both scientists discuss small comets rather than large meteors, so the observation of the large meteor would not affect their viewpoints. Eliminate (G), (H), and (J). The correct answer is (F).

33. **D**   The question asks which region astronomers should focus on to take pictures of small comets with enhanced imaging technology, according to Scientist 1. Scientist 1 claims that *about 30,000 small comets enter the Earth's magnetosphere every day*. Based on Figure 1, the magnetosphere is more than 600 km above sea level. Eliminate (A), (B), and (C), which all discuss altitudes below 600 km above sea level. The correct answer is (D).

Passage VI

34. **G**   The question asks how the amount of hydrogen peroxide changed during the elongation period of S2. Tables 1–3 show Day 1 of the elongation period, the midpoint of the elongation period, and the end of the elongation period, respectively. Look at each table to find the amount of hydrogen peroxide for S2. Table 1 shows that S2 had 6.0 µmol/mg of hydrogen peroxide on Day 1. Table 2 shows that S2 had 5.3 µmol/mg of hydrogen peroxide at the midpoint of the elongation period. Table 3 shows that S2 had 0.2 µmol/mg of hydrogen peroxide at the end of the elongation period. Therefore, the hydrogen peroxide only decreased over the elongation period of S2. The correct answer is (G).

35. **A**   The question asks for the dependent variable of the experiment. This question requires outside knowledge of dependent variables. An independent variable is a variable the scientists manipulate and a dependent variable is a variable whose value depends on the independent variable. A dependent variable is measured, but not directly manipulated or controlled by the scientists. Use POE. Eliminate

(B) and (D) since scientists selected the type of plant and directly manipulated which type of superoxide dismutase each strain could produce. Eliminate (C) as the point in time during elongation did not depend on anything. The introduction of the passage states that *scientists wanted to study whether the level of hydrogen peroxide affected the length of the cotton fiber.* Therefore, the length of the cotton fiber is a dependent variable that was measured but not directly manipulated. The correct answer is (A).

36. **F** The question asks which type of cell does not have a cell wall. This is an outside knowledge question. The Animal kingdom is the only kingdom in which cell walls do not exist. The correct answer is (F).

37. **C** The question asks for the most likely description of a plant with a fiber length of 0.6 cm and an average amount of hydrogen peroxide of 5.9 μmol/mg. Use POE. For (A), use Table 2 to find that S1 at the midpoint of the elongation period had a fiber length of 2.7 cm and 4.1 μmol/mg of hydrogen peroxide. These numbers are not close to the ones given in the question, so eliminate (A). For (B), use Table 3 to find that S1 at the end of the elongation period had a fiber length of 3.6 cm and 2.1 μmol/mg of hydrogen peroxide. Eliminate (B). For (C), use Table 1 to find that S2 at the beginning of the elongation period had a length of 0.5 cm and 6.0 μmol/mg of hydrogen peroxide. These numbers are close to the ones in the question, so keep (C). Check (D). Use Table 3 to find that S2 had a length of 1.4 cm and 0.2 μmol/mg of hydrogen peroxide. These numbers are not close to the ones in the question, so eliminate (D). The correct answer is (C).

38. **J** The question asks which strain was used as a control. Outside knowledge is needed here: control is the strain that was not changed and serves as a basis of comparison. The introduction says, *The gene for SOD1 was active in S1, the gene for SOD2 was active in S2, and the gene for SOD3 was active in S3.* The fourth strain, S4, is not mentioned as having an active gene. Therefore, S4 is the control. The correct answer is (J).

39. **A** The question asks how to characterize the slope of the line in a graph with the time of the elongation period on the *x*-axis and the length of the cotton fiber on the *y*-axis. Compare Table 1, which shows Day 1 of the elongation period, with Table 3, which shows the end of the elongation period. For each strain, the length of the cotton fiber is longer in Table 3 than Table 1. Therefore, as the time of the elongation period increases, the length of the cotton fiber increases. Since the relationship is direct, the slope is positive. The correct answer is (A).

40. **F** The question asks how the amount of hydrogen peroxide and the length of the cotton fiber compare between S1 and S2 after 4 days. Day 4 for S1 is shown in Table 2. On Day 4, S1 had 4.1 μmol/mg of hydrogen peroxide and a length of 2.7 cm. Day 4 for S2 is shown in Table 3. On Day 4, S2 had 0.2 μmol/mg of hydrogen peroxide and a length of 1.4 cm. Therefore, S1 had more hydrogen peroxide and a longer length. The correct answer is (F).

COLLEGE ADMISSIONS INSIDER

Admissions and Financial Aid Advice

While *ACT Prep* will prepare you for your exam, *College Admissions Insider* will help you navigate what comes next. The bonus materials included here contain invaluable information about finding your best fit college, wending your way through the financial aid process, figuring out post-college plans, and more. We wish you the best of luck with your studies and preparation for college.

Part 1

26 Tips to Help You Pay Less for College

by Kalman A. Chany, author of
Paying for College Without Going Broke

GETTING FINANCIAL AID

1. Learn how financial aid works. The more and the sooner you know about how need-based eligibility is determined, the better you can take steps to maximize such eligibility.

2. Apply for financial aid no matter what your circumstances. Some merit-based aid can only be awarded if the applicant has submitted financial aid application forms.

3. Don't wait until you receive an acceptance letter to apply for financial aid. Do it when applying for admission.

4. Complete all the required aid applications. All students seeking aid must submit the FAFSA (Free Application for Federal Student Aid); however, other forms may also be required. Check with each college to see what's required and when.

5. Get the best scores you can on the SAT or ACT. They are used not only in decisions for admission but they can also impact financial aid. If your scores and other stats exceed the school's admission criteria, you are likely to get a better aid package than a marginal applicant.

6. Apply strategically to colleges. Your chances of getting aid will be better at schools that have generous financial aid budgets. (Check the Financial Aid Ratings for schools on **PrincetonReview.com**.)

7. Don't rule out any school as too expensive. A generous aid award from a pricey private school can make it less costly than a public school with a lower sticker price.

8. Take advantage of education tax benefits. A dollar saved on taxes is worth the same as a dollar in scholarship aid. Look into Coverdells, 529 plans, education tax credits, and loan deductions.

SCHOLARSHIPS AND GRANTS

9. Get the best score you can on the PSAT: it is the National Merit Scholarship Qualifying Test and also used in the selection of students for other scholarships and recognition programs.

10. Check your eligibility for grants and scholarships in your state. Some (but not all) states will allow you to use such funds out of state.

11. Look for scholarships locally. Find out if your employer offers scholarships or tuition assistance plans for employees or family members. Also look into scholarships from your community groups and high school, as well as your church, temple, or mosque.

12. Look for outside scholarships realistically: they account for fewer than five percent of aid awarded. Research them at **PrincetonReview.com** or other free sites. Steer clear of scholarship search firms that charge fees and "promise" scholarships.

PAYING FOR COLLEGE

13. Start saving early. Too late? Start now. The more you save, the less you'll have to borrow.

14. Invest wisely. Considering a 529 plan? Compare your own state's plan, which may have tax benefits, with other states' programs. Get info at **SavingforCollege.com.**

15. If you have to borrow, first pursue federal education loans (Perkins, Stafford, PLUS). Avoid private loans at all costs.

16. Never put tuition on a credit card. The debt is more expensive than ever given recent changes to interest rates and other fees some card issuers are now charging.

17. Try not to take money from a retirement account or 401(k) to pay for college. In addition to likely early distribution penalties and additional income taxes, the higher income will reduce your aid eligibility.

PAYING LESS FOR COLLEGE

18. Attend a community college for two years and transfer to a pricier school to complete the degree. Plan ahead: be sure the college you plan to transfer to will accept the community college credits.

19. Look into "cooperative education" programs. Over 900 colleges allow students to combine college education with a job. It can take longer to complete a degree this way, but graduates generally owe less in student loans and have a better chance of getting hired.

20. Take as many Advanced Placement (AP) courses as possible and get high scores on AP Exams. Many colleges award course credits for high AP scores. Some students have cut a year off their college tuition this way.

21. Earn college credit via "dual enrollment" programs available at some high schools. These allow students to take college-level courses during their senior year.

22. Earn college credits by taking CLEP (College-Level Examination Program) exams. Depending on the college, a qualifying score on any of the 33 CLEP exams can earn students 3 to 12 college credits.

23. Stick to your major. Changing colleges can result in lost credits. Aid may be limited/not available for transfer students at some schools. Changing majors can mean paying for extra courses to meet requirements.

24. Finish college in three years if possible. Take the maximum number of credits every semester, attend summer sessions, and earn credits via online courses. Some colleges offer three-year programs for high-achieving students.

25. Let Uncle Sam pay for your degree. ROTC (Reserve Officer Training Corps) programs available from U.S. Armed Forces branches (except the Coast Guard) offer merit-based scholarships up to full tuition via participating colleges in exchange for military service after you graduate.

26. Better yet: attend a tuition-free college!

Part 2

7 Essential Tips for Writing Your College Essay

Most selective colleges require you to submit an essay or personal statement. It may sound daunting to represent your best self in only a few hundred words, and it will certainly take a substantial amount of work. But it's also a unique opportunity that can make a big difference at decision time. Admissions committees put the most weight on your high school grades and your test scores. However, colleges receive applications from many worthy students and use your essay (along with your letters of recommendation and extracurricular activities) to find out what sets you apart from the other talented candidates.

1. What Sets You Apart?

Your background, interests, and personality combine to make you more than just a GPA and a standardized test score. The best way to tell your story is to write a personal, thoughtful essay about something that has meaning for you. If you're honest and genuine, your unique qualities will shine through.

2. Sound Like Yourself!

Admissions counselors have to read an unbelievable number of essays. Many students try to sound smart rather than sounding like themselves. Others write about a subject they don't care about, but that they think will impress admissions departments. Don't write about the same subjects as every other applicant. You don't need to have started a company or discovered a lost Mayan temple. Colleges are simply looking for thoughtful, motivated students who will add something to first-year students.

3. Write About Something That's Important to You.

It could be an experience, a person, a book—anything that has had an impact on your life. Don't just recount—reflect! Anyone can write about how they won the big game or the time they spent in Rome. Describe what you learned from the experience and how it changed you.

4. Be Consistent and Avoid Redundancies.

What you write in your application essay or personal statement should not contradict any other part of your application, nor should it repeat it. This isn't the place to list your awards or discuss your grades or test scores. Answer the question being asked. Don't reuse an answer to a similar question from another application.

5. Use Humor with Caution!

Being funny is a challenge. A student who can make an admissions officer laugh never gets lost in the shuffle. But beware: what you think is funny and what an adult working in a college thinks is funny might be very different. We caution against one-liners, limericks, and anything off-color.

6. Start Early and Write Several Drafts.

Set the essay aside for a few days and read it again. Put yourself in the shoes of an admissions counselor: Is the essay interesting? Do the ideas flow logically? Does it reveal something about the applicant? Is it written in the applicant's own voice?

7. Ask for Feedback!

Have at least one other person edit your essay—a teacher or college counselor is best. And before you send it off, triple check to make sure your essay is free of spelling and grammar errors. We recommend asking a second person to proofread your essay, as spellcheck and grammar software won't pick up every typo. It can be tricky to spot mistakes in your own work, especially after you've spent so much time writing and rewriting.

Feel free to check out our book *Complete Guide to College Essays*.

Part 3

The Right College for You

By The Staff of The Princeton Review

COMMON MISTAKES TO AVOID
WHILE CHOOSING A COLLEGE

The college admissions process may seem like a minefield of advice. College counselors, parents, teachers, friends, and even representatives of the colleges themselves all have admonishments to "be sure to…" and "don't ever…." Unfortunately, these tidbits, while intended to be helpful, can often contradict one another, giving students a picture of the process that looks more like a booby-trapped labyrinth than a map of a clear and straightforward path to success. In order to avoid adding to the confusion of the college selection process, here are just a few very important mistakes to avoid.

Get Started Now!

The biggest pitfall is probably the most obvious. Don't procrastinate! Getting started can be difficult, and there are plenty of places where you can get hung up or feel overwhelmed. Procrastinating can create undue stress and probably won't allow enough time to visit a campus so that you can get the most out of each college visit. And of course, there is also the ultra-last-minute procrastination of the applications themselves, which can cause you to make careless errors that could jeopardize your admissions chances. The bottom line here is that being prepared in advance for each step of the process can make the whole college admissions timeline much more manageable.

You have to take this process seriously. Which school you end up attending is the biggest factor that will shape your college experience, but many students don't put that much time or effort into this consideration. Don't make a decision without spending time researching colleges and finding out what you want. Because students don't often invest much time in exploring their options for different colleges, they can fall into the trap of assuming the best colleges are the most familiar ones. If you don't spend enough time thinking about the kind of person you are so that you can come up with a more appropriate "fit" instead of just getting in to some "brand name" institution, then you may not be able to realize your full potential, or you may just end up switching colleges after the first year because the experience wasn't what you dreamed it would be.

Schedule a College Visit

Part of taking this process seriously and doing your research properly is visiting as many colleges as you can. Often students and parents put this off, thinking it's either a waste of time or too expensive, but visiting at least a few schools is almost always worth it. Nothing can give you as much information about how a school "feels" and how you'll feel at it as actually walking around campus and getting a sense of its atmosphere. If you have the time and ability, visiting multiple schools early in your application process can help you narrow down which schools to apply to. If your candidate schools aren't local or you have limited means, it can be helpful to wait until you've received acceptances and weighed aid offers, and visit only your top two or three schools to aid in your final decision. We have multiple strategies and tips about planning an effective college visit in Part 3.

DOs	DON'Ts
Do it early, as soon as possible, or right now.	Don't procrastinate.
Do consider many schools you haven't heard of.	Don't choose a school based on name recognition alone.
Do listen to professional advice.	Don't neglect school visits.
Do it yourself!	Don't let your parents make all the decisions.
Do your research.	Don't let a school's "sticker price" scare you.

WOULD YOU RATHER?

Now that you know some of the key factors and some of the mistakes to avoid, it's time to really start figuring out what you want from colleges. Read through each question and write down your answer without thinking about it. You might be surprised what you learn about your college expectations.

Would you prefer a school that...

- is big (10,000+ undergrads), medium (4,000–10,000 undergrads), or small (fewer than 4,000 undergrads)?

- is close to home, or as far away as you can get?

- requires you to live on campus, or off?

- has an ivy-covered campus, or looks modern?

- has a set, structured list of academic requirements, or grants total academic freedom for all four years?

- is in a city, the suburbs, or a cornfield?

- is warm and sunny 340 days a year, or cold and snowy from October to April?

- has many of your high school friends as students, or is full of total strangers?

- has plenty of fraternities and sororities, or no Greek scene at all?

- has a dry campus, has somewhat of a social atmosphere, or is a party school?

- has 400 students in lecture classes, or six kids in a small class?

- is populated with liberal hipsters, or young Republicans?

- has professors who will know your name, or will refer to you by your social security number (in paperwork, since they probably won't call on you in their large classes)?

- has mostly students who live on campus all four years, or is mainly a "suitcase" school where people travel to and from campus?

- assigns lots of homework and readings, or hardly any of the same?

- is bureaucracy central, or a well-oiled machine?

- has a politically active student body, or one that never reads a newspaper?

- has tons of things to do off campus, or where the school itself is the center of all fun activities within a 20-mile radius?

- has a diverse student body, or has a fairly uniform student body?

- is very accepting of gay students, or has a "don't ask/don't tell" policy?

- is a "jock" school, or is full of students who rarely participate in sports?

- enrolls mainly pre-professional students, or kids who will "figure it out after we graduate"?

- sends almost every junior abroad for a semester or year, or where everyone stays on campus all four years?

- doesn't consider environmental issues as a top priority, or recycles everything possible?

There you have it: a few ideas about how to start your search for the college that will fit your needs.

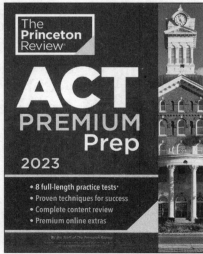
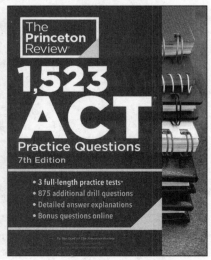